THE CHAMP
& THE CHUMP

THE CHAMP & THE CHUMP

JAMES McNICHOLAS

H

HEADLINE

First published in 2021 by
HEADLINE PUBLISHING GROUP

1

Cataloguing in Publication Data is available from the British Library

Hardback ISBN 978 1 4722 8037 4

PICTURE CREDITS
All photographs © James McNicholas apart from:
Section 1, p3 © The SF Experience, p6 (bottom) © Ben Carpenter,
p7 (bottom) © Central Press/Getty Images.
Section 2, p1 (bottom) © Popperfoto via Getty Images,
p7 (top left) © ANL/Shutterstock, (top right, bottom) © Murdo Macleod,
p8 (top) © David Montgomery/Getty Images.

Typeset in Monotype Sabon by CC Book Production
Printed and bound in Great Britain by Clays Ltd, Elcograf S.p.A.

Headline's policy is to use papers that are natural, renewable and recyclable
products and made from wood grown in well-managed forests and other
controlled sources. The logging and manufacturing processes are expected
to conform to the environmental regulations of the country of origin.

HEADLINE PUBLISHING GROUP
An Hachette UK Company
Carmelite House
50 Victoria Embankment
London EC4Y 0DZ

www.headline.co.uk
www.hachette.co.uk

For my world champion grandma, Barbara
The toughest fighter I've known

CONTENTS

PROLOGUE   1

RING WALK   15

THE TALE OF THE TAPE   19

ROUND ONE: BEGINNINGS   21
  IN MY CORNER   45

ROUND TWO: EVACUATION   49
  IN MY CORNER   69

ROUND THREE: FIGHTING   71
  IN MY CORNER   89

ROUND FOUR: AMERICA   99
  IN MY CORNER   119

ROUND FIVE: MARINES   123
  IN MY CORNER   155

ROUND SIX: BARB   159
  IN MY CORNER   177

ROUND SEVEN: THE RISE   181
  IN MY CORNER   211

ROUND EIGHT: WINNING THE TITLE   215
  IN MY CORNER   239

ROUND NINE: CELEBRITY   243
  IN MY CORNER   271

ROUND TEN: LOSING THE TITLE   273
  IN MY CORNER   297

ROUND ELEVEN: THE COMEBACK   299
  IN MY CORNER   313

ROUND TWELVE: CONSEQUENCE   317

THE SCORECARDS   333

ACKNOWLEDGEMENTS   340

PROLOGUE

Do you remember the last time you were on a boat?

I do. It was 7 January 2018, and my wife Camille and I were on honeymoon in Sri Lanka. We had got married the previous September, but delayed our trip to Asia by a few months. Travelling in January allowed us to avoid both the Sri Lankan rainy season, and the grey monsoons of the English winter.

It was not the blissful interval we had hoped for. The honeymoon period, in as much as there was one, lasted thirty-four days. After the joy, grief: five weeks after my wedding day, my world champion grandfather, Terry Downes, died. Our beginning was his ending.

It was, by that stage, no great surprise – this once indefatigable fighter had been ill for some time – but anticipation does not cushion the blow of loss. You can't duck grief or feint past mourning. The death of a grandparent is crushingly inevitable. You see it coming all the way, but it still hits you like an ice-cold scything uppercut.

My wedding day adhered to the cliché of being the best of

my life, but nonetheless it was not perfect: Terry wasn't there. A few weeks before the big day, a period of poor health saw him admitted to hospital for closer supervision. My grandma Barbara had insisted that he'd make it, that this man who'd fought at arenas on both sides of the Atlantic had one more grand occasion in him. In the end, however, he was too weak to attend. It was my grandma who, a few days before the nuptials, threw in the towel: an act of kindness for the husband she adored. And so, on my big day, there was an empty seat at ringside.

His absence left a void. Terry was the figurehead of the family, the pugilist patriarch who presided over Christmas dinners, summer barbecues and everything in between. He was at the centre of our identity, the star around which we orbited: to many people, I was just 'Terry Downes' grandson', just as my mum had been 'Terry Downes' daughter'. I'd spent my whole life overshadowed by his achievements, his bristling masculinity, the sheer force of his personality. I'd always envisaged him there at my wedding day, heckling from the back row just as he did at boxing halls up and down the country – and this hapless performer would never have been more happy to be upstaged.

But it wasn't to be. The count had begun, and this time Terry no longer had the strength to beat it. His final days were spent at Watford General, the same hospital where I'd been born three decades before. My birth and my marriage seemed tied inextricably to his death. Endings and beginnings, jumbled into one.

Within hours of his death, obituaries started appearing – not of the growling grandfather I'd known, but of the boxer who conquered the world in 1961. The cockney kid who became a US Marine, the whirlwind middleweight with the flying fists and barbed tongue, the champion of the world and conqueror of the great Sugar Ray Robinson. It was a reminder of his celebrity and his success, the heights he scaled and the glory he won. As I grappled with the loss of a family member, the sport mourned a legend.

There was some comfort in that. Everyone loses grandparents; not everyone gets to open the newspaper and read about it. The celebration of his achievements offered real consolation, and perhaps staved off the grief. In his old age, Terry had not been a public figure – this larger-than-life character had been content with, simply, living. Now, he was a star again, the black-and-white film footage of his fights flickering into life for the first time in decades. In death, he suddenly seemed more alive than ever.

And so perhaps it didn't hit me, right away. Perhaps my pride outweighed my grief – perhaps I was so caught up in the passing of 'Terry Downes, world champion', that it took a little time to register the loss of my grandfather, the man I knew simply as 'Pop'.

For my entire life, at his insistence, I've called him by that name. I believe this is fairly unusual – you hear 'Pops' a fair bit, but a singular Pop? Use of that term is reserved for fizzy drinks in the north, and – if nursery rhymes are to be believed – the sound a weasel makes. He in turn insisted on calling me 'Bosco'.*

---

* Or at least that's what we thought. After about thirty years, we finally deciphered via the spidery hieroglyphs in his diary that he was actually writing 'Bossgo'. When confronted with this, he explained that the name derived from the fact that when I was a baby, I was the 'boss' and everyone had to 'go' where I said. It's as good an excuse for a spelling mistake as I've heard.

When I knew him, Pop was no longer a champion but a cantankerous charmer, a man who wore gardening gloves rather than boxing gloves, and who prized a cup of tea over any title. It was the loss of this man I had yet to reckon with.

Until, that is, that boat in Sri Lanka. Maybe the intervening weeks had given me time to process things. Maybe the relaxation and the space afforded by a trip abroad allowed my thoughts to rise to the surface.

Ostensibly, we were there to watch whales, although as I'll explain later, that activity is one fraught with difficulty. But as I stared out at the vast, seemingly empty ocean, suddenly I understood: Pop really was gone.

And that was not all. As the sadness washed over me, as the waves rocked the little boat from side to side, I found myself reflecting on the disparity between Terry's life and my own – that of a world champion boxer and a world-class buffoon.

I suspect most people of my generation feel that their grandparents were tougher than them. Terry's story seems to take that divergence to ludicrous extremes. Terry grew up in a world war, I grew up playing World of Warcraft. He was a US Marine, I was mummy's little soldier. He honed his punches while I crafted punchlines, using humour as a shield to avoid real confrontation. Terry was an all-forces champion, a British champion, a world champion – barring bureaucracy, he might well have been an Olympic medallist. The only prize I've ever won was for a story I wrote aged five about a particularly hubristic mouse.

The Indian Ocean was rocky that day. As the waves grew bolder, my mind was tossed back and forth, caught in comparisons. I was thirty-one at the time, juggling twin careers in comedy and journalism, not successful enough in either to set the other aside. Terry had retired from boxing at twenty-eight, a self-made millionaire with a business empire already established. How could I live up to this legacy? When I died, how might my obituary read?

I could always see that Terry and I were different – in fact, growing up, that was one of the few things I could see. When you wear glasses, fighting isn't really an option. I got my specs when I was seven. My teacher, Mrs Fielding, told my mum I needed glasses because I couldn't see the whiteboard from my seat at the back of the class. She was right. My inability to keep up led me to resort to cheating: I once copied a boy called Robert Gilbert's maths answers so diligently that I accidentally wrote his name at the top of the paper. This could only have been an act of pure desperation: Robert Gilbert was not good at maths.

The problem was that my mum, Wendy, didn't want a little specky kid. Who can blame her? This was 1993. It wasn't fashionable then. Jerry Maguire was another three years away; children with glasses were still creepy not cute. 'He's fine,' insisted my mum, as I continued to stumble through education and into walls.

Things came to a head a few weeks later. At the time we lived in a village called Letchmore Heath in Hertfordshire. I say 'village', it's basically a pub, a war memorial and a pond surrounded by a few circuitous lanes lined with houses with antiquated exteriors and immaculate interiors – Range Rovers outside, and Agas within. It's the very middle of middle England.

One day, Mum and I were driving along one of those lanes.

They're narrow roads, the kind that mean cars frequently have to edge forward and back to squeeze past each other, like two office workers awkwardly caught in a corridor. On one side, there was a row of houses – on the other a fence and a field. As mum's 4x4 roared incongruously through the countryside, I turned and pointed to the fence, less than six feet away.

'Look mum, a sheep!' I shouted gleefully.

Mum turned and looked. But I was not pointing at a sheep. It was a bag of cement.

We went to the opticians that same afternoon. The integrity of Robert Gilbert's appalling mathematics was preserved, and the integrity of my face forever compromised by a pair of spectacles.

Suddenly, I had a stigma (also, as it happens, astigmatism). Obviously, glasses aren't the worst thing that could happen to a comfortably-off little white boy growing up. That, of course, would be someone treading on my Warhammer models. Nevertheless, I did occasionally feel like an outsider. I was the first person to get glasses in my class, and it's probably no coincidence that, more than a decade later, I'd be one of the last to lose my virginity.

Wearing spectacles puts a very literal polycarbonate pane between you and some of the more primal aspects of life. You can't really have sex in glasses, nor can you fight in glasses. Well, you can, but in both instances it doesn't look right and is liable to end badly. When it comes to fighting, glasses rob you of any peripheral vision. You can only see directly ahead of you, like a horse wearing blinkers. The 'blind spot' accounts for about sixty per cent of your field of vision. The big fear, of course, is that the glasses come off. In any high-stakes situation, that's game over. You never see guys kicking ass and taking names while squinting through a pair of specs.

People say that if you're short-sighted you can't see things that are far away, and if you're long-sighted you can't see things that are close to you. I don't know what I'm supposed to be because I can't see either. I'm an evolutionary aberration. In a pre-spectacles world, I would not have survived.

Consequently fighting, physicality and even sport have always felt somewhat like things that other people do. There's a perception that people with glasses are somehow cleverer. That's clearly wrong, but I think the basis of that idea comes from the fact people with glasses are forced to make different choices. No war games, just word games. Less football, more FTSE. Academic pursuits become the consequence of physical fallibility.

In most families, that'd be fine – celebrated, even. The problem is: I was supposed to be good at sport. My dad was fairly good at it, even if he dreamt more of being a rock star than a rugby player. My uncles were really good at sport, representing the county in cricket and athletics. And my grandad? Well, my grandad was the middleweight champion of the world. I grew up to be a comedian, an actor and writer. I haven't just fallen far from the tree – I'm in a whole different orchard. It's apples and oranges.

As whales surfaced and dived again, tourists lurched from one side of the boat to the other, camera flashes reflecting off the water's surface, creating a dizzying spectacle. When the boat pulled into harbour, my head was awash with the thought of Terry's life measured against mine, two lines on a graph with one easily outstripping the other. I cursed how I'd inherited the weight of legacy without the boon of talent. I should have felt like I was standing on the shoulders of a giant, yet instead I was perpetually in one's shadow.

In that, there was the germ of an idea. What if I were to retrace Terry's steps? To study his life to see what I could learn of my own? To throw myself into his world of men and see if I could remain afloat? I was at once the last person who should be talking about boxing, and yet the only person who could tell this story. No one could be closer to Terry, and yet no one could be further away.

And then, something quite extraordinary happened – the reason that I remember so clearly the last time I stepped off a boat. I disembarked, changed. I returned to dry land, only to find it moving beneath my feet, replicating the slosh and swell of the tumultuous ocean. The sand of the Sri Lankan beach seemed to give way as I walked, the ground disturbingly pliant below me.

I struggled to keep my balance, swaying like drunk Bambi, and leaning on my wife Camille for support. Now this, I have since learned, is not especially unusual. Lots of people have that sensation after getting off a boat – it can last for anything from a few minutes to about twenty-four hours.

It was only when I woke up the next morning, still feeling for all the world that I was cast adrift at sea, that I began to worry. Everyone I spoke to offered reassurance, insisting things would get better in an hour, or a day, or a week. I rang my mum, I rang my grandma. This, they were certain, was normal. 'You go on the boat, you get your sea legs; you get back on the land, you need your land legs back.' They made it sound like bowling, where you just swap your shoes.

As the hours, days and weeks rolled on, the ebb and flow of the tide unrelenting, nothing about this experience felt normal. The sense of motion was constant, and violent. Staying still brought no respite. Every seat was a rocking chair, every bed a hammock. The ground seemed to shift beneath me; it felt a little like walking on a trampoline – but more than anything, it felt like I was still aboard that boat, still bobbing and swaying to the rhythm of the Indian Ocean.

The rest of my six-week honeymoon was spent ashore, but I wouldn't have known it. Twenty-four hours a day, seven days a week, I had the sensation of being rocked violently side-to-side. I had Camille for company, but it felt for all the world like I was lost on a solo sailing mission.

And it got worse. As time wore on, as weeks turned to months, my symptoms increased. The dizzying effect of the waves became entrenched, aggressive. My head pulsed, my temples throbbed, my neck ached as it futilely fought against the phantom motion. My ears were ringing, my vision blurrier than ever before. I fought so hard to stay upright that I could not focus on anything else. Relaxing, working, continuing began to feel impossible.

With the physical symptoms came psychological scars – the trauma of a honeymoon ruined, the guilt of burdening Camille, the feeling of being cast helplessly adrift. By the end of 2018, I was an emotional and physical wreck, a cocktail of guilt and dizziness and confusion left me in a state so vulnerable I could be moved to tears by anything from self-pity to the climax of Tyson Fury's first fight with Deontay Wilder.

I hadn't even intended to watch it. It was December 2018, almost a year into my landsick nightmare. The fight took place at the Staples Centre in LA. I've never been a particularly big boxing fan, but given the familial ties, I've always kept half an eye on it, which is easy for me on account of the aforementioned astigmatism.

I had woken up in the middle of the night, head pounding and ears ringing, the familiar percussion that had begun to underscore every day. After stumbling into the living room, I collapsed into the sofa. I'm a subscriber to the old house-husband's tale that when you can't sleep, the best thing to do is get up for a bit. Fight fire with fire. It's a hard reset on the whole 'going to bed' process: by getting up for an hour, you can trick your body clock into thinking it's bedtime. Sometimes I clean my teeth again, to solidify the conceit.

Flicking mechanically through the channels, I concluded that there's not much on at 3 a.m. on a Sunday morning: rolling news, old films. ITV were showing something called *ITV Nightscreen*. The info button told me it was a 'text-based information service'. By day, just an ordinary television channel; by night, Wikipedia. A few nudges down, sibling station ITV2 were showing reruns of a programme called *River Monsters*. This is a show where a bloke goes out to some distant waterway where the locals are being terrorised by a mythical fanged beast. It's always, always a catfish.

On one of Channel 4's many, obscure offspring (4 Fucksake, or something like that) there was a documentary about the world's fastest tractor.

I kept flicking: *Brit Cops*, *Criminals Caught on Camera*, *Motorway Patrol*. I guess crime never sleeps. My thumb found an easy rhythm, steadily drumming me up into the higher reaches of the TV guide. We were in the 900s now: this is Babestation territory, these are the murky realms of pay-per-view. Eventually I settled on a different kind of sweaty, topless action: a boxing match.

A big boxing match, in every sense: six-feet-seven tall Deontay Wilder against the six-feet-nine Tyson Fury. In the dim light I experienced flickers of recognition – this is, after all, the sort of heavyweight title bout that will occasionally penetrate popular culture. Big-time boxing is pervasive – we know the major personalities, their foibles and their fearsomeness. You don't have to be an ardent fan to know that you don't make fun of Mike Tyson's lisp.

My grandad used to say that boxing was about showmanship, which I always felt overlooked the critical ingredients of 'punching' and 'being punched'. Elton John is a great showman, but I wouldn't fancy him over twelve rounds. In the film *The Greatest Showman*, there isn't a bit where Hugh Jackman uppercuts an elephant.

Personalities sell fights though, and these two are characters colourful enough to light up any arena. Wilder by name, wilder still by nature: a snarling slab of Alabama muscle dripping with charisma. Wilder styles himself as 'The Bronze Bomber', and with good reason: his right hand is as violently explosive as a cat in a microwave. Forty fights, all victories, thirty-nine knockouts – twenty of them inside the first round. It made my pounding headache worse just thinking about it.

Then there's Tyson Fury, with a name like a comic-book character and a personality that's just as implausible. Fury personifies that conflict so many feel about boxing: viscerally unpleasant yet somehow captivating. Flamboyant and inflammatory, a class warrior with less than classy conduct. For some, he is an inspirational figure who highlights mental health issues. For others, he's one of the world's best boxers, but one of the UK's highest profile homophobes; The Gypsy King of bigoted Britain.

I started watching quite late in the fight, the ninth round of twelve. That Fury was still going was arguably something of a surprise – he'd spent two years out of the sport suffering a host of physical and mental problems, and had been stripped of titles, dignity and muscle definition. Fury had spoken openly about his suicidal thoughts and pledged to donate his entire fee for the Wilder fight to mental health charities. He'd shaved both head and beard, monk-like penance as he looked for redemption.

Here he was back in the ring. This was the prize after the fight for his life: the prizefight of his life. And he was winning. Fury was defying the odds, defying gravity as his huge frame ducked and weaved like the boxers of legend. What do they say? 'Float like a butterfly, sting like a bee'? Or just be a jellyfish and do both. Here Fury was, re-established as ringmaster. Hugh Jackman would be proud.

I couldn't help but be drawn in. Boxing is unlike almost all other sports in that you require no understanding of its laws to engage with the concept. People bang on about the Queensbury Rules but let's be honest: it's two blokes hitting each other in the face until one of them can't stand up anymore. What rules exist are pretty self-explanatory: no punching in the balls, no biting, etc. These are the rules of the street, they barely need to be written down.

And it is mesmerising. It's like watching Richard Madeley present live television: you can't look away for a moment because there's always a chance that something truly horrifying might happen.

And then, in the final round, as Fury looked poised to crown his comeback with victory, it did. Wilder landed a right-left combo of such force it would have sent a shatterproof ruler scattering into a thousand tiny pieces. The fight was over, Wilder celebrated, and even the commentators proclaimed him the winner. Fury was flat on his back, the giant felled, his eyes rolling back in his head as if even they could not bear to watch.

The ferocious force of that punch, the way it sent Fury sprawling to the floor, resonated with me. That was how I felt: flattened by fortune, seemingly out for the count.

As I considered my situation, there was, among it all, an inescapable irony. Bereft of balance, senses dulled, grasping desperately for a secure footing, I thought again of Pop – the man who fought for a living, while I found myself fighting to reclaim my life. And suddenly, perhaps for the first time, I felt those two lines on a graph meet. There was a convergence. There was no getting away from it. I – the quintessential coward, the man who'd never really been in a fight in my life – had been knocked down, and with my senses betraying me, was all but out. Coming back from this seemed inconceivable. I was punch-drunk.

RING WALK

Long before Tyson Fury rode through the crowd on a giant throne to the strains of Patsy Cline's *Crazy*, before Prince Naseem Hamed floated to the ring on a flying carpet, there was Terry Downes' war dance.

When a young Terry made his debut in the 1950s, there was not so much of the showmanship we associate with boxing today. In those days, there were no pyrotechnics, and no show-boating: you walked to the ring solemnly, with your hood up and your head down.

Not Terry. During his time training in America, he'd been taught the importance of limbering up, and getting loose. And so, on the occasion of his first professional fight, he duly danced out to the ring, shadow-boxing his way up through the Harringay crowd.

Well, this exuberant warm-up was not warmly received. The traditionalists saw this cockney's capering as mere showing off. Terry had not long since returned to the UK and must have hoped for a hero's welcome. Instead, boos rained down from the balcony. He was inadvertently cast as the villain.

But he didn't let it phase him. The more they booed, the more he'd dance – it must've been like watching a misguided *Britain's Got Talent* audition. Terry's only chance of turning the tide of opinion was to win the fight, and win in style.

He did. By the end of the night, the dazzling debutant was the talk of the arena. After the setback, the comeback. So it is with boxing stories.

As far as I can see, anyway. Truth be told, the little I know about boxing comes from the movies. There's certainly been plenty of them – eight *Rocky* films, for a start. When Thomas Edison unveiled his kinetoscope back in 1891, the first thing it showed was footage of a boxing match. Even today, boxing films far outnumber any other sports films, and *Rocky* remains the only sports movie to take the Oscar for Best Picture (although I think we can all agree that *Space Jam* was robbed.)

Part of that is simply down to the fact that cinema-goers love violence – and film-makers love trying to capture it. There has been a variety of approaches to achieving this. Michael Mann shot from multiple angles in *Ali*, using slow-motion to exaggerate the quick feet and flying fists of his star subject. In *Creed*, Ryan Coogler used single takes for each round, ducking and weaving between fighters to capture the intensity and intimacy of the contest. In *The Fighter*, David O. Russell perfectly recreated the HBO television boxing broadcast style, even down to the grainy footage of the era – boxing, after all, is something most people have only seen on a screen.

But there's more to this cultural obsession than a fixation with violence. There's something in these stories that fascinates us, that connects with us on a primal level. Perhaps it's because there's such a clear trajectory to the boxer's journey – he's fighting for something. Sometimes it's something as literal as a title, other times it's more abstract. In Ali's case, he's fighting for his civil rights. In Rocky's case, he's fighting for self-respect. In George Foreman's case, he's fighting to sort distribution for his grilling machine, and to see off increasing competition from startups like Deliveroo and Uber Eats. He's got his hands full, to be honest.

The boxing narrative grabs our attention because it's dramatic, it's gripping, it's entertaining. It's two blokes hitting each other in the face. What could be more entertaining than that? But the reason we care about it is because we invest in it, we empathise. The boxer can be a surrogate for something else: his struggle represents our own. You can't uppercut oppression; you can't shatter prejudice's nose; you can't knock Deliveroo's teeth out – but by God we'd all like to sometimes: earlier this year I waited 75 minutes for a KFC. It probably would've been quicker to work out the Colonel's secret recipe myself.

Anyway, you can't punch *those* things. But you can externalise that feeling and prove to the world that you still have some control, some power. When we see a man without money, freedom and self-respect – or with a collapsing grilling empire – throw a stiff jab, it gives us hope. None of us have the money, freedom and self-respect we want. The jab though . . . well, in theory, you could learn that. That's comforting, because we're all fighting something, but most of us are fighting something you can't hit. Whether in fiction or reality, on film or on pay-per-view, boxing stories crystallise something fundamental to the human experience: the importance of getting back up after being knocked down, of moving forward in the face of adversity, of being booed into Harringay Arena for dancing about but then pushing on to win anyway. Fighting is sometimes about glory; more often it's about guts. These stories are really about comebacks.

And so to my ring walk. I'm following Terry's path, shadow boxing, and boxing shadows. I'm going to track his life and do my best to tread in his dancing footsteps – to learn about where I'm from and understand why I don't fit. They say that styles make a fight, and mine and Terry's couldn't clash more.

Perhaps I'll encounter a few boos along the way, but that won't deter me. An unhappy crowd is nothing new: I once played the titular role in a theatre-in-education production of Shakespeare's *Macbeth* where a boy shouted 'Gay!' at me every time I came on stage.

We're seconds out from seconds out. If I had cornermen this is where I'd usher them from the ring – looks very much like a square to me, but then who am I to say? This is my fight to get to grips with a world where I've never belonged. Let's just hope my glasses don't fall off.

Here we go: round one. Ding Ding.

THE TALE OF THE TAPE

In the red corner, a working-class hero.
In the blue corner, a privately educated man of privilege.

In the red corner, a man of honour.
In the blue corner, a man with an MA (Hons).

In the red corner, a record of forty-four fights and thirty-five wins.
In the blue corner, a record of sixty-seven auditions and four jobs.

Five-feet-ten of muscle and sinew against fifteen stone of flab.

Twenty-twenty vision against a bespectacled boy in 2020.

The pugilist and the pacifist.

The fighter and the writer.

The champ and the chump.

Round One
BEGINNINGS

In West London, in the district of Paddington, is a street called Westbourne Terrace. It runs north to south, slicing this chunk of Westminster in two. For the most part it is a tree-lined parade of stylish nineteenth century homes. At the southern end is the elegant Sussex Gardens – at the other, the highway narrows into what is known as Westbourne Terrace Road, terminating on the bank of Regent's Canal in Little Venice. And it is on this street that both our stories begin.

Westbourne Terrace bisects more than just the map. Sandwiched between two Royal Parks, Paddington is an area of sharp contrasts: looming apartment buildings cast long shadows over million-pound mansions. Less than two miles away, the burned-out sarcophagus of Grenfell still stands.

For this part of London, glamour and morbidity have long lived side-by-side. Paddington is where Queen Victoria arrived after her first rail journey in 1842. More recently, it was the venue for the birth of Prince George at St Mary's Hospital. Historically, however, this region had the dubious honour of being associated with hangings – 'to dance the Paddington Frisk' is a euphemistic term for the jerks and twitches of a body dangling from a noose.

It has always been a cultural melting pot. French Huguenots settled in the village of Paddington in the eighteenth century, and subsequent generations have seen arrivals from Greek, Jewish, Irish and Asian communities. The nearby Edgware Road brings a flavour of the Arabian Peninsula to this corner of England's capital. There is everything here. It is pretty and rough, expensive and tatty. Cultures and social strata collide like tectonic plates, levering volcanic tower blocks into a grey sky.

At the heart of it all stands the station, a towering cathedral of iron and glass, erected by the celebrated engineer Isambard Kingdom Brunel in 1847. The train rattles in and out of Paddington station like a current, bringing with it an ebb and flow of newcomers, of possibility. Paddington is where Nobel Prize winner Sir Alexander Fleming discovered penicillin. It is home to the most high-security police station in the United Kingdom, Paddington Green. It is synonymous with the world's most famous bear. And for the Downes family, it is something like home.

A canal meanders through the area known as Little Venice. No gondolas here, but on the day I visit a discarded shopping trolley bobs along the water's surface. This fashionable enclave makes for an oasis of beauty in the midst of the humming metropolis.

At the Venetian end of Westbourne Terrace stands The Bridge House pub, and above it the Canal Cafe Theatre. It is home to the News Revue cabaret night that has helped launch the careers of Rory Bremner, Reece Shearsmith, Bill Bailey, Sara Pascoe and more besides.

And it is a few hundred yards away at 162 Westbourne Terrace that Terry Downes, my world champion grandfather, grew up. It's on this street where the fighter was forged. And it is here that almost a century later, in a little theatre by the canal, blissfully ignorant of the biographical synchronicity, I had my first comedy gig. Two lives, inextricably linked, operating in perfect parallel.

Terry would not recognise the area from his childhood of the Thirties and Forties. His Paddington was a London that's been long since lost, a London of fable and memory – little kitchens coughing out engine smoke and washing lines strung up everywhere like makeshift bunting. Gone are the pie and eel shops, whose wriggling wares once littered the streets. The public's appetite for its slithering speciality has crashed in tandem with the Thames population. Gone is the old Coliseum cinema, affectionately nicknamed The Fleapit, where fleas were frequently the least of your problems: my grandma Barbara remembers films regularly being interrupted by water rats from the canal creeping across the screen.

In the space of a square mile, Terry had his family home, later a nightclub, and later still a betting shop. All are long since gone. On Westbourne Terrace Road, the crime fiction writer Margery Allingham's ten-year residence is marked with a blue plaque. There is no sign of Terry Downes.

But talk to people who grew up in this part of town, and his memory is still alive. Some recall him training at the Stowe Club on the Harrow Road; others cite him sparring with Portobello Road associate Lenny Cain. Some remember him opening his first bookmakers just along from the Queens Park Estate; one person has a story about him filming a commercial back at the Lee Lighting shop on Kensal Road.* A milkman tells me that on his early rounds, he once found a worse-for-wear Terry passed out on a huge pile of rubbish. We all create our own myths around our families, but in the case of Terry Downes, the reality requires little embellishment.

Every hero has his origin story. A portentous prologue that informs their identity and motivations. Superman arrived from outer space; Spiderman was bitten by a radioactive spider; Batman was very rich and sad. Terry's own origin story is beautifully efficient: it's the story of a cockney boy getting into a fight.

He was born in 1933, just a couple of years after Paddington station's digital clock first flickered into life. They say to be a true cockney you need to be born within the sound of Bow Bells. Terry would've taken issue with that: he was born six miles away in Paddington Hospital, but he couldn't have been more cockney if he'd been born in the bell tower itself.

The Downes clan were well known in that particular nook of West London. Terry's dad Dick hailed from a Catholic family, and the Pope would've been proud of them – Dick was one of 16 brothers. I guess Dick's mum and dad, Walter and Ellen Downes, must've loved each other almost as much as they hated contraception.

---

* The advert was apparently for the 'Raving Bonkers Fighting Robots' toy, a 1970s classic which saw two plastic boxers square off in a ring. You had to press a 'punch' button with your thumb until your fighter caught the opponent with an uppercut, at which point his head would crank upwards, accompanied by a strange grinding sound. I'm assured almost exactly the same thing happens in real life.

It was a huge family. 'My grannie had more than a hundred grandchildren and it seemed we all lived within a stone's throw,' Terry told *The Times*. 'Like all good relatives, we fought like wild cats.'

Dick married Hilda Harwood – reportedly of Romany gypsy descent. Dick had been a soldier and done a stint with the Red Cross. He seemingly managed to get by working almost any job that didn't include doing office hours – a philosophy I came to identify with. 'I wouldn't say the Downeses were rich,' explains Terry's widow Barbara, my grandma, 'But I didn't know any that were poor.' If you were feeling mean-spirited, you might say that's not a particularly helpful description. For God's sake Grandma, be more specific. But I think what she was alluding to is the fact that the Downes family were, by nature, grafters.

They were wheeler-dealers, and as many of them were in the car trade, sometimes just wheel dealers. About a year ago I was chatting to a friend who said they'd been to a party where they'd met someone they thought might be a distant cousin of mine. I asked what they had said they did for a living. The friend said they hadn't mentioned any specific job, but at one point in conversation, apropos of nothing, they'd offered to sell them their watch. I told them we were almost certainly related.

Paddington lies in the shadow of the train station. Pop used to tell me he'd climb the old railway wall to watch the trains chuntering in from the West, bringing 'all sorts of interesting people into London'. 'And,' he'd add with a wink, 'the occasional Welsh bloke.' God love the mischievous xenophobia of the older generation.

From an early age, he had a tendency to end up in scraps. As the oldest boy of his generation, the Downeses would regularly turn to 'our Tel' when there was trouble. It's funny to think of a nine year old as a local enforcer. In reality, Terry admitted that at that age he was no tougher than anyone else. It was the exposure to conflict that hardened him, and the law of averages that meant he ended up with a decent record of wins.

In between brawls, he found time to attend St Saviour's School. It was there he encountered a teacher called Mr Beal – the Mickey Goldmill to this nine-year-old Rocky – and there that Terry's origin story was spun. After yet another playground scrap, Mr Beal was weary of tearaway Terry getting into trouble, and so challenged him to clean up his act and channel his anger into sport – 'If you're going to hit people, learn to do it properly, make something of yourself'. It's questionable advice, really – 'You know that illicit activity you're doing? What if you learned to become really proficient at it?' If he'd caught him pickpocketing, would he have urged him to start planning large-scale bank robberies?

One of the things that really motivated Terry to get into boxing was that Mr Beal kept waxing lyrical about Terry's older cousin, Ronnie Grogan – himself an aspiring pro. Grogan would ultimately have a journeyman career, winning exactly half of his fifty-two professional bouts. His last fight, in 1953, saw him suffer a knockout defeat to an up-and-comer from Liverpool called Pat McAteer. Five years later, Terry would beat McAteer to claim the British middleweight title. Ronnie served to inspire Terry, but ultimately the younger cousin far surpassed him. Grogan was destined to remain the Salieri to Terry's Mozart, the Joe Frazier to his Muhammad Ali, the Dan Walker to his Gary Lineker.

And so the young Terry wandered down to the local Pembroke boxing club, where a trainer showed him the ropes (presumably literally as well as figuratively). He ducked out of trouble and weaved his narrative into the world of boxing, and there you have it. It's a story that gives you everything you need to know: here's a scrappy kid with an attitude, who finds sanctuary and discipline in the sweet science of boxing. Fighting is his way in, and his way out.

My origin story, in its own way, tells you everything you need to know about me. It takes place not in West London, but in Gibraltar, during a typical summer sojourn to the south of Spain.

I was with my mum and my grandma Barbara. Although holidaying in Marbella, we'd ventured out on a day trip to Gibraltar. For the uninitiated, Gibraltar is an outcrop of land at the tip of the Southern Spanish peninsula that is a British overseas territory. It remains some corner of a foreign field that is forever England, and presumably from whence the steady British invasion of the Costa del Sol was launched. First we took Gibraltar, then we took the sunbeds.

Gibraltar is one of those curious outposts that doesn't seem to particularly want independence. They had a referendum in 2002 in which the British government offered to share sovereignty with Spain. Less than one per cent of the population voted in favour. Imagine wanting to be British rather than Spanish. I can only attribute it to some Mediterranean equivalent of Stockholm Syndrome. Call me an EU-flag waving liberal nancy (Terry probably would have done), but I just can't countenance choosing to be a Brit over being a Spaniard.* Their country is

---

* I do remember rumours in 2008 that the then Arsenal goalkeeper Manuel Almunia was considering exchanging passports so he could play for England, but he didn't actually go through with it, did he? He was a bad goalkeeper but he wasn't insane.

better. The most obvious piece of evidence is the fact we're so desperate to go there: there's a reason the coasts of Britain aren't packed with Spanish ex-pats angrily demanding a paella and a sangria. It's tempting to wonder what on earth the Gibraltans* are thinking – until, that is, you remember that 2002 was a hell of a year for the UK: Girls Aloud were formed, we won a gold at the winter Olympics *and* the foot and mouth crisis was declared over. No wonder they wanted to stick around.

Anyhow, Gibraltar is populated by monkeys. Not exclusively, to be clear – there are also approximately 34,000 humans there, living their bizarre British-Spanish hybrid existence, eating a Manchego ploughman's and tucking into tapas-sized portions of roast dinner. But there is also a population of Barbary macaques, ostensibly there to entertain tourists. Like many of Spain's migrant workers, they originally hail from North Africa. Their presence dates back to when Gibraltar was under Islamic rule – in fact, they predate the British. If anything, it's more their territory than it is ours. There are about 300 macaques in the colony, the last defenders of what was once their land.†

There's a local legend that says when the monkeys disappear from Gibraltar, so will the British. Apparently during the Second World War, when the numbers were dwindling,‡ Churchill sent to North Africa for replacements. It's those imported immigrant

---

* Just looked it up. Apparently, it's 'Gibraltese' but I honestly think Google is having a wind-up.

† Three hundred, eh? Imagine them all on the ramparts in little helmets, armed with spears and shields, shouting 'This is Gibraltar!' Now that is a movie.

‡ Due to imperial conscription, presumably. Brave underage monkeys signing up to fight for king and country.

monkeys who now engage with the tourists, doing the jobs Spanish monkeys don't want to do.

Gibraltar's legislation states that if you're caught feeding a monkey there's an instant £500 fine. But given what people will pay to swim with dolphins, £500 to feed a monkey doesn't sound so bad. Ultimately it comes down to how much you like monkeys. For some, it's a risk worth taking.

I just want to deal with this up front: I have until now and will henceforth be referring to the macaques as monkeys. Maybe they're not – people seem to love pointing stuff like that out. It's a particular kind of pedantry. 'Actually, a spider isn't an insect.' 'Actually, Sydney isn't the capital of Australia.' 'Actually, a chimpanzee isn't a monkey.' Isn't it? So if I've got a bloke with a pathological fear of monkeys, and I lock him in a cupboard with a chimpanzee, he'll be fine? I don't think so, mate. You know what I meant, stop being a dick.

So these 300 monkeys occupy what's known as 'The Rock' – a craggy outpost at the end of the peninsula. Naturally, it has become something of a tourist attraction. After all, where else in Britain can you see a load of monkeys in the wild?

You can visit the monkeys in a cable car, but I'm not surprised my mum and grandma refused to do that. They think the tube is dangerous. Instead we drove around The Rock, on a kind of low-rent safari. Speaking of rent, we were in a hire car, and Mum was behind the wheel. Given that I was just under a year old, I was strapped into a baby seat in the back.

Now it's important to mention that the rental car in question had a sunroof. Neither my mum nor grandma can recall what the weather was like that day, but that doesn't matter: we were Brits on holiday, and therefore the sunroof was open. I know, you're already there. You have the image in your mind. I won't delay unnecessarily, there's no tantric benefit to deferring any longer: a monkey got into the car. It climbed through the sunroof and dropped down onto the back seat.

And what did my own mother and grandmother do, when this animal interloper clambered into the back next to my helpless infant self? Did they fight off the intruder, rescuing the distressed child from his simious tormentor? Did they fuck. They ran, flinging open the car doors and sprinting to sanctuary, engine still running, baby still screaming.

My hypothesis is that every idiosyncratic quirk of my personality, my need to perform and impress and seek assurance and be loved, could very well stem from this one incident in my first year on the planet: my mum left me in the car with a monkey. Let's say that again, in bold: **my mum left me in the car with a monkey.** I've spent the last eighteen months in therapy, discussing the intricacies and complexities of my emotional inner life, when really all I needed to do was turn up on day one and say, 'By the way, just so you know, my mum left me in the car with a monkey', and I would've saved myself the best part of five grand.

I was completely helpless. Even if I were older and capable, I am not sure I would have had it in me to thrash out, to fight back. All babies are born with their fists clenched, but not all babies are born fighters. Terry may well have emerged using his umbilical cord as a skipping rope, with the placenta as a punchbag, but our stories are fundamentally divergent from the point of birth.

I did once see a grown man punch a monkey. I was on a trip to Sri Lanka – the aforementioned honeymoon – and one that confirms my position plumb in the heart of the middle classes. We were visiting Sigiriya, another 'mountain rock' inhabited by Temple monkeys. When one pinched a crisp from a Russian tourist, he turned and hit the monkey with a firm right hand. The monkey looked cross, in as far as that's possible, and then to my considerable surprise and delight hit the Russian right back. It was like a Simian remake of *Rocky IV* – and absolutely fair enough in the circumstances. Now perhaps that monkey should learn to hit people properly, become a boxer, make something of itself, etc.

Back in 1987, I did not strike out at my monkey. They are family, after all. Unlike Terry, our protagonist, I have been a pacifist since my dribbling days. Instead I did something that, in fairness, seems entirely natural – and the same thing I'd presumably do if you asked me to step into a boxing ring. I cried. I'm a blubberer, not a fighter. Terry's the type to fight back; I'm the type to fight back tears.

I speak to my grandma about this incident, and she has a good old chuckle about it.

'All I can remember is that we ran over and hid near these American tourists,' she guffaws. 'I remember this one woman shouting, "Oh my god, look at that poor little guy, he's terrified!"' And with that she dissolves into more laughter.

As for my mum, her own attitude toward monkeys appears to have done a full 180. She absolutely loves them. A couple of Christmases ago she was insistent that she wanted a monkey wrapped under the tree as her present. She texted me saying, and I quote: 'Please Jamie, I will look after it so nicely. I could keep it in the garage' – a message in which the second sentence really undoes any confidence inspired by the first. As a conservational consolation prize, I recently adopted an orangutan in her name.* As far as I'm concerned, Mum and Grandma are

---

* I know an orangutan is not a monkey, you miserable pedants. Also, when I say 'adopt', I mean in the 'she got a certificate' sense, not in the 'she now has an orangutan living in her garage' sense.

both very fortunate to have avoided a £500 fine for trying to feed a monkey a baby.

It's not my mum's fault that she has a misguided idea of what constitutes an appropriate pet. When she was a little girl, Terry bought her a lamb. Now, it's important to point out: they weren't living on a farm. They were living in Mill Hill, a suburb of north London. 'He just turned up with it one day,' recalls my grandma. 'He called it Poofy.'*

Poofy the lamb formed part of the Downes family life for a brief window in the 1960s. 'We used to feed it with a bottle like a baby. He used to come in the kitchen, or I'd feed it through the window,' says Grandma. 'He used to escape and run over the road to your mum's school. The school would ring me up and say, "Mrs Downes, your lamb's over here."' And so my grandma would head over to the school to collect the wandering Poofy.

'I worried about it,' she admits. 'It got a bad leg; we had to have the vet out to it. It had been running around the garden. Too much gamboling,' she explains – an apt choice of word, for as you'll discover, gambling runs in the family.

Eventually the sheer absurdity of the situation brought things to a head. It transpires that it is quite difficult to housetrain a sheep. 'And I'm not being funny,' says Grandma. 'I was starting to get a bit fed up of chasing it up Milespit Hill shouting, "Poofy! Poofy! Come back, Poofy!"' Quite the image.

As the man who had brought the lamb bleating into their lives, it was Terry's responsibility to rid them of it. 'He told us he took it back to the farm, but I took that with a pinch

---

* Named, I am reliably informed, on account of its cloud-like shape, rather than any homophobic insinuation.

of salt,' admits Barbara. 'Maybe it became roast lamb, you know what he was like. You can't put that in the book though.' Too late.

I know what happened to me with the monkey might not seem so bad. 'Oh no, the poor little rich boy got scared during his safari.' But just imagine for a second that you are me, a baby. Do you want to be in a car with a monkey? I didn't think so. A quick google of what macaques eat tells you they 'occasionally eat small vertebrates'. As someone who was a) small and b) had a spine, I was justifiably terrified.

Quite the moment though. Quite the origin story. Face to face with a monkey, staring back into our beginnings. Two creatures, two individuals, tied by a shared genetic history, yet utterly alien to each other. The perfect prelude to how my life has unfolded – and indeed to this book.

It is tempting to romanticise Terry's working-class background, to lean into the rags-to-riches story. Pop was always at pains, however, to point out he never considered the way he grew up to be any kind of hardship. 'My dad made sure we never went short of a crust or clothes on our backs,' he wrote in his 1964 autobiography,* which conjures the intriguing image of a family attempting to wear bread.

Nevertheless, as well as Terry was fed and dressed, West London was not somewhere laden with opportunity. 'You read about Paddington, where I was brought up,' Terry told the *Sunday Mirror* that same year. 'It's a bit of an asphalt jungle. Grim, grimy, smoky . . . the pounding of railway engines. You

---

* The superbly-titled *My Bleeding Business*.

live there – so put up with it. Or fight your way out of it. With bare fists, gloves, brain, pen, tongue, anything.'

For Terry, autobiography aside, it was never likely to be the pen. Pop always said that he 'wasn't no good in school', which came as no surprise given his rudimentary understanding of double negatives. I once asked him what he would've been if he hadn't made it as a boxer. 'A gangster,' he said. It was delivered with an intonation that suggested it was a joke. I'm not so sure it was – and neither is my grandma. 'He told me that if he wasn't a fighter, he would've been a criminal,' she recalls. 'And he meant it.' Terry was uncompromising in his pursuit of success. He was determined to change his circumstances; it just so happened that the fight game proved the most pragmatic way to do so – and what's more, he loved it.

Just two generations down the line, my own attitude to education was somewhat different. I went to a school where we were encouraged to wear academic successes like title belts, even if anything we achieved was marred by the financial doping that is the private school sector.

The village where I grew up, Letchmore Heath, is just a few miles from London yet looks and feels like a remote hamlet – commuters playing at countryside living. It is probably best known for the fact that in 1973, Beatle George Harrison built the huge Bhaktivedanta Manor there, and gifted it to the Hare Krishna movement. The selection of the site was no coincidence. The founder of the International Society for Krishna Consciousness, A.C. Bhaktivedanta Swami Prabhupada, once said that the beautiful forest surroundings of Letchmore Heath reminded him of Krishna's birthplace, Vrindavan. And so it was that this facade of English country life was occasionally interrupted by shaven-headed monks chanting their fealty to Krishna atop a cart pulled by a huge Rajasthan Ox. Some way to puncture counterfeit countryside.

That, in some respects, sums up my childhood: a veneer of middle-class regularity, interspersed with outbreaks of oddness. My upbringing was unconventional, my siblings strange. My brother Charlie, just fifteen months younger than me, was a curious child. For the first few years of his life he was effectively mute: the only way in which he'd communicate was by whispering demands into my ear to be relayed to the family. The demands, invariably, were for Kelloggs Frosties. He was so obsessed by the cartoon *Bananaman* that he once forced an actual banana into the video machine in an effort to make it appear on the screen.

My sister Rose, five years younger, had unusual habits of her own. While still a toddler, she was discovered at a family friend's house, having opened and eaten the contents of a large bag of coal. By her own admission, Rose has always had a tricky relationship with food. We once saw her walking round with what she claimed was a kale smoothie. We later found out it was a Mint Vienetta she had put in the blender.

When my youngest sister Ella was five, she was sent for an interview at the posh private school down the road. When they asked her what she wanted to be when she grew up, she said: 'A hound.' Suffice to say, she did not get in. Ella was a mucky, unwashed child – one seemingly shrouded in the distinctive smell of a hamster cage.

My own childhood was punctuated with trying moments and unwelcome aromas. I once pooed myself in an art lesson. Unwilling to admit my shameful excretion, I pretended the smell emanating from my corner of the classroom was in fact coming from my new wooden pencil case. In a desperate attempt to distract my classmates from the truth, I was passing said pencil case around going, 'Oh my god, smell my new pencil case, it smells just like poo.' They played along, but they all knew the truth. My plan had a singular but ultimately fatal flaw: I had failed to consider that wooden pencil cases do not actually smell of human faeces. So near, yet so far. Oh Icarus, you flew too close to the sun.

Monkeys weren't the only animal causing me grief. In 2012, when I was fourteen years old, the family dog Flora committed suicide by eating an entire bag of salt. Apologies to anyone out there who's upset by that, but it is true. Maybe we should put a sticker that says 'Trigger warning: dog suicide' on the cover. Flora was a beautiful golden retriever, named after the Latin term for flowers rather than the butter-esque spread with which she shared her colouring (and which, ironically enough, is celebrated for its relatively low salt content).

I recognise this is a story that requires some unpacking. Essentially, Flora (also fourteen) was found severely dehydrated with the remnants of a packet of salt scattered around her. She was rushed to the vets, but it was explained that at her age and with her general health in decline, there was only so much they could do (as so often, the 'only so much' constituted a lethal injection). We were devastated. Rose was perhaps most upset of all – not because she had wanted to eat the bag of salt (although given her coal exploits who would put it past her?), but because she had left it at an attainable height on the bottom shelf of the larder.

So why the verdict of suicide? After all, it's not like Flora left a note. Well, the vet calmly explained to my mum that, 'No sane dog would have done this'. He cited a cocktail of dementia and depression. I've spent years pondering it, but to this day I honestly don't know if Flora was depressed. After all she had a sizeable garden, in an idyllic country village, surrounded by perpetually friendly Hare Krishnas. I guess money can't buy happiness. The moral of this story is that middle-class comfort is not always everything it seems.

I got into a few scrapes of my own – just very rarely on purpose. I was born with the trait of being incredibly accident-prone. I know Freud said there are no accidents, but it's worth remembering he never got to spend an extended period of time with me. At times my life has felt like one long game of Mousetrap, an endless assault course, a never-ending slapstick sequence where the joke is squarely on me. At the time of writing, I've got a sore knee from falling accidentally down the stairs, a sore arm from accidentally getting it trapped between a van and a car, and a sore head from accidentally agreeing to write a book. I can't even disembark from a boat safely.

My privileged pursuits were subsequently laced with danger. A skiing holiday to Chamonix in France ended with me spending several days in hospital. I had agreed to race my brother down a slope, declaring that the winner would be the first to touch a particular tree at the foot of the mountain. Suffice to say, I won – emphatically so, finishing with my arms and legs wrapped around the tree in cartoon fashion having collided with it at considerable speed. I spent a couple of days in a French hospital. I remember neck braces and brain scans and a little box television showing endless cycles of international news, the morphine and monotony blurring my recollections. To be honest, I was probably lucky not to be more seriously hurt.

One thing I do remember clearly is being urged by doctors, nurses and my dad not to look in the mirror. This advice would frankly have stood me in good stead throughout my adolescence, but was particularly pertinent in this instance because the top few layers of my skin were still embedded in the bark of that unfortunate tree.* Their intention was to spare me the trauma of that sight. Overcome by curiosity, I staggered to the bathroom in the middle of the night, only to look up at a face which looked, for want of a better description, like an as yet uncooked pizza. When I returned to school a few weeks later, none of the boys would even sit next to me as my face resembled one big scary scab.†

Remarkably, that was not the last time I defaced myself so substantially that I was urged to avoid my own reflection. There was another incident in which I fell off my bike – not in itself particularly noteworthy, children fall off their bikes all the time. As it happens, it was Terry who first 'taught' me to 'ride' my bike. He did this in his own uncompromising fashion: by sitting me on one, then continually pushing me down a hill and shouting at me, until I learned to stay on.

Despite this remarkable education in the art of the bicycle, I still suffered the occasional tumble. I must've been about ten when this particular incident occurred. I came off the bike, and in doing so somehow managed to jab the handlebar into my eye. At this point, and I'm afraid there's no particularly pleasant way to say this, I tore my eyelid in half. I remember being hurried into a toilet so tissue could be applied to stem the flow of blood, and once again being urged to avoid looking in the mirror while plans were made for me to be taken to hospital.

---

* Perhaps millions of years from now, scientists will recreate me by extracting my DNA from chunks of flesh still trapped in the sap.

† This was not helped by the fact that I'd insist on picking and eating it.

I should have listened, but a morbid curiosity once more got the better of me. When I looked in that bathroom mirror, I saw the gory mask that would become Terry's trademark. And how did I react when I saw myself in this state, a bloody reflection of my grandfather's crimson-splashed courage? I immediately fainted. This multitude of mishaps meant that by the time I reached puberty I'd taken more bangs on the head than some professional fighters.

It is said that everybody has their vice. While this expression stems from the Latin word '*vitium*', meaning a failing or defect, it could just as well refer to the unflinching grip it can hold on your life. In both mine and Terry's childhood, the spectre of addiction hung over the household.

Terry's dad was a mechanic but also a chronic gambler – so one way or another, he was always trying to fix stuff. 'He'd bet on anything,' says my grandma. 'It was compulsive, and it was sad. He couldn't control it.'

Dick was a terrible gambler, in every respect: he did it a lot and he won very little. He'd place a wager on any contest, but it was the greyhounds that really got their teeth into him. If he wasn't gambling, he was spending money rearing or training potential winners. It was an obsession that toppled over into addiction, one costly in every respect.

Both my parents became addicts too. Perhaps in a childhood where I was privileged to have so much, it was inevitable we'd encounter the issue of excess. For my mum and dad it wasn't the dogs, but booze. Both parents, in succession, crossed the line from social into dangerous drinking. The bucolic setting of my childhood was marred by an alcoholic scourge. As much as my life may sound like a succession of hilarious scrapes, there have been harder times too. Perhaps it's those moments that forge the comic instinct. The act of reframing your life as a comedy is, in part, a way of disguising the pain. A friend once told me he believed that funny things just happen to me. Maybe that's true. Maybe it is some sort of comedy curse. More likely, it's because I seek to consciously foreground the funny in the narrative of my life. I shine a light on the stupidity to detract from the darkness.

The young Terry and I both lived in the shadow of that chaos, that uncertainty, that shame. A natural response is to apply self-discipline, to exert control on your own life. The rigorous training schedule Terry adopted from his earliest days suggests someone seeking order, rules, structure – perhaps that's what ultimately drew him to the military, too.

My way of imposing discipline was to be voluntarily teetotal until the age of twenty-four. I guess I lived with the fear that I was an alcoholic-in-waiting. Having addicts as parents is unnerving – you live your life waiting for that all-conquering craving to kick in. Terry, for his part, was always very wary of gambling. He even opened a chain of betting shops, so mindful was he of the fact that the bookie always wins. As it happens, I'm still waiting to find out what it is I'm addicted to. Current contenders are Ginger Nuts, Options Hot Chocolate, and TV's *Homes Under The Hammer*.

Having two addicts as parents did feel like bad luck, I'll admit a – jab-hook combo that offered little respite. It was my dad, Barry, who confronted and then exorcised his demons first, getting sober thanks to some professional help when I was in my mid-teens. His sobriety came at a price for the family unit: as is often the case, his personal journey saw him drift away and ultimately separate from my mum, whose drinking then became problematic in its own right.

I honestly don't know if she always had a problem and my dad's drinking obscured it, or whether their subsequent divorce drove her to that point. I remember the feeling of exhaustion, having shown patience and forbearance with one parent as we helped them back to health, of having to undergo the same process again. It was arguably all the more difficult the second time around too. There was a vulnerability to my mum that was never quite present in my dad. I was occasionally scared of him, but constantly scared for her. I lived in fear that she would kill herself – not because I was paranoid, but because, in her despair, she frequently told me she would. I remember my therapist's face when I casually told her that, while still at school, I'd regularly check on my mum in her bed in the morning, not entirely sure whether she'd be alive or dead.

Where I can identify most clearly with Terry is that the responsible adult in my home was not always a particularly responsible adult. Addiction has a way of subverting priorities: having a drink, or having a bet, comes first. Inevitably, that has knock-on consequences for any kids in that environment.

Some literature in the field suggests that the children of addicts 'become approval-seekers who lose their identities while trying to please others – not feeling that they are getting adequate support at home in childhood may lead to an ongoing need for praise from others in adulthood. It may even become more important to be liked than to be authentic to oneself.' Could that hunger for recognition drive someone to become a world champion or, even more preposterously, a professional comedian? I couldn't possibly comment.

It wasn't all bleak. People hear the term 'alcoholism' and

certain associated images come to mind: a man alone at a bar, a vodka bottle under the desk. What they don't tell you about is some of the absurdity: trying to boil an egg in the microwave; breaking down crying at the beauty of Frank Bruno's world-title win. At one stage I swear my mum got stuck in a rut where she served us chicken kiev every day for a year. She served it with Alphabites or, if we were lucky, potato smiley-faces. But they were the only smiley faces in our house.

The same delirium applied to Dick's gambling. A familiar family anecdote tells of when Terry's parents had a three-piece suite delivered, only for his dad to sell it to fund his gambling habit before they'd even had a chance to sit on it. His wife Hilda was devastated and furious in equal measure – but there is a comic bathos to it all. Growing up in a house like that, you certainly learn to find the funny. So much comedy is born of trauma. Terry was one of the most naturally funny people I've known.

As I've already mentioned, I've been going to therapy. It's fine, I'm going to charge it all to the publishers, because most of the time has been me talking about this book. It won't come as any great surprise to learn I approach the sessions from a somewhat performative perspective. In Lockdown London, those sixty minutes have been the closest I've come to doing a proper gig. During one such session, I recently asked my therapist if there was anything she was hoping for me to say I hadn't said yet. The insecurity of the performer there, evident even in a situation where I am literally paying the audience to attend. What she said in response took me aback: 'I'm waiting for you to get really angry with your parents.'

It feels like she'll be waiting a long while. Any burning resentment that was there has long since fizzled out. I like my parents – and I really respect how they've managed to exorcise their demons. After all, I love a comeback story.

I bear no grudges. Their actions were the consequence of illness, not ill will. Dad is a gentler, happier man than ever. The manner in which he has seized control of his life is remarkable. My mum too seems more content and more whole than she has ever been. She is someone who struggles with boundaries; who doesn't know when to stop. Like Dick, her use of family finances was at times questionable: she once spent more than £40 trying to save *Big Brother*'s Jon Tickle from eviction. But she is also someone who is incapable of partitioning her love, who cannot help but give. There is kindness even in her flaws.

What's interesting is that, despite his travails, Terry's father remained his hero throughout his life. There was no one whose approval he sought more vehemently; no one who inspired him to greater feats. He feared him and revered him.

I've never felt quite like that about either of my parents. I love them, and admire them, but the conventional hierarchy is not intact. I have seen them too low, too broken, too human. I've come to understand them as people, rather than venerate them as idols. The pedestal has crumbled. In a sense I have come to know them too well. That nigh-mythical status, that hero worship has, until now, been reserved for Terry.

IN MY CORNER

Between each round, between merciful bells and heavy breaths, the fighter retreats to his corner. It's an opportunity for the trainer to check in with his charge – to make sure he's still focussed, still in the game, that he hasn't quite glazed over, and that he still wishes to go on. Helpfully, this space provides me with a chance to do the same with my reader.

This is the place where cuts and scrapes are attended to, where Vaseline is liberally applied to eyebrows already slick with blood. It's where fighters are patched up before being pushed back out into combat, futile instructions yelled into sore, swelling ears. And it's here that I will deal with how I began to patch myself up; to tell the story of how I set about dealing with the physical and mental blows dealt to me on that boat in Sri Lanka.

The first step I took was perhaps the most obvious: I went to see a doctor. They fobbed me off with some painkillers and seasickness tablets. Even as he wrote out the prescription, I knew they would not work. After all, it wasn't the sea making me sick – it was the land.

The next leg of our journey saw us head north from the coast towards Kandy, camped among the misty hills in the centre of the island. Here we stayed at a place called the Samadhi Centre, a leafy retreat that rises up out of the surrounding forests. You enter through a huge stone doorway, guarded by a statue of a Hindi goddess, half-woman and half-horse, an equine beauty hewn from stone. From there, steps lead you up towards thirteen linked pavilions, each leaning out of the hillside. It is a miniature town among the trees, populated by friendly staff and, somewhat terrifyingly for me, a good few monkeys.

The Samadhi Centre is a temple of tranquillity, and consequently an obvious retreat for artists and creatives. In our time there, we befriended a woman who was writing a book about her own family. The thought, at that point, could not have been further from my mind. My brain ached so acutely that I had enough trouble stringing together a coherent sentence.

This hillside haven did, however, provide some welcome respite. There was no television, no alcohol, and the kind of faint, intermittent Wi-Fi that, for a customer of Virgin Broadband, provided a flavour of home. There were no sounds other than the chirping of crickets and the distant hum of a waterfall. If there was a place where my mind might settle down, might somehow recalibrate itself, then this was surely it.

There was also a medicinal dimension to the retreat. Upon arrival, you meet with a doctor who is a practitioner in Ayurveda, the alternative medicine system that has thrived in the Indian sub-continent for more than 5,000 years. 'Ayurveda' is a Sanskrit word, with a meaning roughly equivalent to 'knowledge of life and longevity'. The practice is dedicated to the holistic treatment of mind, body and spirit. The theory goes that in order to be truly healthy, the patient must achieve equilibrium among the dosas – the three substances that are believed to be present in a person's body: vata, pitta and kaffa – loosely wind, bile and phlegm. This is similar to the European idea of 'the humours'. Essentially, it's all about balance – and for a man who could barely walk ten yards without feeling like the world might capsize, that held an obvious appeal.

The doctor asks you if you're suffering with any illness. I said I thought I might be, but I couldn't be sure. If I was it was unlike any I'd ever experienced. They take you through a long questionnaire which includes queries about your dietary tendencies and defecation habits. They then prescribe a course of 'treatment' – effectively a controlled vegetarian diet and some unusual types of massage. In the shirodhara, medicated oil is poured slowly over the forehead – think of it as the Ayurvedic equivalent to petroleum jelly in a gash. In the swedhanam, you're effectively encased in a box while the body is given a herbal steam bath. They tried to talk me into a virechanam treatment, essentially an Ayurvedic colonic, but that was a bridge too far even for me. Call me a cynic, but I didn't see how clearing out my bowel would clear out my head.

It's worth saying that Ayurveda, like many alternative treatments, is considered by modern medicine to be pseudoscientific. Western science regards its practices as quackery. However, it has been reported that around sixty to seventy per cent of Sri Lanka's population still rely on traditional, natural methods such as Ayurveda for their primary health care. What's more, I was desperate enough for my customary scepticism to be overcome. What was happening to me felt so out of the ordinary, so supernatural, that I was open to anything as a potential cure. Having politely declined the hippy laxatives, I went ahead with the massages, and the diet – after all, everyone loves a massage, and veggie curries are famously delicious.

And the food was lovely, and the massages were largely pleasant, even if the drip-drip of oil onto the forehead during the shirodhara does bear a striking resemblance to Chinese water torture. My pulse slowed, my muscles relaxed, yet at the end of my week-long stay, I was no closer to finding the balance I craved. I had been soothed but not cured, and now more challenges lay ahead of me – more journeys, more trains, more planes. I had the bustle of India to contend with, where I would go on to enjoy the quintessential Indian experience by shitting myself in the Taj Mahal.

I returned to the UK, and in the weeks and months that followed had countless people recommend alternative treat-ments – everything from acupuncture to yoga, craniosacral therapy through to reiki. I gave most of it a whirl. For someone who didn't take either biology or chemistry through to GCSE, I am surpris-ingly committed to science – but my experiences seemed to defy logic, so I was open to the idea that the solution might too. I tried meditation, downloading that app with the nice voice, but it didn't work for me. I didn't want to be present, I didn't want to be here in the now and, above all else, I didn't want to be in my useless body. I wanted to be back in the summer of 2017, about to get married, ideally in the body of Dwayne 'The Rock' Johnson.

None of these methods provided anything other than tem-porary relief; at best they were pleasantly distracting, never decisively purgative. Meanwhile, I was getting worse. I'd hoped that returning to home soil would steady the shifting ground beneath me, but I was more unstable than ever. Physically and emotionally, it felt as if I was caught in quicksand.

I was still staggering around – vision blurry, ears ringing, temples pulsing – like a fighter who'd been caught with a big right hand and hadn't yet recovered. Any respite I received was temporary, and before long, life's bell rang out again, and I stumbled back out into the fight.

Round Two

EVACUATION

The drive from London to Cornwall is one flanked with incongruity.

In one respect, the A303 appears to take you back in time. Once you break free of the Home Counties, the conurbations dissolve into countryside. At one point, you even pass Stonehenge – a set of perfectly arranged monumental milestones to chart your journey through the ages.

You also pass, however, more than one Starbucks. Quite a few in fact: on this journey I count as many as four. Just as the monoliths at Stonehenge have been delicately placed to align with the movements of the sun, so the mighty conglomerate has intelligently deployed its drive-through coffee shops, to synchronise with the stomachs and bladders of the A303's drivers. There are also several branches of Greggs, two Costas and a Costcutter – a cavalcade of consumerism lining this road that stretches out into the past.

I am en route to Newbridge, a tiny hamlet in the west of Cornwall, around nine miles from the very end of Land's End.

It is the same journey Terry would have made, albeit with less frequent access to a frappuccino, in 1940. For my grandfather's childhood did not take place exclusively in London. When the man he referred to in his autobiography as 'that mug Hitler' set about starting World War Two, the boy from West London was uprooted to the most westerly point of this isle.

Now of course, I have never been evacuated from the place I called home to escape the threat of bombing. I was however sent on a week-long French exchange trip by my school – and my hypothesis is that these two events were essentially identical.

Much like on a French exchange, evacuees experienced tearful farewells, before being ushered onto cramped transport, and then subjected to regular roll calls as they saw the comfort of home disappear into the distance. Much like on a French exchange, the parents of evacuees were issued with a list of items all children had to take with them, delicately labelled and yet doomed to be lost. And much like on a French exchange, children were packed off to somewhere with food that they didn't like and accents they didn't understand. As I think back to the feeling of being stranded in Strasbourg,* attempting to make polite conversation in a language I categorically could not speak, I can almost feel Terry's spirit move within me.

It is claimed that the mass evacuation of World War Two remains the single greatest mobilisation of the urban public in British history. Anyone who says that clearly didn't witness Mrs Robson attempting to assure the safe passage of my Year Ten French class to Alsace. That is surely a feat of human organisation that will remain unsurpassed.

---

* Incidentally, 'Stranded in Strasbourg' was one of my alternative titles for this memoir.

Maybe there are some among you reading this thinking how horribly entitled it is to talk about such a horizon-expanding trip with such a negative taint. Perhaps you think, had you only had the opportunity, you would have loved to go on a French exchange.

You are wrong. At least the evacuees enjoyed the mercy of remaining in a country they knew and understood. To comprehend the full horror of my plight, you have to remember this was the early Noughties, when globalisation was still in its infancy. It's not even like I could shelter in the familiar embrace of a Starbucks. I was a stranger in an alien world. The Austrian philosopher Ludwig Wittgenstein once said that if a lion could talk English, we still could not understand each other, as the frames of reference would be so different. That was broadly how I felt about the prospect of talking to a bunch of French teenagers. What's more, lest we forget, I was still emotionally reeling from a tragic episode of canine suicide.

More of that anon. Terry, I am sure, must have felt similarly displaced. At three years old, he was settling into life at his tin-roofed nursery school on Harrow Road, when that moustachioed mug started ramping up things in Germany, and Britain began preparing for the horrid inevitability of a second world war.

The Government evacuation scheme was first developed in the summer of 1938. It involved the nation being divided into three zones: 'evacuation', 'neutral' and 'reception'. The parallels with the British government's tripartite response to the second wave of coronavirus are, frankly, unavoidable. As Terry lived in a built-up area, close to amenities like hospitals and of course the train station, his neighbourhood was very much a 'Tier 3' concern.

Over 100,000 teachers were tasked with gathering millions of children and transporting them out of London to the seeming safety of the countryside. This mass migration was referred to as 'Operation Pied Piper' – a questionable choice of name given that in the associated legend the titular character uses his pipe-playing powers to abduct and effectively murder a town's entire child population. He isn't a good guy; he's a creep with a recorder and a vendetta. They might as well have called it 'Operation paedo-with-a-whistle'.

Schools went as far as staging rehearsals for the eventual evacuation, offering children lessons on why it was important not to cry and how to wave goodbye, even specifying that clean hankies were preferred. Parents faced agonising decisions on whether to stick or twist; a game of chance where the stakes could not have been higher. My grandma Barbara is very proud of the fact that her family remained in London throughout the Blitz, although the fact they survived is arguably as much down to luck as judgement.

Terry's family took a more conservative approach, and arrangements were made for the children in the Downes family to move en masse to Cornwall. Paddington itself became a bit of a hub for the evacuation programme, catapulting kids from the train station out into the wilderness of the west.

It was in the early hours of 1 September 1939 that the Government's plans for evacuation swung into action. The majority of schools, teachers and mothers were moved before the war was formally declared on 3 September. Two weeks later Mr James Ede, the MP for Southshields, told Parliament that 'we have during the past few days seen the most remarkable movement of the civil population ever recorded in history'.

When the decision was taken for the Downes children to leave

London, they did so as one – a rag-tag bunch of kids being shunted out as near to nowhere as possible. 'One push, and we'd all be in the sea,' as Terry used to say. For kids used to shuttling a couple of stations along the tube, the train journey would have felt impossibly long. Cornwall must have seemed another world to them, rife with exoticism. Tucked away on a southwesterly peninsula and seemingly defined by a pastry, Cornwall is very much the Portugal of England. It's difficult to imagine how a cockney kid from the smoke would have coped in Cornwall, just as it's difficult to imagine the nightmarishly mangled accent they would eventually return with.

Terence Frisby, the playwright, was evacuated from his home in Kent to Dobwalls in Cornwall, about sixty miles inland from where my grandfather was based. In his book *Kisses on a Postcard*, he writes: 'About sixty of us were herded into the centre of the main schoolroom, and the villagers crowded in after us and stood round the walls. What a scene, this auction of children with no money involved. The villagers slowly circled us and picked the most likely looking. They used phrases strange to us in thick accents we could barely understand. "Hallo my beauty", "There 'y're me handsome." "What be your name then?" "This one here will do."

'Inhuman as it could all be judged now, I can think of no quicker, better way of dispersing us. At least our new guardians were given some sort of choice in who was going to share their homes, even if the children were not.'

I find these accounts of families picking children out of a line-up – identifying the ones that looked most handsome, healthy or helpful – absolutely terrifying. Thankfully I didn't suffer that humiliation on the French exchange. It's a sense of peril I have only really experienced in the school playground when captains set about picking football teams. While I have grown to love football, I adopted it late. My mum remembers taking me and my brother to play for a local team, and us insisting in playing central defence together – not because of our intuitive tactical understanding, but so we could hold hands. I don't know precisely how old we were, but if I had to hazard a guess, I'd say it could be anywhere between the ages of four and seventeen.

Part of the reason I was so bad at sport is that for much of my childhood I was very overweight. I remember when I was about thirteen, my school PE teacher Mr Long told me that if I 'carried on like this' he expected me to be dead by the time I was twenty-three. I'd love to say I lost weight thanks to self-discipline and hard work – in reality, the true catalyst to my body transformation was my parents' divorce. They separated when I was seventeen, sending me into a six-week stupor from which I emerged substantially thinner, largely due to having forgotten to eat. Even then, I knew that was not an optimal or healthy way to lose weight, but it provided me with a little kick in the right direction. It got the big round ball rolling.

Strangely, in what was to become something of a forerunner for how their relationship would play out, Terry and his sister Sylvia were separated. Instead, Terry was housed with his cousin – although fortunately the Downes generation were largely living within walking distance of each other. The little village was overrun. A new dawn had come to Newbridge, one greeted with the chirping of cheeky cockney children.

At least there, they were out of the firing line. Terry's time in Cornwall is reminiscent of my own upbringing in Hertfordshire, where the closest we got to hearing an air-raid siren was the faint tinkle of an ice-cream van on the wind. I'm not sure how

I would have handled being similarly uprooted from everything I knew. I didn't like leaving home much. My mum and dad used to threaten me with going to boarding school, which may be the most privileged 'threat' imaginable. 'You better behave yourself or you'll be sent to an elitist establishment almost guaranteed to improve your career prospects!' 'No, please!' I'd shout. 'I don't want to be Prime Minister!'

For some in wartime Britain, the fear of separation out-weighed the fear of being bombed. There are reports of children who walked fifty miles in an attempt to return home. Occasionally parents' resolve would break, and they'd bring their children back to London – only for tragic consequences to follow. On 20 September 1944, *The Times* reported: 'Children who had only just returned from evacuation were among those killed by flying bombs which were sent over the southern counties, including the London area yesterday. Two months ago, when flying bomb attacks showed no sign of slackening, a little girl named Margaret, aged five, and her two sisters were evacuated from their home in southern England to Birmingham. Then a few days ago the menace seemed to be ending and their parents, who now had also a baby boy, decided to bring the children home. On Friday there was a family reunion. Now only Margaret is alive. The others were killed while they slept.'

Even for children who stayed clear of the major cities, there was no guarantee of safety. On Sunday 30 July 1944, two boys were killed when they climbed through barbed-wire fencing into an anti-tank minefield on a beach near Gunwallow in Cornwall – just twenty-five miles around the bay from where Terry was staying.

✳   ✳   ✳

I am, by nature, a homebody. My school was within walking distance of my house. Even when I eventually went to university, I chose University College London, a mere twenty-five minutes by train from my Hertfordshire home.

I'm the sort of person who, when they arrive at a holiday destination, immediately turns on the TV to see what English channels they have.* I become instantly sentimental about reminders of home, watching BBC World News on loop and trawling Spanish supermarkets in search of Marmite. I measure the exoticism of a destination by how difficult it is to acquire a full English breakfast.

It's not that I'm a ferocious nationalist – this sentimental homesickness is generally a temporary state. I don't think I'd end up like one of those people who moves to the south of Spain but spends their time exclusively watching English football, eating English food, drinking English beer and attempting to alter their skin colour to better reflect the lobster red and tan-line white of the St George's flag. I just love the comfort of the familiar.

And so a French exchange – a trip abroad, without my family – was therefore a daunting prospect for me. My first worry was the food. At this time, I was widely regarded as one of the fussiest eaters in Europe. I had a decidedly anti-EU palette. You are reading the words of a man who claimed, until the age of eighteen, that he did not like pasta.

The list of food I've taken against is a long one. It includes tomatoes, mushrooms, strawberries. At one point I claimed to be allergic to bananas just to avoid questions over why I

* Perhaps out of some latent nostalgia for that heady period recovering in a French hospital.

refused to eat one. At the time of writing, I have still never eaten a pear.

Consequently, the very prospect of a week with only access to home-cooked French cuisine was enough to fill me with dread. As far as I could tell, the French were obsessed with eating things more conventionally found in a witches' brew: frogs' legs, snails, quiche Lorraine. I vaguely remember my mum giving me a pack of Mars bars before we departed. I distinctly remember eating them all before we even arrived.

My issue, by and large, was texture – or, as the French say, 'texture'. I didn't object to the taste of most of these things – in truth, I either couldn't remember what they tasted like or simply didn't know. It was a suspected squishiness that I found so off-putting. I remember watching in horror as Terry gulped down his beloved jellied eels.

The exchange saw me paired up with a boy from Strasbourg called Edouard. Edouard was like me in every way, except he was French, handsome, thin, spoke several languages, and wasn't afraid of girls. Picture, if you will, an adolescent Arsene Wenger. His parents owned the Meteor brewery in Strasbourg. As far as some of my mates were concerned, I'd hit the jackpot: a wealthy family putting me up in a big house, and as much beer as I could drink.

At this time, as you know, I did not drink – not because I was obsessed with dutifully following the letter of the law, but because of my parents' alcoholism. I felt sure that if so much as a drop of alcohol passed my lips, I would undergo a horrific transformation from Dr Jekyll to Mr High-dependency.

There was also the language to contend with. Edouard's English was immaculate, whereas I was out of my depth in French as soon as I had to ask for anything other than directions to the *bibliothèque*. For some reason, the main phrase I seem to recall covering in French lessons at school is '*le petit cheval est sous la table*'. It rolls off the tongue beautifully. Unfortunately, what it means is 'the little horse is under the table', which is often difficult to work into a conversation.

Anyway, during this French exchange, all the English and francophone kids went to a big house party. Now here was where *la merde* hit the proverbial fan. While I attended a boys' school, Edouard was, in classical Euroliberal fashion, at a mixed school.

It's not that I never encountered girls – I had two sisters, and the boys' school I attended neighboured a girls' school. While lessons were separate, we would mix for extra-curricular activities (hence the considerable lure of a school play) and at lunchtimes. The two schools were separated by a pair of wrought-iron gates, and so it became customary to arrange to meet a group of girls 'at the black gates' – an activity which sounded to me every bit as intimidating as being asked to enter Mordor.

On one such occasion, I reluctantly agreed to accompany a fellowship of friends on the quest to the black gates. Like the certified stud I was, I had taken some unfinished chemistry homework with me to complete during the lunch break. At some point, a girl called Zosha playfully snatched my answer-sheet away from me and pretended to put it in the bin. On reflection, this was potentially an early attempt at something like flirting. My response? To burst into tears and angrily call her 'a bastard'.

I was never good with girls. I say that: I had friends who were girls, but no girlfriends. As a flamboyant theatre kid with long hair, I think it was generally assumed that I was gay. In fact, I was one of the few people I know who had to come out as heterosexual. The first time I admitted I liked a girl, it was greeted like a titillating novelty. People were shocked.

If I was bad at talking to girls in English, imagine me in French. It was a nightmare: none of them knew where the library was, or why the little horse was under the table.

I do however remember France, and specifically that house party, for the first compliment I ever received from a member of the opposite sex. I was fifteen at the time and had adopted a dress sense that is best described as 'circus chic': baggy patterned trousers, huge black shoes with spikes on, topped off with a flowing perm that cascaded over my shoulders like recycling escaping an overflowing wheelie bin. I thought I looked like Jesus; I actually looked like Krusty the Clown. Strangely enough, photographic evidence suggests Terry briefly adopted a similar look in the 1970s, when it was arguably substantially more appropriate.

Anyway, France did not know what had hit it. As far as they were concerned, I had strutted straight off the London catwalk and into Strasbourg's cobbled streets. I was, for that brief period, an icon. If there followed a period of appalling fashion among the youth of Alsace shortly after 2002, I apologise – it's entirely my fault.

For my entire adult life, I've treasured the moment one teenage French girl remarked with an intake of breath, 'Quel look!'

This translates roughly as 'Wow, what a look!'

'Finally,' I thought, 'Someone who gets me.'

Writing that now, it strikes me that perhaps a degree of irony may have been lost in translation. Either way, the damage was done: what I'd taken as a compliment strengthened my resolve. The hair got bigger, the trousers got baggier, the jewellery got banglier. The best way I can sum up my dress sense in this period is to suggest imagining what might happen if Stephen King's It got into LSD.

Of course, I am grateful for the generosity Edouard *et la famille* showed in welcoming this awkward, antisocial child into their home. In that, there are echoes of the spirit of camaraderie than underpinned the evacuation project. In his book, a grateful Terence Frisby wrote: 'Ten shillings a week per evacuee was the official allowance, and in return they'd given themselves without stint. Was there ever such a bargain? They were without guile and without self-interest. The salt of the earth, is the saying.'

After visiting their children, one group of London mothers from East Ham placed a letter in a local newspaper to thank the families of Truro for the hospitality they'd shown the evacuees:

'After visiting our children on 3 August we must send at once our heartfelt thanks and appreciation for all that the mothers of Cornwall are doing to mother our children. We all noticed how clean, well-kept and happy the children all were and how well they looked. We also wish to thank the foster mothers for the kind way they welcomed us into their homes and looked after our welfare until we had to leave. We are sure the time will come when we can repay the hospitality.'

But of course, the difference with the French exchange is that there is a guaranteed, fixed appointment to 'repay the hospitality'. Edouard's family weren't acting entirely 'without self-interest' – they knew that in just a few months' time, he would return to visit me in London. My positive experience in France was effectively a down payment on his stay in the Home Counties.

It felt as if almost as soon as I was home from Strasbourg, the tables were turned and I was playing host in London. I was only in my early teens, but I remember being embarrassed by the banality of my life. I went to school, played Playstation and consumed white bread products. Even then, I felt self-conscious about seeming somehow ordinary.

I did my best to be a good host, even if it goes against every antisocial instinct I have. I took him to Camden, the sort of place that feels very 'London' and yet isn't very much like the rest of London at all. It's almost a theme park, like trying to suggest EuroDisney is somehow typical of Paris. Still, I showed him where I bought my ridiculous clothes. He took a suitcase full back to Strasbourg. 'Quel look' indeed.

Despite everything, I hope Edouard reflects on his time in England fondly. I doubt he remembers very much at all. If anything, he may remember a Sunday roast we had when my whole family got together. On that day, he met a world champion.

The Downes kids flooded tiny Newbridge. I remember Terry talking about his memories of his time there. His primary concern was the food. He insisted the people of Cornwall subsisted on a diet consisting entirely of 'cold custard, or bread and jam'. The memory stayed with him: if we misbehaved as children, he'd threaten to put us on the same rations. Frankly, as a kid with a sweet tooth, that sounded alright by me.

After a few weeks, Terry began to acclimatise. The sea air washed the smoke away from his lungs, and his ear attuned to the bewildering accent. One day, Terry and Sylvie were out peering into a shop window, when they spotted their mum asking some strangers if they'd seen a couple of cockney kids knocking about. Terry cried out to Hilda, and the happy trio were reunited. No mobiles, no Google Maps, just taking a chance and having a chat was enough to unite the family.

As soon as they were together again, it was immediately clear to all of them that this separation lark had to stop, even if it wasn't yet safe to return to London. And so they hatched a plan: they had taken the boy out of the city; now it was time to bring the city to the boy. Terry's mum and aunt went off to talk to a local farmer about taking over the farmhouse. If there's one thing cockneys can do, it's talk, and before long thirty-odd Downes children (and a few parents besides) were living under one roof on a farm called Higher Tregerest.

Higher Tregerest is no longer a functional farm. The farmhouse and outbuildings have been converted into homes – and one barn in particular, I am delighted to discover, into a bed and breakfast for passing tourists.

It is there I am headed for the weekend, to stay in the very place where my grandfather lodged during the Second World War. I know I will be hosted by Trudi and Scott, but don't discover their surname until I spot the sign at the entrance to their drive.

When I do, I double-take: the sign reads 'LOWNDES' – eerily close to an anagram of Terry's family name. Take away the 'L' for London, jumble the letters up a bit, and you've got everything you need to spell out 'DOWNES' – the name of the evacuees who briefly called this place home.

I'm instantly glad I came. It's difficult to imagine how strange and shocking the countryside must have been for Terry, until you experience the juxtaposition for yourself. Although I have lived in London for more than fifteen years, I grew up surrounded by greenery – yet even to me the space and the tranquillity is startling. This could not be further away from the smoky, swarming environment Terry would have known. From the farm, fields spill away towards the sea, the only blight on the vista the telephone wires that run like some cable car down to the ocean. It was the beauty of the West Country that inspired William Blake, another Londoner, to pen the lyrics to *Jerusalem* – to ponder whether Christ's sacred feet had ever walked upon England's green and pleasant land.*

The past is somehow tangible here; the speed of change seems slower than in the cities. History is behind every hedgerow. Records show that a farming settlement has existed at Tregerest since 1302. Two miles away is Bosullow Trehyllys, a small settlement of houses from the fifth or sixth century, arranged around the Iron Age fort of Chun Castle.

Within walking distance are two chambered tombs or 'quoits' from the Neolithic period – Chun Quoit and Lanyon Quoit. These huge stone structures resemble great granite toadstools, with one huge boulder laid horizontally across other vertical rocks to form an enclosed space. They are believed to have been used for burials or religious rituals, and date from 3000-1500 BC. In another direction lies the Tregeseal Stone Circle, another Bronze Age relic that has inspired tales of meddling fairy folk.

At the B&B, the history on show is more recent: tucked into the welcome booklet is a DVD documenting the lives of William and Rene Tregear, the last people to work the land

---

* Incidentally, *Jerusalem* was also my school hymn – I suppose if Jesus had got all the way from Jerusalem to Cornwall, then practically speaking the chances are he might well have come via Hertfordshire.

here using traditional methods. Filmed in the 1970s, the grainy footage still feels an age ago.

The barn I am staying in would once have been the threshing shed for the farm. The garden, where once stacks of corn would have been kept, is now decorated with trinkets collected from a life of travelling.

Trudi and Scott, originally from Manchester, say they try to live as sustainably as they can. They have their own water supply from a borehole, which taps into the aquifers 100 feet down – 'The water pressure doesn't stretch to a power shower,' Trudi tells me. 'But the taste more than makes up for it.'* The slates from their old roof have become raised beds for the vegetable patch, a copper hot-water tank has become a flower container, as has the stainless-steel drum from a disused washing machine. They keep two Arab horses and a Shetland pony, almost a nod to the multiculturalism of modern Paddington.

They say their neighbours have spoken about evacuees living on the farm during the war, but they don't know the specifics. I stroll up to the old farmhouse, peering in at windows, wondering which of the little rooms might once have been Terry's. At breakfast I have bread and jam: a tribute to the food Pop ate as a boy, and subsequently spent the better part of a century complaining about.

I nip down to Newbridge. To call it a village would be a vast exaggeration – even a hamlet feels generous. It makes Letchmore Heath feel like London. It is difficult to overestimate how foreign this would all have felt to Terry's eyes, to his lungs. In this world war, he was a world away from everything he knew.

I visit Cornwall on the weekend that would have marked

---

* Obviously, like all water, it tastes of nothing.

Terry's 85th birthday. When I wake up on Sunday 9 May 2021, I see that my grandma has posted on her Facebook wall: 'Miss you x Love you x Happily heavenly birthday.'

Although comfortably into her eighties herself, Barbara is pretty handy on social media. She has an iPad which increasingly represents her window on the world. Predominantly she has used it to play FarmVille, an agriculture-simulation game which was released in 2009. More than once she's told me she needed to get off the phone so she could 'go and feed her sheep'. At one point, FarmVille had more than 34.5 million active users. In the decade following its launch, the number of players steadily declined. By 2020 it was pretty much just my grandma, building her huge farming empire in a world bereft of competition, herding thousands upon thousands of sheep and harvesting tonne upon tonne of grain. Next to her sprawling fiefdom, Higher Tregerest begins to feel somewhat inconsequential.

As has become tradition, I call her up to see how she's handling Terry's birthday. 'I'm alright,' she says. 'It's harder because of how he was on birthdays. He was such a nutter, he loved all the fuss. He loved a day that was all about him.'

I go for a final walk around Newbridge, then head back to the B&B. As I pack my things, the BBC local news broadcast runs a story about two beachgoers spotting a pair of killer whales swimming off the Cornish coast.

Maybe I hadn't even needed to go all the way to Sri Lanka after all. Fuck.

Having been a regular soldier during peacetime, Terry's dad Dick was unsurprisingly called into action when the war broke out. He joined the REME (Royal Electrical and Mechanical Engineers), and spent some time serving in Africa and Italy. Being separated from the family can't have been easy. After all, this was the olden days: you couldn't just WhatsApp your dad a TikTok dance or Uber Eats a letter home. When they were on home soil, Dick and his brothers would creep out of their barracks and hitchhike down to Cornwall in the dead of night, just for a glimpse of their kids. It's a truism that for cockneys, family comes first.

All in all, Hilda, Terry and Sylvie spent the best part of a year in Cornwall. I'm sure they adjusted. It is, after all, an area of spectacular natural beauty. Prior to the war, the only animals Terry and Sylvie would have encountered would have been dogs, cats and pigeons. Thanks to their evacuation, they would have been able to add to their scrapbook such exotic creatures as cows and sheep.

Despite all this excitement, they did decide to return to London. There's only so many pasties you can eat before you long for the slither of an eel down your throat. The war was still raging at this point – if anything the worst bombing was still to come – but the family opted to take their chances and moved back to Westbourne Terrace. The degree of risk was emphasised when a bomb landed just a few streets away, the force of the impact sending Terry's mum Hilda tumbling down the stairs.

Returning to London was no guarantee of happiness. One evacuee, Dorothy King, did not experience the elation she had anticipated. 'It wasn't the joyous homecoming I'd waited for over all the years. Our school building had been bombed and we had to make do with inadequate, patched-up classrooms. Our homes were shabby with war damage and neglect.'*

This was not the London people had left behind. This was

---

* Gillian Mawson, 2020, *Britain's Wartime Evacuees*, Frontline Books, UK

a London ravaged by war and collapsing into recession. As Terry stepped off the train, the familiar sights of Paddington scorched and scarred, perhaps there flickered in him the dream of something better. His childhood had not been one of great hardship, but now circumstance had destroyed much of what he had known. Perhaps it was in that moment Terry sensed that his destiny might lie, quite literally, in his own hands. Somehow, amid the debris, he saw a way forward.

I did not return from Strasbourg with the same degree of clarity. My parents' divorce was not far away, an unexploded bomb still buried beneath the surface, bringing with it the implosion of our family life. Even now as I sift through the wreckage of my adolescence, I find it difficult to pinpoint a direction. I had privilege but no plan. For all my big hair and swollen body, I felt small. For all I had, I felt lost. Also, I was still incredibly bad at French.

And yet, as he arrived back in London, Terry's path was becoming clearer and clearer. A generation returned to a capital full of rubble and bereft of job prospects. What else to do, then, but fight your way out? What else to do but be a boxer?

IN MY CORNER

I remember describing my symptoms to a friend: the phantom motion, the excruciating headaches, the sensitivity to noise and light. And I remember them looking at me and asking politely, carefully, if I had considered the following: 'Maybe it's all in your head?'

While they may have been the only one to ask, I sincerely doubt they were the only ones to think it. I'm blessed with an overactive imagination and a propensity towards anxiety – it was undoubtedly a very reasonable question. In fact, it's one I asked myself time and time again, almost wishing for my experience to be some dark fantasy conjured from the recesses of my subconscious, a nightmare from which it might be possible to wake. I'd begun to hear of people who had suffered with similar symptoms and then experienced 'spontaneous remission' – an instant and unexplained subsiding of the waves. Every night I went to bed hoping that tomorrow might be the day. It is a horrible thing to wake up every morning, disappointed. I felt that way for months and months.

And here's the thing: as more time passed, I became increasingly convinced it was 'all in my head'. After all, that's where the pain emanated from. Whatever was affecting my relationship with the world, I figured, it was most likely my inner ear, my eyes or my brain. The symptoms were all emanating from the neck up.

It's wild when you start to distrust the very part of your corporeal form where your personality, your essence, your being is contained. Your head is essentially you, right? It's got the face, it's got the brain – all the key stuff. You wouldn't recognise many people without one. The bit that was most fundamentally me was going fundamentally wrong.

And sometimes, I'll admit, I wondered whether perhaps this was all a fiction. Or worse, was it somehow self-inflicted? Perhaps my symptoms were simply a figment of my depraved imagination, a psychological cry for help with some surprising physiological side-effects? Was I ill, or was I just depressed and unable to properly process it? Ultimately, I decided, it didn't really matter. Whether the depression was borne of the illness or vice versa was irrelevant: what was certain was that I was now fighting both – and both were now feeding each other in a vicious cycle.

With such a mysterious set of symptoms, diagnosis was done principally by elimination. I saw an eye doctor, who saw nothing untoward in my vision, beyond the crippling short-sightedness of which my mum had been so ashamed. An ENT specialist said my ears were all-clear, bar the inevitable wax. It was then I was packed off to see a consultant neurologist.

My friend had been right: perhaps it was all in my head after all.

Round Three

FIGHTING

I don't want to mislead you: mine has not been a life entirely bereft of violence. While it would be conceptually tidy if I'd never been involved in any sort of physical altercation, it's not strictly true – and I am determined to apply a policy of strictness to truth.

I have punched three people in my life, the how and why of which I will unfold to you now.

1) Dean Jacobs and the rough book
At school, we used something called a rough book. The idea was that children would take notes in the rough book during a class, and then transfer this newly acquired knowledge in a more polished form to their exercise books later. The reality, of course, is that rough books were usually filled with suspicious stains, unfinished games of hangman, and pornographic doodles.

My rough book, however, was a portfolio of artwork which demonstrated a transcendental genius; an insight into a dark, warped mind; i.e. it was filled with a lot of little doodles of goblin-men. It was precious to me, providing an opportunity for procrastination and distraction, which is effectively how I survived science lessons.

Now, in one such lesson, a boy called Dean Jacobs saw fit to put my rough book under the laboratory tap. Dean was and is a quintessentially nice boy. There is nothing bad to say about Dean Jacobs. He probably thought I'd find it funny. For some reason, on this day, I did not. To my mind, this act was akin to a vandal breaking into the Louvre and slashing through the Mona Lisa with a knife. I sprung off my stool and landed a right-hand square on Dean's jaw. In my memory he flies back into several racks of test tubes, lying crumpled amid broken glass and scattered Bunsen burners. In reality, I'm sure he basically just said 'Ow' and told the teacher.

Nevertheless, it was indicative of something: a latent anger with no outlet. Even then, I knew it wasn't Dean Jacobs that caused me to get so angry, or the demise of the rough book. Even though that was bloody annoying.

I wasn't disciplined by teachers for my misdemeanour – or indeed, for anything I did wrong. I imagine they spoke in hushed tones of 'problems at home' and declared a moratorium on punishing me. School became a refuge for me, a safe place. I'm just sorry I couldn't say the same for poor Dean Jacobs.

2) The boy in the rugby match
In my early teens, by some miracle I managed to wobble my way into the school rugby team. This owed more to the simple laws of physics than any real talent – once a boy my size gathered momentum, he was difficult to stop. I was a gelatinous juggernaut. The beauty of rugby as a school sport is

that it quite literally takes all shapes and sizes. You need pace and agility in the backs, and you need some immovable lumps among the forwards.

As lumps went, I was perfectly immovable if worryingly immobile. I was, however, a trier (notwithstanding the fact that in six years of competitive activity, I never scored a single try). We started playing when I turned eleven – until then it had been football, and I was astonishingly bad at that. I knew my dad and my uncles had all played rugby for the school, and that it had jobs for bigger boys. This, I thought, might be my shot at sporting success, or at least acceptance.

When the first trial day came around, I did okay – it turns out that enthusiasm and size counts for a lot at that age. I was asked to come back the following week for a proper training session. For someone who'd spent years as last pick, that meant a lot. I had a spring in my step as I went home to tell anyone who'd listen about my newfound love for all things rugby.

When the practice session came around, however, I was found out. My inability to a) run and b) catch proved quite significant obstacles to my future as a rugby player. At the end of training, the rugby coach Mr Metcalfe unfurled a piece of paper and addressed us thus: 'The following players will be cut from the squad, and need not attend next week: James McNicholas . . .'

I don't remember the rest of the list. I remember I was first though. It hurt.

I was disappointed but not surprised. This was to be expected. The fact I'd somehow fluked my way through the trial was the anomaly here. As was so often the case in those school days, I trudged off to the tuck shop, seeking solace in a Chelsea bun. My sporting future looked bleak, unless of course they had plans to start a school sumo team.

But at some point in the following few days, something happened I still find difficult to believe. From somewhere, I summoned up the courage to go back and ask the teacher in charge, Mr Metcalfe, whether he'd consider giving me another chance.

I don't know what possessed him to consider my request. Maybe he felt sorry for me. Maybe, as is tradition among PE teachers in the private school sector, he admired my balls. Whatever the case, he acquiesced, and allowed me to start training with the squad again. The initial understanding was that I was only there to make up the numbers for practice, that I wouldn't be considered for selection – but within a few weeks I was starting for the First XV. I think I was possessed by a determination to be acknowledged, particularly in a sporting sense – the weight of failure, of being a disappointment to my family, was simply too great to bear. I don't think I had the heart to tell them I'd been dropped, so I made sure I wasn't.

Consequently, rugby came to mean a great deal to me. I took it seriously – in as far as it's possible for a sixteen-stone child to claim they're taking any sport seriously. Every September, upon returning to school, the entire year would be made to run a horrendous cross-country course called 'The Donkin Cup'. There was a longstanding decree that any members of the first-team rugby squad had to finish the race in the top thirty of the 150-odd boys competing, or else they'd be dropped from the team. I finished 133rd.

And yet still they persisted with me. Maybe I was a kind of mascot for the team. Maybe they admired my dual dedication to both competitive sport and chocolate Hobnobs, who knows? Either way, I managed to hang around. Like I said: immovable.

I must have been about fourteen – by then, a grizzled veteran of the school rugby scene – when the infamous punch occurred. I was sprinting* away from some artless melee when an opponent reached out a leg to trip me. Embarrassed and enraged, I sprung† up and threw my best attempt at a punch. This manifested as a sort of upwards thrust with the heel of my hand – quite Jackie Chan, if Jackie Chan had been an obese boy covered in mud. I was promptly sent off. I strode from the field, nauseous with adrenaline, pride and shame.

3) The Scottish man at Edinburgh Festival

As a comedian, the beauty of the Edinburgh Festival is that it provides you with three million punters who are all potential audience members. Or, in my case, people you might punch.

It was 2016, and I had just come off stage after performing with my sketch group, BEASTS. My mum had been in the audience that day, as had my younger cousin Lucy and her then boyfriend, and when I joined them in the bar they explained that they were having some trouble with one of the locals. Edinburgh folk have decidedly mixed feelings about the festival: they basically loathe it, but to a certain extent their practical life depends on it – it's similar to how I feel about Amazon Prime. Anyway, this particular lad had been aggressively 'flirting' with Lucy and goading her boyfriend in the process. When he tried it again, I gave him a wee whack in the face.

Wee is the right word. The problem was that, as my father-in-law later explained to me over the phone, I 'didn't hit him hard enough'. I had neither the experience nor the courage to really commit to the punch; I threw my fist out in defence rather than with any real intent to cause damage. I struck him

---

* trotting
† hauled myself

around the cheek. He was shocked, he was angry, but I'm not sure he was ever really hurt.

Fortunately, security dashed over to intervene before he could retaliate. I blame the rush of being on stage for instilling that false feeling of temporary invincibility. I was giddy with applause. Do not clap me, I could turn violent.

So that's it: the three times I've ever punched someone. Oh, and I've punched my brother loads obviously, but I'm not sure that warrants inclusion. Brothers bickering is a tale as old as time: just look at Cain and Abel, Noel and Liam or Paul and Barry Chuckle.

Not everyone is so accepting of that kind of sibling rivalry. Between 1999 and 2015, heavyweight boxing was dominated by two brothers: Vitali and Wladimir Klitschko. Wladimir claims Don King once made a $100 million offer for him to fight his older brother, to no avail. 'A billion wouldn't help,' said an unwavering Wlad. 'Money is not everything in life. I understand that people are excited and driven by money, but no. Between two brothers? I love my brother too much.'

They sparred together in their youth, but when Wlad suffered a broken leg during one session he took it as a sign from God that the two brothers were not meant to fight. However, there was something else that forced them to stop, something even more compelling than divine intervention: they'd promised their mum. 'We were asked many times if we are going to fight each other or not, but we made a promise to our mother that we will never fight each other,' Wlad explains. 'She asked us . . . "You can box, you can both be involved in boxing – which I don't like – but you have to promise me one thing: no matter what you won't fight each other."'

Wlad sounds like a good son. There are plenty of promises I've made my mum, and I broke them for a lot less than $100 million.

One such promise was that my brother and I would behave ourselves on the first occasion she asked us to babysit my youngest sister Ella. We would've been in our mid-teens, and Ella would have been about three. My mum and dad were only popping out for a couple of hours – to Pizza Express, as I recall, a restaurant somehow emblematic of my middle-class origins. High streets round me were populated almost entirely by Pizza Express, Zizzi, Prezzo, Ask – a cavalcade of faux-Italian eateries – aspirational, unoriginal and, in the case of their garlic dough balls, absolutely irresistible.

Shortly after they went out, Charlie started shooting petits pois at me through a plastic straw. As the elder brother, I took authoritative action and confiscated said straw, threatening to throw it away. It was at that point things escalated quickly: my brother retaliated by pulling out one of my mum's kitchen knives and 'playfully' swiping it in my direction. As I remonstrated with him, the blade playfully sliced through my little finger. As the blood poured out, I asked my brother what I should do. His advice: 'Run it under the tap.'

Now. 'Run it under the tap' is, in some medical emergencies, good advice – if, for example, you have a burn. It is not great a great course of action for an open wound. If you put a gash that's pouring blood under a tap, I'll tell you what happens: more blood comes out. It was at this precise moment that Ella toddled into the room, screaming as a crimson waterfall of blood cascaded into the kitchen sink.

Reluctantly, my brother and I placed a sheepish phone call to my mum and dad, solemnly explaining that they had to abandon their American Hot because Charlie had sliced Jamie's finger off.

Incredibly, the McNicholas brothers did not take this as a sign from God that they were not meant to fight, and there were further incidents:

I once showed surprising strength to push over a sofa while Charlie was stood on the top, leaving him bloodied and bruised.

We played indoor rugby using an infant Ella as the ball.

An impromptu wrestling match in a corridor resulted in me being unable to move from the neck down for a full fifteen minutes. On that occasion, as I lay there, paralysed, the words I managed to utter were not 'Help!' or 'Call an ambulance' but merely a plaintive cry of 'Don't tell mum'. I wonder if the Klitschkos ever did the same.

But that's it. Other than that, I have shied away from conflict. It's not that I'm particularly good at working problems out verbally, but I know I'm especially bad at solving them physically.

It's a far cry from Terry's place as his generation's enforcer. As the oldest boy, he was forever being thrust to the front when some cousin was caught up in a row. It's not that he was especially big. Here's a curious thing: if you looked at me and Terry side by side and were asked which was the boxer, there's actually a decent chance that you might choose me. Set aside my glasses and my growing gut, and I am taller, broader – I've even got a nose that looks like it might have been through a few wars. I am a big guy: six feet one with shoulders broad as my comedy and thighs like doner kebabs. I look like I should be able to handle myself. But as the old saying goes, 'It's not the size of the dog in the fight, it's whether or not the dog is a big geeky coward.'

On the subject of my geekdom, I co-host a podcast about my beloved Arsenal, the ludicrously titled Arsecast Extra. Seemingly every time a listener recognises my distinctly nasal tones in public, they'll remark that I'm 'taller than they expected'. It is the most backhanded of backhanded compliments. 'Oh, you're more physically imposing than your pathetic personality suggests.' They expected that audibly palpable chip on my shoulder to be at a more accessible height.

I guess what Terry had – and it's something that never left him – was that innate physical confidence. He wasn't an idiot; he didn't go around fighting kids from a whole other weight division. He knew how to pick a fight – a crucial art in any boxer's career.

At that early stage, Terry had no real aspirations of a life as a professional boxer – even after Mr Beal's intervention at St Saviour's School set the schoolboy on the straight and narrow. Until the age of thirteen or so, it was all playground scraps. Pop used to tell the story of the day his dad found out he'd developed an interest in boxing. Dick Downes did what any sensible father would do: stripped the floor, got down on his hands and knees and asked his son to fight him. Terry shed tears of frustration as he failed to beat his father's guard. It pushed him. It motivated him to get better.

It was when Terry moved up to St Augustine's School in Kilburn that he began to pursue fighting as a sport, rather than just *for* sport. When football was rained off, benches would be laid out in a square and two boys pushed into the makeshift ring to take swings at each other. Must've been a great laugh for the PE teachers: 'Looks like the pitch is waterlogged again. Oh well, how about we force some children to fight?'

Well, the standard of entertainment was seemingly suffi-

cient for the staff to suggest entering a team into the national
schoolboy championships. Terry and a boy from his class, a
lad called Charlie Canavan, started attending the Pembroke
Boxing Club in North Kensington to pick up a few pointers.

And then the championships rolled around, and Terry had
his first real fight. He weighed in at a meagre six stone and
eight pounds, roughly the same as a full-grown octopus. Despite
his bravado, there were nerves – his stomach only settled by a
pre-match meal of spaghetti on toast.

Terry skipped through his first two bouts with ease. He
moved on to the next regional round at Camden Town, then the
next at Lime Grove Baths. As he progressed, more and more of
the Downes family began turning up to support him. It makes
me think of all the cold, wet Saturday mornings Terry stood
on the sidelines watching me play rugby, growling instructions
for a game he barely understood.

He learnt the taste of defeat too. At Lime Grove, Terry was
scheduled to face a kid called Grout. He pulled out, meaning
that ironically enough it was someone other than Grout who
had to fill the gap. The new opponent was a boy called Hillier –
Terry fancied his chances, but ultimately took a beating. He
was inconsolable until someone presented him with a schoolboy
boxing manual, and Hillier was the guy posing for all the pictures. He'd been boxing for years and was literally the poster
boy for the sport. It was an honourable loss, at least.

But a curious thing happened. As Terry began to find success
in the ring, it cured him of his tendency to fight outside it. It
was as if knowing he could do it was enough. He had proved
something to himself.

*   *   *

From the inception of this project, I always planned to test myself out in the ring a little. While it made some narrative sense, I also considered enlisting for training a clever insurance policy against my proclivity to eat lots and lots of cake. If I contractually guaranteed to embark on an exercise regime, it might offset my dreadful diet.

Then coronavirus happened. For those reading this book hundreds of years in the future, probably as part of GCSE English Literature or something,* coronavirus was this thing that meant everyone had to stay home, drink alcohol and gain weight. For some people this was disruptive and disconcerting. For me, it was far too comfortable.

When it came to my training, however, the pandemic presented a problem. My plan had been to lurk at the back of a few boxercise classes, maybe see if I could learn to skip. Now, gyms were shutting down left, right and centre. The grim reality steadily set in: if I was to do this, I would need someone who was prepared to train me one on one. Someone who wasn't scared of coronavirus, or anything else for that matter. Someone like Rowan Katzew.

The story of how I found Rowan Katzew is a story like so many others: I clicked on lots of things on the internet until I ended up on his website. It's easy to see how he turned up in the search engine: his 'About' section is basically a series of macho fight-y keywords separated by a bare minimum of conjunctions. Here we go:

---

* I reckon the set texts are probably this book and *The Catcher in The Rye*. That's always in there. Kids just love catching that sweet, sweet rye.

'Rowan Katzew is a respected hand-to-hand combat coach and experienced security professional. He specializes in coaching boxing, MMA, kickboxing and Self-Protection Combatives. Prior to founding Top Primate Academy, a highly successful MMA gym in Cape Town, South Africa, Rowan was an active fighter in his hometown of Johannesburg, competing in boxing and K1 kickboxing. He is an experienced boxer as well as a multiple-time national and international Shotokan karate champion.

'Over the years Rowan's coaching systems have helped produce several world-class athletes as well as countless everyday warriors and self-protectors. His coaching continues to evolve as he travels and trains with some of the best combat sport athletes, martial artists, military, law enforcement and security professionals around the globe.

'In addition to coaching, Rowan is a highly experienced security professional specialising in Hostile Environment Close Protection and operating as a security consultant in Africa and the United Kingdom.'

At this point I didn't know Rowan Katzew personally, but I did know I wanted to watch a movie about his life. It was a biography to rival even that of Terry Downes.

I emailed Rowan and arranged to meet him at his studio in Wood Green. 'Good news,' I told him: 'I've already got a gumshield.' I wear one every night, due to grinding my teeth with anxiety.

Before heading over for my first session, I gave Rowan's social media a final, apprehensive glance. His latest Instagram post is not a picture, but a slogan – a motto which presumably underpins his personality and his practice. It reads simply: 'Your wokeness won't fix your weakness.'

I am in trouble here. I am in big, big trouble.

For Terry, suffering his first loss stung – especially because it meant that, unlike his friend Charlie Canavan, he returned to school without a medal. Canavan's medallion, emblazoned with the image of a boxer, was the talk of the playground.

In a desperate attempt to remedy things, Terry organised a couple of fights down at the Pembroke boxing club. After he punched his way through some inexpert opponents, he was led over to the prizes table, where he pleaded for a medal. 'Sorry son,' he was told. 'No medal.' Terry scoured the prizes table desperately, looking for something shiny to take home.

He ended up with a teapot – a little china thing he presented to his mum. Terry always told the teapot story like the prize was a punchline, but the fact that he held onto it for the rest of his life shows just how much it meant to him. Medals, trophies and title belts were all to come, but in that moment it just meant enough to be recognised. To be acknowledged.

Rowan is a sinewy, tattooed South African with steely eyes and a bristly red beard. He has the quiet assurance of a man who knows he could kill you. When I arrive, I'm anxious about whether he'll shake my hand – not because he might transmit the virus, but because he might crush it.

His first combat sport was karate; he was a black belt by the age of thirteen. 'Then I walked into a boxing gym,' he says. 'I thought I knew how to fight, but like everyone does in their first session, I got the absolute shit kicked out of me.'

'Yeah, sure,' I gulp, wondering if I should tell him I've got a veneer on a front tooth I'm worried might come off, making a mental note of all available exits, and hastily sellotaping my glasses to my face.

Although Rowan is coaching me specifically in boxing, he works across various fields: personal training, professional coaching and self-defence classes. I ask him if he sees a correlation between what are ostensibly sporting pursuits and the ability to handle yourself on the street. 'Of course,' he says. 'The base skills, the motor skills, the muscle memory is all the same.

'If you want to learn self-protection, I think you should first be able to do what we're going to do: learn to move like a boxer, throw a punch, slip a punch – and you should be able to do this continuously under pressure, under duress, for a decent amount of time while you're tired.'

Something moves in my stomach. It feels a little like nausea, and a lot like regret.

Rowan believes that most people can learn to fight – more than that, he believes they should. 'Especially if you're a man,' he says emphatically. 'I think it's very important that everybody tries to get to some decent level of competency. I just don't see how any man can say, "Okay, I want all the spoils of life – I want a woman or a partner, I want kids" – and not want to know how to just have some level of competency to defend them against the worst of people. Because coming from where I come from, I know how bad people can be.'

What if, I posit, you don't believe in violence?

'That's nonsense,' he smiles. 'It doesn't matter what you

believe in. There's no two ways about it. Violence is the golden standard. It's the universal language. It's the thing that rules everything. Order is kept because of the threat of violence. At the end of the day, if you break the law, you will be arrested – and in many cases, they will do that physically. That is a form of violence. I'm not glorifying it. But it is what it is.

'I'm not saying everyone should learn to fight so that if someone talks shit to you, you can stand up to them. Nothing like that. If someone talks shit to you, you stand up, they pull out a knife, you're dead. So no, I'm just saying, what about when you don't have a choice? I'm talking about having to deal with non-consensual violence. You are relying on the mercy of your attacker, which is not a good thing to rely on historically. Or you're relying on someone else, the authorities, or you're okay with being violently assaulted.'

'Am I okay with it?' I ask myself. Not really: I have been the victim of a violent assault myself, as you will discover. I wasn't okay with it then, nor am I now. Equally, I'm not ready to embrace violence as the solution. It still feels alien to me, still feels like it just doesn't suit me.

There's only one way to find out if I'm right, and that's to get started. Rowan's philosophy is to train everyone – competitive athletes or private clients like myself – using the same drills and principles. 'I'm going to do exactly the same with you as I would with the professionals', he reassures me. Oh good.

Terry would have approved of that. This isn't a sport you can really do recreationally. 'With boxing you can't mess around,' he once said. 'You can't be a bit of a fighter. You can be a bit of a football player or a bit of a cricketer. You can play a game of tennis for a lark. But you can't have a bloody lark at boxing.'

At first I don't say who my grandfather is, because, frankly, it would be so embarrassing. If I'm going to be a disappointing boxer, let me at least be a disappointing boxer on my own merit. We begin with some skipping – an activity easily mastered by little girls in school playgrounds, yet utterly mystifying to me. Rowan then leads me through the basics of boxing movement.

As he helps me shift my weight side to side, forward and back, a thought forms in my mind.

'It's just like a dance,' I say.

'Exactly,' he affirms.

What I don't tell him is that I can't dance.* In fact, the very exercises we're doing take me back to an agonising term at drama school when I had to learn to schottische, jive and merengue as part of a 'period dance' course. I did not fare well. Choreography is my kryptonite. For the first dance at my wedding I refused to attempt anything remotely graceful, instead insisting on choosing the Ini Kamoze track *Here Comes The Hotstepper* so I could bust out my own freestyle moves. I'm not sure it's quite what every bride dreams of.

Rowan teaches me the basic punches: jab, cross, hooks and uppercuts. He gives each punch a number, so he can call out combinations in sequence, like a mathlete eagerly reciting decimal places of Pi. I'm lost amid the algebraic instruction: where's Robert Gilbert when you need him?

Rowan explains how the power behind the punches lies in the stance. Much like the dancing, it's all in the hips.

'It's tricky explaining it to people in this country,' he protests.

Why's that?

'Well, none of you have guns.'

Another gulp.

---

* In fairness, this may be so apparent as to not require saying.

'Back home people understand what it is to hold a loaded weapon. That's how it should feel before you punch.'

I'm sweating profusely, and I've barely exercised yet.

Rowan says he thinks I have a natural stance and 'good balance' – the latter of which obviously comes as a surprise to me. Even the gentlest exercise has me feeling that familiar dizziness. I don't feel able to tell this stranger that I feel like I'm rocking and swaying before I've even taken a punch, but I don't want him going easy on me, either.* To my complete surprise, he appears relatively impressed. Maybe it's flattery, maybe it's pity, but it's enough for me. Rowan asks me if I've boxed at all before. I say no, and he raises his eyebrows, suggesting that I have a 'natural aptitude'. Perhaps, he posits, it's because I'm an actor. In some way I am inhabiting the role.

I'm flattered, of course: actors love playing boxers. I think it's partly because it's difficult to be a performer and be conventionally, traditionally masculine. Portraying a boxer is a suitable antidote to the prevailing idea that actors are somehow effeminate. And all the big stars have played fighters: De Niro, Denzel, Russell Crowe, Marky Mark, Christian Bale, Will Smith. They relish the physicality. They get to work out and tell reporters they're in 'the best shape of their life' and that their trainers really thought they 'probably could've been a decent fighter'. It's the ultimate alpha role. It's *Gladiator* with gloves.

It's a nice theory from Rowan, but I have to admit I'm not sure this is a role I'd ever be cast for. In fact, the very day we first meet, I'm waiting for news on an audition I've just done for a French advert in which I would play an aspiring boxer.

---

* Correction: I actually *do* want that, but I recognise that it may not be the best thing for the book.

I leave the session to an email from my agent explaining that while it was a close fight, the other guy won on points. 'Just not quite believable enough,' says the feedback.

No lucrative commercial for James, and no medal either. Not even a teapot.

IN MY CORNER

The question took me aback. After countless GP visits and fleeting access to specialists, I had become accustomed to being subjected to an exhaustive survey on my health and well-being. But not once had this particular query come up.

'Have you ever sustained any concussions?' asked the neurologist.

'Any what, sorry?'

'Concussions. Bangs on the head. Have you ever been in any fights?'

I explained that I've never been much of a fighter. I'd punched three people, but since then I'd kept my hands to myself. This, of course, was 2017 – pre-Rowan, pre-training, pre-transformation into 35-year-old boxing wunderkind. I was still being described in reviews as a 'doughy Alan Carr'.

'But,' I offered, 'I did ski into a tree once.'

And then I remembered: I had been in a fight of sorts. Although it wasn't much of a contest. Tuesday 19 November 2013, was one of the worst days of my life. It started with a hospital appointment. I'd been afflicted with some bizarre symptoms – a frequent need to urinate, and pain in my pelvis. It was therefore decided that I should be booked in for a cystoscopy – or, in layman's terms, a camera up the knob.

This was far from ideal. For those lucky people who have until now escaped this fate, let me elucidate: you're asked to lie down in a hospital gown that is hitched crudely above your waist. A nurse (female, in my case, which adds a touch of sexual jeopardy to the whole enterprise) rubs some anaesthetic gel on the end of your penis, as if lubricating you to make love to a Breville sandwich maker.

Then in goes the camera. I imagine most men have, at some time or other, wished for a larger penis. In this case I did so purely for anatomical reasons – I prayed for everything to be sufficiently scaled up, so that I had a wide enough urinary tract for the camera to slip in and out with ease.

It's a difficult sensation to describe. There isn't anything quite like it. If you are a man, perhaps imagine someone attempting to put a camera up and into your penis. If you are a woman, imagine you have a penis, and then do the same. Alternatively, imagine you have been abducted by an alien, but with a twist: this alien is a fucking pervert.

The first half of the procedure is surprisingly okay. The cystoscope is shaped somewhat like an arrowhead, allowing it to disappear up the urethra like the proverbial rat up a drainpipe. Once inside, they pump water through the cable to inflate your bladder from within, allowing them to examine the internal walls. The doctor seemed keen to show me this on a grainy monitor, as if we might find cave paintings there hinting at ancient life within. Crucially, we didn't find any indicators of malignancy. Result.

The problem comes on the withdrawal. Suddenly, that arrow-head shape isn't quite so convenient. It's essentially like hauling a wrought iron anchor up out of your John Thomas, scraping the walls of your urethra as it goes. The camera feels a lot bigger now, and it feels like they've squeezed in a boom mic and film crew too.

The second issue is all that liquid they've pumped into you, blowing your bladder up like a water balloon. What goes in, must come out. A cystoscopy is an outpatient procedure – you're probably inside the hospital for about twenty minutes, all told. They kick you out before any pain really kicks in. I was headed towards the exit when I was overcome by an urgent need to go to the loo. I ducked into a cubicle. Patients in the adjoining waiting room must have wondered what was going on in there – I screamed bloody murder as I weed out of my freshly-raked urethral tract. It was as if I was pissing an eruption of liquid hot magma. I staggered out to the car park, where I folded myself gingerly into my mum's car.

There was a diagnosis. It turned out that, at just twenty-seven, I had the grossly enlarged prostate of an elderly man. For the first time in forever, Terry and I really did have something in common. In my case, the doctors suggested it might be due to the fact I'd recently started cycling around town to try and lose weight. I knew exercise was bad for me.

The cystoscopy alone would be sufficient to make this dark November day one to forget. But fate had more up its mucky sleeve. Later that evening, not content with the medical assault on my genitalia, I managed to get myself actually, properly assaulted too.

I'd love to say it happened in one of London's crime hotspots, in an area rife with gang warfare and violent acts of retribution.

It didn't. It happened in West Hampstead, one of the sunniest, leafiest, most affluent neighbourhoods in north London. They have a Gail's Bakery: that's about as middle class as it comes. Only I could get assaulted somewhere with a Gail's.

I still don't know quite what happened (smashed over the head with a seeded sourdough?). I was leaving West Hampstead station, making my way up West End Lane, staring intently at my phone in a manner which quite frankly asked for trouble.

Trouble duly obliged. Details are admittedly hazy: I was hit over the back of the head by *someone* with *something*. It might have been a fist – it's surprising how much damage a good straight punch can cause if you're caught completely off-guard. It might have been something else. My foggy memory recalls something that looked like a briefcase swinging in my direction – that would be a suitably middle-class weapon of choice.

It felt like a baseball bat. The blow caused me to fall and hit my head on the pavement, knocking me out and fracturing several teeth. While on the ground I took a couple of kicks to the head for good measure.

Once I'd hauled myself to my feet, I made the clearly concussed decision to pursue my attacker. Only one problem: my glasses had come off – without them, as discussed, I am powerless. What's more, I'd been struck from behind – I couldn't have picked the assailant out of a line-up. To be honest, I'm so short-sighted I probably couldn't see as far as the line.

Plus, there were bits of my teeth scattered all over the ground, like my head was just a pinata full of little enamel sweeties. One of my front teeth was crudely snapped off near the gumline. Somehow, groping around the pavement, I found it. Now my priorities changed: vigilante justice was beyond me, but I could still save the tooth.

From deep in the recesses of my mind came the idea that I should put it in milk. It's one of those bits of received wisdom that had seeped into my brain via osmosis, like peeing on a jellyfish sting, using white wine to combat red wine stains, or practically any application of baking soda. And so, I staggered up the street, bleeding and blind, towards the nearest super-market. I grabbed a pint of milk – semi-skimmed, out of pure instinct – and hurried to the front of the self-checkout queue. I remember a woman on the phone saying under her breath, 'A drug addict has just come in and pushed in front of me.' I smiled back, and she flinched at my gruesome grin. And then I popped the tooth into the chilled milk, a cryogenic carton keeping the fractured incisor tooth in suspended animation.

All in vain, as it turns out. While there is some truth in the 'keep it in milk' legend, it only works for an entire tooth, root and all. It does not apply to chipped off portions of teeth, however large. According to my dentist, the best thing to actually keep a lost tooth in is your own saliva. Just swill it around your mouth like a Werther's original until you can get an appointment.

It was as I came out of the supermarket that I was fortunate enough to bump into a policeman. He called me an ambulance, as by this time blood was dripping from inside my earhole. Now I'm no medical man, but I knew that wasn't good. And so, that night, I was back in hospital again, this time in a wheelchair, for stitches and brain scans. It wouldn't have surprised me if they'd decided to have a little check in the old bladder again, seeing as I was there.

The whole thing was compounded by the fact that I was due to film the next day. I wore foundation to cover the bruising, and my dentist was kind enough to temporarily glue the broken front tooth back together to help me survive the shoot. If anything,

I was probably grateful for the immediate distraction filming provided. At first at least, I had no time to dwell on what had happened.

I wasn't robbed. They took nothing; not even the phone I'd had in my hand. The police explained there was no CCTV covering the location, and that no witnesses had come forward. I'd never know who attacked me, or why, and they'd never face justice.

It does strange things to you, being attacked. The idea of a random assault is so bizarre, so unfortunate, that it's difficult to comprehend. Instead, you start trying to piece together a narrative that justifies or explains what happened. Had I absent-mindedly bumped into someone or tripped them up, causing a retaliation? Was it some guy whose girlfriend I'd kissed in 2009? Was it Dean Jacobs, finally seeking revenge for the rough book incident?

My fantasies were fed by the fact that around this time I had become a sort of 'public enemy' in South Korea. The whole kerfuffle came about because of a Korean footballer called Park-Chu Young, who was performing poorly for my beloved Arsenal. In what had been intended as a piece of light-hearted ribbing, I released a parody version of the P Diddy track *Bad Boys 4 Life*, adapting the lyrics to the ingenious 'Bad Buys 4 Life', framing Park as one such disappointing purchase. This seemingly inconsequential video ended up getting around half a million worldwide views and was shown on national television in Korea. This led to a considerable degree of online abuse and even death threats. A Korean rap duo released a retaliation video in which they set fire to and then stamped repeatedly on a picture of me. They subtitled their diss track in English, but had clearly only run the lyrics through Google Translate, leading to some ominous but curiously worded threats. The song criticised my 'bulky useless actions and boldness', before things got really personal:

> *Look your goofy head,*
> *You better have hair loss surgery now,*
> *Because you will be bald to get so riled up,*
> *So Fuck You.*

> *Besides you never ever tried to apologise a thing,*
> *You were proud of becoming a hot issue in Korea,*
> *I'll give a lesson to your gabbling mouth,*
> *You listened ROYAL but you still spill out POOR,*
> *YOU ARE AN OVERLOAD.*

A devastating takedown – and when it comes to my hairline, disconcertingly prescient. Somehow, this video got over 70,000 views. Now granted, if you're going to fall foul of a Korean nation, let it be the southerners, but this was still less than ideal. Was it all just coincidence? Or had I been taken out by the South Korean secret service, or just a vigilante Park Chu-Young fan?

The authorities were kind enough to put me in touch with a victim support charity that offered me a few free counselling sessions. I was embarrassed to attend them, really – I knew my own experience was child's play compared to the ordeals they must sometimes hear about. But these sessions helped me come to terms with the fact that it just happened – it wasn't my fault, it wasn't a vendetta, it wasn't something I had provoked or deserved. The police concluded it was most likely the actions of a dare-driven gang inductee – I believe Hampstead gangs are the toughest of all – or simply a passing madman (not their exact words). The counselling helped me accept that. It quietened the conspiracy theorist in me and, crucially, taught me to trust the Korean people again.

The charity also showed me how to apply for a government grant which is awarded to the victims of violent crimes. Compensation for crimes is a funny idea really, as it appears to be based on the premise that psychological trauma is in some way assuaged by cash. Not that I was complaining: as I recall, I was awarded about £1,000, which, handily, was just enough to pay for the first round of dentistry. I've required several procedures since, with fees spiralling into the thousands, but it was the mental rather than physical or fiscal cost of the assault I felt most keenly. Every time I left the house, I took extra precautions, extra glances over the shoulder. For a few months, I admit, I was jumpy. If a stranger touched me on the arm to ask for directions, my heart leapt into my throat – and not because of my woeful geography. I was in a state of perpetual high alert. It felt as if disaster might be waiting for me around every street corner. At the time I was living in Elephant & Castle, hardly London's most salubrious neighbourhood. If I wasn't safe in West Hampstead, presumably I wasn't safe anywhere.

On the outside, at least, it got better quickly. Bruises faded, cuts healed, the dentist did a remarkable job. I'll always remember the first time he popped my new front tooth in, and then immediately said, 'No – if it's going to match we need to make it more yellow.'

Unfortunately, the amount of painkillers I was on made it difficult to voice the contention: 'Why not just make the others more white?' Alas.

But inside, behind the gleaming if expensive veneer, something lingered. Yes, there was the emotional aspect: the humiliation of physical assault; the brutal emasculation. I could console myself that I was attacked from behind, but despite my best attempts, I could not convince myself I would have fared any better from the front. What would Terry make of a grandson who couldn't defend himself?

And what about the physical aspect? Was there some link between old head injuries and present-day dizziness? I'd never been much of a fighter, but my life has been a long litany of accidents: skiing into trees, falling off bikes, getting beaten up in wealthy suburbs. On their own, these incidents may not have meant much. But was the neurologist getting at something more disturbing? Could a series of inconsequential accidents have, in the end, some serious consequences?

Round Four

AMERICA

All my life, I have believed I was Terry Downes' first and eldest grandson. It is only in the process of writing this book that I have discovered I was wrong.

I was visiting my dad, Barry, at his home in Bristol when his wife Helen asked me to help her with something on her laptop. I have become accustomed to serving as IT support to my entire family – when you wear glasses, it's just assumed you'll understand computers. In my case, it's not an unfair assumption: if it looks like a nerd, talks like a nerd and fights like a nerd, then it probably is a nerd.

Anyway, once we flipped open the screen, I noticed that she was logged into ancestry.com.* She showed me the basic functionality of the site – that it enabled you to build out a family tree, and to search public records for corroboration, using birth, marriage and death certificates. In fact, she even showed me that two of those documents appeared under my

---

* Other genealogy-based subscription sites are available.

own name (birth and marriage certificates, obviously. If she'd shown me a copy of my death certificate that would have been freaky as hell.)

Now, given the fact that I was in the process of researching a book on a family member, the possible benefits of an ancestry. com subscription were immediately apparent to me. I am, however, notoriously reluctant to sign up for anything with a recurring fee, because I instantly forget about it and end up with a financial commitment that will follow me to my grave. At the time of writing, I still have unwanted direct debits in place to Vimeo Pro, Disney+, and an orangutan adoption agency. So, when Helen nipped out the room, I seized the opportunity to quickly type 'Terence Downes' into the search box.

And what I found came as quite the surprise.

In some ways, I probably have more in common with Terry's sister Sylvie than with him. She was always in the entertainment business. As soon as she could walk and talk, she was dancing and singing. As a girl she was part of famous dance troupe Terry's Juveniles,* crossed paths with a young Julie Andrews, and trod the boards in pantomimes across the capital.

Her dream, however, was to join the circus. She got her break in London, as part of theatre impresario Tom Arnold's extravaganza, staged at the Harringay Arena – later the scene of Terry's first professional fight. It was fourteen-year-old Terry's job to meet her at the station after every show, with two of his dad's prized greyhounds straining at the leash for company. It was a natural progression from childhood enforcer to teenage

---

* The name is pure coincidence. And pretty creepy actually.

bodyguard. While her brother acted as minder, Sylvie was part of a trapeze act called 'The Abbott Sisters', five supposed siblings who in reality had come from all over England.

In 1952, this young acrobat soared to greater heights: The Abbott Sisters were cherry-picked to cross the Atlantic and join up with the world-famous Ringling Brothers and Barnum & Bailey Circus. Ringling Brothers was a family business which had begun as a five-cent show in rural Iowa, before expanding to form a travelling railroad production that became famous across the world. In 1906, they acquired and merged with the Barnum & Bailey Circus made famous by Hugh 'Jazz Hands' Jackman in camptacular smash hit *The Greatest Showman*.

After a winter training camp in Sarasota, Florida, Sylvie headed out on the road to take her place in 'The Greatest Show on Earth'.* She even pipped Terry to appearing at some of America's finest fight venues. She performed at New York's Madison Square Garden, and Boston Garden – the 13,000-capacity arena where Terry would later fight twice for the middleweight championship of the world. As well as the trapeze, she was also juggling family matters: for a short time while she was in America, parents Hilda and Dick were separated – and all their correspondence went through Sylvie. While Dick scoured London looking for his wife and son, Hilda took Terry and hid out in Taunton, Somerset. Sylvie became a human

---

* Impressively, this circus conglomerate actually managed to trademark the name 'The Greatest Show on Earth', even suing Kid Rock when he called his 2018 show by the same title. Frankly, I'm surprised he wasn't done for false advertising too: imagine the disappoint of buying a ticket for 'The Greatest Show on Earth', then realising you're just going to see Kid Rock.

switchboard, mediating their marital troubles via letters sent from 5,000 miles away.

It was in Taunton – almost another evacuation for Terry – that the young fighter acquired his first significant scar. When a bumptious teacher doled out some corporal punishment to one of his new friends, Terry made the mistake of flashing a disapproving look. The teacher strode over and ordered him to get back to work, accompanying the command with a back-hander across the ear. Terry shot up out of his seat, but before he could fight back was struck with an uppercut that sliced through his lip like my brother's knife through my finger. For all his fighting career, this is the one scar that remained visible on his face until his final days – one acquired not in the boxing ring, but in the classroom. No wonder he didn't like school.

On the other side of the ocean, Sylvie's tour was due to reach New York on April Fool's Day – and sadly, a cruel trick was indeed around the corner. The circus arrived in Baltimore, just forty miles from the nation's capital, Washington DC. It is a quintessentially American city: the birthplace of Babe Ruth and the Star-Spangled Banner. For show people, Baltimore was known to be a jinxed town. In 1948, a Ringling 'elephant man'* was killed by a tractor while the big top was being taken down. To be fair that really does sound like the greatest show on earth. In 1949, Ringling trapeze performers The Geraldos fell and were seriously injured during a show. In 1951, a seventeen-year-old aerialist fell to her death while performing with the Shrine Circus. In the same show, just four days later, a fire burned two performers and killed a chimpanzee and two monkeys.†

---

* It's unclear whether he looked after elephants or simply resembled them.
† i.e. three monkeys, see Round One.

In 1952, the jinx came for Sylvie. She was riding the number 23 Baltimore Transit Company bus* through town, with her elbow leaning out of the open window. As they turned from Lexington Street into Liberty Street, they jumped the kerb, crushing Sylvie's arm between the vehicle and a steel telephone pole at roadside. 'I felt a bump and heard Sylvia scream,' fellow Abbott sister Brenda Goring told local newspaper *The Evening Sun*.

The bus lurched to a halt. Eye-witnesses spoke of Sylvie calmly lifting her arm back inside, hanging as if by a thread, and placing it in her lap, like a fisherman winding in his catch. She was grateful for critical interventions from two passing patrolmen. First, John Sinnott used his handkerchief to stem the flow of blood. The sight was so gruesome that newspaper reports said 'three women and one man in the crowd fainted'. For all Terry's gory exploits, in his entire fighting career he never had four people pass out at ringside. Then another passing patrolman, William B. Clayton, stripped off his belt to use it as a tourniquet. In doing so, he most likely saved Sylvie's life.† When Sylvie arrived at the Mercy hospital, they had no choice but to amputate her arm above the elbow, with surgeons saying it was 'too badly mangled' to be saved. She was only eighteen.

---

* Interestingly, I have lived my whole life with a superstition about the number 23, without knowing this fact. In my teens I noticed the number seemed to be occurring with frightening frequency in my daily life – a phenomena known by some as having an 'angel number'. Jim Carrey had the same experience, and later made a horror film called *The Number 23* in which he was haunted by those two digits. Obviously, as someone who was already convinced the number was somehow after me, this really freaked me out.

† The poignancy of that moment presumably only undermined by his trousers immediately falling down.

Back in Paddington, on 7 June 1952, a telegram marked 'Downes' arrived at 162 Westbourne Terrace. By now Dick had tracked down Hilda in Taunton, and the family had reunited back home in London. At this moment, however, sixteen-year-old Terry was home alone. He tore the telegram open, before breaking down in tears at the necessary brutality of the message: 'Sylvia in bus accident lost right arm above elbow. Mercy Hospital, Baltimore, Maryland. Our legal department making arrangements for attorney to represent Sylvia. Everything possible being done for her. Signed: Ringling Circus.'

Sylvie's last letter home was still on the sideboard. It said, 'Mum, you mustn't worry if you don't hear from me as regularly as you would like. There's nothing to worry about. Nothing can ever happen to me.'

Scant consolation, perhaps, but the Ringling's attorney did a good job. Sylvie's accident was part of a spate of injuries that occurred aboard these buses. Over the next two months, a further three passengers broke their arms in similar incidents. Sylvie ultimately sued the Baltimore Transit Company for $250,000. The claim was settled out of court – and the offending pole was removed.

Arrangements were made for Hilda to fly to Sylvie's bedside. As the family scrabbled to afford a plane ticket, she pawned her wedding ring. Given her marital troubles with Dick, perhaps that wasn't quite as painful a sacrifice as it sounds. Hilda arrived in Baltimore fearing the worst. As she approached the hospital room where Sylvie was recovering, she caught sight of some frolicking feet beneath the door. It flung open, to reveal Sylvie. As soon as she was walking again, she was dancing again. The girl who sashayed through the air raids was soft-shoeing through another crisis.

Baltimore accepted Sylvia into its heart. 'I pictured her lying in a hospital alone while the show had to keep going on the road,' Hilda told a local newspaper. 'But when I came here, I found her with friends all around her. Everyone has just been wonderful.' Brenda Goring, her circus sibling, even took temporary leave from the roadshow to remain by her bedside.

Before long it was decided that the whole family should be reunited in America. Terry and Dick scraped together enough cash to cross the Atlantic by boat. When they stepped onto the dock in New York, Hilda and Sylvie were there to meet them, three hands enthusiastically waving a welcome. The Downes' American adventure was underway.

Like a cat with buttery paws, the Downes family always seem to land on their feet. After a farmhouse in Cornwall, they took over a townhouse in Baltimore. A wealthy local woman, the allegorically-named Mrs Pennyman, offered up her residence to them while she went travelling in Europe. Another generous local gifted the family a car. Terry didn't have a licence, but he didn't let a minor detail such as that stop him driving round town.

Before long, it was suggested that Terry should enlist in school. That didn't hold much appeal – if his accent had raised eyebrows in Somerset, imagine how it might have gone down in Maryland. By this stage, Terry was more interested in earning than learning. He eschewed education, instead joining the *Baltimore News-Post* as a copyboy. Copyboys (and girls) were charged with moving written copy between desks, then helping with the physical task of assembling the newspaper via the printing press. They were also responsible for any number of errands within the office building: heading to the nearby coffee shop, accompanying photographers on assignments or sometimes even carrying bets to the local illicit bookie.

I didn't realise until researching this book that Terry had worked for a newspaper. It shouldn't surprise me: he always seemed to have a knack for publicity. A boxer's career depends on a degree of fame, or even infamy. Ultimately, people have to want to watch you fight. That might be because they want to see you win in style; equally it might be because they want to see you get your comeuppance. Terry was a dedicated athlete, but he also had an intuitive understanding of his role as an entertainer. He knew that meant taking the rough with the smooth. And he had a touch of vanity to go with his valour. At the very start of his professional life, he marched into the *Boxing News* offices to tell them he knew he was a good fighter, but he wanted other people to know about it too. At the height of his boxing career, it was not uncommon to see him descend on Fleet Street the day after a big fight, either to confront his critics or collect copies of the best photographs.

Journalism is one of the careers that I have accidentally stumbled into. Something which started as a pastime has become a profession. In 2004, inspired by the achievements of Arsenal's legendary 'Invincibles', I started a website called 'Gunnerblog'. For the best part of a decade, I recorded my observations about the team on an almost daily basis. I earned almost nothing from the site in this period, but I enjoyed the exercise and catharsis of writing.

People who don't know me are often quite surprised I'm into football – and I get it. I don't exactly match the stereotype. I don't even like beer – my teetotal adolescence meant I never quite acquired the taste. I think I owe my football fandom to one man: Arsene Wenger, the former Arsenal manager. I was ten years old when he was appointed, this gangly foreigner in glasses. Suddenly a sport from which I had felt alienated, that

I had associated largely with outdated ideals of masculinity and drinking culture, became accessible and beautiful to me. It inspired me to write.

Over time, I began to pick up bits and pieces of freelance work as a footballer writer. I became co-host on Andrew Mangan's 'Arsecast Extra' podcast, opening up a big new audience of readers and listeners, before eventually taking on a role covering the club for *The Athletic*. I have interviewed people who were heroes of mine – the likes of Ian Wright, Tony Adams and Thierry Henry. I'm incredibly fortunate to call that work, but the performative part of me still wrestles slightly with my position as a football writer. Sometimes I fear I have become what comics hate most – an unqualified critic, passing judgement on work that I don't have the capacity to do. Still, that clearly hasn't troubled me sufficiently to put me off writing a book about a sport I know literally nothing about. Onwards!

Terry never intended to pursue a career in the world of newspapers – it was simply a way of earning a wage. His heart was still set on being a boxer, and so it was that he went down to the local YMCA gym for a tryout.* This mouthy cockney must have initially wondered if he'd bitten off more than he could chew. In his first sparring session, Terry – then a scrawny featherweight – was matched with a bristling middleweight, Jimmy Hines. Fortunately, Terry acquitted himself well enough for the gym to offer him a year's free membership, and a first step on the ladder of the American boxing scene. He was so

---

* Although now indelibly associated with the Village People hit, the YMCA was at this point a youth movement with considerable sporting pedigree, and – in Baltimore at least – access to some excellent facilities. Like the song says: 'They have everything for you men to enjoy.'

delighted he even invited opponent Jimmy home for dinner – and before long, Jimmy had married Sylvie. It's quite something to be punching someone in the face one minute, inviting them home for dinner the next, and then within a matter of months welcoming them into your family. From the outside, that's one of the things most appealing about boxing – the mutual respect, even affection, that can exist between combatants. For the duration of the fight, they're trying to render each other unconscious. The bell sounds and suddenly the sluggers turn to huggers. It's all backslaps and cuddles. I imagine the shared recognition of the physical demands, the mutual appreciation of what you have given and what have you risked, creates an inherent camaraderie. Boxing can be a lonely sport, but in those moments after a fight, you see companionship.

Sylvie's injury didn't keep her down long – within a year, she was back in the circus. An article from *The Baltimore Sun*, dated June 1953, reported the show's return to town. 'Included as a performer will be Sylvie Downes, the young English acrobat who lost her arm in a bus accident here last June. Miss Downes will appear as a showgirl in three of the four circus pageants.' It's a touching coda to an article with the spectacular headline: 'Robert the Rhino, Circus Pet, Found Dead in Cage on Train.' Frankly it sounds like the start to the best *Poirot* ever.

After 146 years, the Ringling Brothers Circus closed for good in 2017 – by coincidence, the same year Terry died. The circus had been engaged in a long battle with animal rights activists, and a dwindling attendance could no longer meet the operating costs of 500 circus performers and 100 animals. After a final show at Uniondale's Nassau Coliseum, the big top was packed away one last time. 'The world is losing a place of wonder,' said ringmaster Jonathan Lee Iverson. 'It's the last pure form of entertainment there is . . . It's the last safe space.' Unless you should happen to be a rhino, it seems, in which case it's bloody dangerous.

Sylvie's story is quite something. Really, it warrants a book in its own right. At this stage of his life, Terry had begun fighting but had never really been knocked down. To see his sister triumph over adversity like this, to see her dance in the face of tragedy, taught him the true meaning of strength, the true value of resolve. They say you can't teach grit, that you can't coach determination – but I do wonder how much Terry might have learnt from his big sister. The great Jack Dempsey said that 'a champion is someone who gets up when they can't.' Quite what he would've made of someone, shorn of an arm, who gets up and rejoins the circus, I don't know. There aren't enough titles in the world.

Sylvie is eighty-seven now. She still lives in Baltimore. She came to live in Britain in the 1960s after she and Jimmy were divorced, but returned for a holiday in 1974 and never came back. There is something about this city that feels like home.

For as long as I can recall, Sylvie and Terry were not on speaking terms. Nobody remembers why – it's shrugged off as one of those things that happens in families. 'They were very close,' says my grandma. 'But, oh, they fought like cats and dogs.'

Sylvie's family in America reassure me that whatever went on, she still received a birthday card every year from Terry. 'That's because I remembered and bought it and sent it!' says Grandma, cackling in delight as she shatters the illusion.

Sylvie has lived an extraordinary life, one touched with

tragedy as well as triumph. In 1964, just weeks after her father had died, her two-year-old daughter Judy drowned in their swimming pool. Sylvie was left with the haunting thought of whether, without her amputation, she might have been able to save her. Again, she somehow found a way – to be a mother, to be a wife, to move forward.

She lives in her Baltimore home with her second husband Tom. But even though Sylvie is an ocean away, in her mind she's back in Paddington. In recent years, she has suffered with dementia, and the period to which she perpetually returns is her wartime experiences with her family. Any fall-out with her brother, like most of the relatively recent past, has long been forgotten. 'Her reality is she's in London, and she's much younger,' explains her daughter Jenny. 'And every time I visit her the first thing she'll say is, "Have you seen my Terry?".'

She's still witty, still fiery. She still has the same sandpaper-dry humour that was evident in Terry. 'Even though she has dementia, sometimes you can talk to her and you wouldn't know it,' says Jenny. 'A new nurse practitioner came in yesterday, and asked her, "Sylvia, do you know what year it is?" And she looked at her, paused for a moment, and said, "Do you?".'

She asks after 'her Terry' regularly, even now that he's dead. For a long time, her family couldn't bear to tell her that he'd passed away. They feared causing more upset and confusion. 'It was difficult,' says Jenny. 'At first we'd just say that he wasn't well; that he was in the hospital.' But that only led to more questions – what was wrong? Why couldn't she go to his bedside? 'Eventually we had to tell her that he'd passed away and that he was in heaven, with her mum and dad, and that they would be together soon.'

And then Sylvie would get upset. She would cry. Why, she

would ask, did she not have the opportunity to speak to Terry before he passed?

Only, she did. In the weeks before Terry died, with his health failing, a phone call arrived from Baltimore. It was Sylvie. For the first time in more than twenty years, brother and sister spoke. In the grip of dementia, a precious if unremembered reconciliation.

In the end, I decided to pay up for ancestry.com. I got more than I bargained for: I got a new cousin.

When I logged on to Terry's page, I'd seen the four children I expected to be listed: Wendy, my mum, and her three younger brothers: Terence Junior, Paul, and Richard.* But then there was another, unexpected, entry. A fifth child, by a different mother – Terry's first born. His name, according to the website, was Terence Michael Downes.

At first I thought perhaps it was a mistake. After all, the Downes family are notoriously widespread, perhaps this was another branch. The name felt like a substantial coincidence, but then in fairness the men in the family do all tend to share one of about four names. I know of at least six cousins called Wally. Perhaps this was simply an error. Plus, surely no one could have an ego so large he would name not one but two sons after himself? Could they?

Or perhaps it was someone falsely laying claim to a family link? There are plenty of reasons to want to say your grandfather was a world champion boxer – the bragging rights, the

---

* I never really use those names. As was his wont, Terry Senior insisted on calling them Tel, Buster and Rigo, and the names have stuck.

kudos, the potential book deal. Perhaps this 'Terence Michael Downes' was just an imposter. Where was he even born, anyway?

I scoured the records. 'Baltimore, 1957'. Ah. The odds of this all being a really big coincidence were, by this stage, dramatically diminishing. As you will discover later, we already knew of at least one other child Terry had sired out of wedlock. The claim of this Baltimore boy was becoming more credible all the time. And then, on the cusp of an exciting discovery, a tragic twist. A couple more clicks revealed another entry under Terence Michael Downes' file. A newspaper clipping from October 1980:

'OBITUARY, DOWNES: On October 27, TERENCE, devoted father of Shaine, beloved son of Maria (née Baccala) and Vincent Cala, beloved brother of Victoria, Vincent and Mark Cala.'

If this was Terry's first son, why was this the first I've heard of him? And what caused him to die at just twenty-three?

I've since learned Maria Cala was the married name of the eldest daughter of Sam Baccala, himself a former professional boxer in the Baltimore area, with a record of forty-one wins from eighty fights. Aside from working as a brickmason and taking an active role in local Republican politics, he coached boxing at Baltimore's South Eastern Police Boy's Club. These were summer camps for inner-city kids, funded by local cops. It's presumably through his involvement in the local boxing scene that he encountered Terry.

Sam's daughter, Maria, was five feet two with a shock of red hair and a captivating personality. It seems she and Terry met in 1956. By that time, Terry had been in America for several years, graduating from the YMCA gym to join up with the US Marines. A child was conceived, but before it was even born Terry had returned to the UK to pursue his professional boxing career.

As far as I'm aware, Terry maintained no contact with the son he had with Maria. I have to admit, this sits at odds with my idealised image of Terry as a family man. The pedestal on which I've placed him does not crumble, but creaks. It seems inevitable that the more you discover about a person, the more their imperfections become apparent. I suppose that's why sometimes relationships between grandparents and grand-children feel so easy – because they're spared the exposing, inescapable intimacy of the parent-child dynamic.

But then, in mitigation, there's the fact that the child was named after him. That suggests to me there was at least an initial intent for him to be involved. Knowing what I do of Terry's dad, Dick, it would not surprise me if he had sought to whisk the promising boxer away from the constraints of a young family. He was insistent that Terry's focus should be fighting. Even when Terry met the woman he would eventually marry, my grand-mother, his father expressed concerns the relationship would prove disruptive to his career. Perhaps I am making excuses for Terry. I don't know; it is difficult to reconcile the doting grandad I knew with an absent father – but one was a man of consider-ably more years and experience. Maybe that was a factor too.

I've since discovered Terry and Maria's son preferred to go by his middle name, Michael – perhaps to distance him-self from his eminent yet estranged father. Sylvie's daughter Jenny remembers meeting him once. 'He came to our house, back when I was in high school,' she says. 'He was just a kid, maybe twenty. He knocked on the door, with all this red curly hair, and said, "I'm Terry Downes' son". This must have been around 1977 or '78.'

It's sad to think that just two years later, still no closer to knowing his dad, he had died. And sadder still to look over that obituary again and note that he left behind a son of his own: Shaine.

It all makes sense now. There's a reason James McNicholas doesn't look like the eldest grandson of a world champion boxer. It's because he's not: Shaine Downes is.

I eventually track him down on Facebook. Say what you like about Fake News or social responsibility, that search functionality is still damned useful. How else would you conduct espionage on a prospective employee, ex-girlfriend, or newly discovered distant family member? Crucially, the site also gives me the opportunity to scroll through his pictures and get a sense of the kind of man he is.

The answer: the manliest kind of man. A man's man's man. Shaine is forty-four now, ten years older than me, but is in incredible shape. He is a wall of muscle, shoulders that flank his torso like tyres on a monster truck. His profile is full of photos of gym grimaces and shirtless smiles, flexed biceps and raised beers. He is everything I'm not, and everything a very primal part of me can't help but wish I was.

Finding him isn't entirely straightforward – Shaine has dropped the 'Downes' name from his profile. Given that, I'm not sure how my approach will be received. I send him a message, saying tentatively that we may share a grandfather. That we may be cousins. As those familiar dots appear to suggest an impending reply, I hold my breath.

I needn't have worried. 'Gosh this is awesome!' comes the response. 'I always wondered if my family over there even knew

I was alive <crying laughing emoji>. So very nice and cool to connect with you!'

We arrange to speak via videocall, as is the vogue in 2021, and it turns out to be so very nice and cool indeed. When he answers I notice a striking resemblance to my (well, our) uncle, Terry Junior (the UK edition). He still lives in Baltimore – only twenty minutes or so from Jenny and Sylvie.

'This has been a mystery my whole life,' he says. 'My mom never really spoke too much about it. I think she's been crushed since my father tragically passed . . . She'd always tell me I had a lot of family in England, and maybe in the States, and that one day I'd come across them. But she had no clue where they were.'

Shaine had heard the stories. Uncles would whisper that his grandfather was a world champion boxer – he was once accosted in the gym by someone who claimed to know Terry – but he had no way of proving the link. His father passed away when he was only three. Shaine had no memory of either him or his grandmother, Maria.

'The thing that made it more difficult personally, and for my mother, is that my father was a merchant marine,' Shaine explains. 'So he was all over the place – he was never in one place long enough to form relationships with family. I don't think my mother knew much about it either.'

One reason Shaine didn't pursue his British family is that he suspected he might be an unwelcome surprise. The other was a reluctance to rake up the trauma of his father's passing, particularly for his mother's sake.

The story of Michael's death is, unfortunately, one wrapped in mystery and violence. 'He was in Louisiana, supposedly he was hitchhiking home,' says Shaine. 'No one really knows what happened. They found him on the side of the road – he was either hit and flew at least ninety feet or dragged ninety feet along the pavement. It was pretty much a scrape-up job. They never found who was responsible. That's the part that's haunted me my whole life.

'My uncle, his step-brother, says they don't know if he saw something he shouldn't have seen, or was in with the wrong people . . . He thinks he was ejected out of a car at a high speed and hit by oncoming traffic. These merchant marines go from port to port; you don't know where he might have been coming from. Down in Louisiana there's some shady people, you never know.'

Given Shaine's impressive physique, the obvious question is whether he's a fan of boxing. Of course he is – and he even has plans to step into a ring himself. 'In fact,' he says, 'I was actually in training to be a professional wrestler pre-Covid.'

Of course. Terry's first grandson was never going to be a chubby speccy comedian. Instead, he's the next Hulk Hogan.

I was a fan of wrestling growing up, in the WWF heyday of The Rock, Stone Cold Steve Austin and Triple H, the man whose name sounds like a type of battery. Occasionally I'd watch it at Terry's house. For someone who fought in legitimate competition, he took a surprising amount of pleasure out of the pantomime and pageantry. I think he understood their licence to entertain, maybe even envied it a little. He was a sportsman by trade, but a showman by nature.

For Shaine, stepping between those ropes has been a lifelong goal. 'It's simulated fake violence!' he marvels. 'Your job is to be believable and entertain the crowd. You can't ask for anything more than that.'

Shaine had been planning to enrol with MCW Pro Wrestling –

the Maryland independent wrestling promotion that forms part of the talent pool which feeds the giant WWE. MCW has been graced by greats like Ricky Steamboat, The Road Warriors and Jerry 'The King' Lawler. Shaine was all ready to follow in their footsteps: he'd styled himself as a nefarious persona called 'The Ultimate Ego' and had his uniform and entrance music picked out. 'I've always been a villain,' he says, in a manner so gentle and soft I am tempted to offer him acting lessons. 'I clotheslined the doctor the moment I was born.

'Physically there were things I needed to change,' he says. 'My goal was to be 270 pounds and sustain thirty minutes of cardio at my target heart rate, and I was in a position where I'd achieved that. I was right there – and then Covid happened.'

'It's a three-month training process. They guarantee you at least one match and you talk about a contract from there. I'm forty-four now, but I know I could still do it.'

I tell Shaine there's still time. If I am going to try and learn to box, him learning to wrestle seems like a doddle. And I tell him that when the world reopens, and the time comes, when that entrance music hits and The Ultimate Ego walks down to the ring for his debut bout, I'll be there in the crowd, booing with the rest of them.

It's inescapable that despite growing up almost 4,000 miles away, Shaine has inherited traits of Terry's that I simply haven't: the physicality, the muscularity, the machismo. Maybe his distance, physical and emotional, granted him the liberty to do that. I always knew I was not born to box – but the scale of Terry's achievements made trying to seem pointless. I always knew that I could never match him. Why fight, when I can only lose?

As we go to finish the call, Shaine says he has one last thing to show me. On the wall in his apartment, he has framed pro-grammes from two of Terry's most famous fights – victories over world champion Paul Pender and all-time great Sugar Ray Robinson. In our family homes in the UK, we're lucky enough for this kind of memento to be relatively commonplace. They've been handed down through the generations, memorabilia of the family myth. Shaine bought his on eBay. It's a touching tie to a family he never knew, and a grandfather he never met.

I put him in touch with Jenny and send him some more memorabilia in the post. It's the least I can do. He's family.

IN MY CORNER

They call it brain fog; a cognitive mist that rolls into your life, causing the sensation of impaired cerebral function.

You have to grasp for thoughts, for memories, for answers. Sometimes for spellings or simple calculations. Everything is slower. Imagine, if you will, that your brain synapses run on broadband, but you're unfortunate enough to be a subscriber to Virgin's internet service.* It feels a little like being drunk, only without the fun bit. Perhaps a better analogy is waking up every day with an unexplained hangover – paying the penance but without savouring the memory of the night before.

I found it hard enough to walk straight, now I couldn't think straight either. Sometimes it felt as if the tinnitus I could hear was the cogs and wheels of my mind, squeaking and grinding rustily as I fought to get my brain in gear again.

---

* The observant among you will notice that the pandemic lockdown period has left me with a considerable axe to grind regarding declining broadband speeds. Hell hath no fury like a nerd denied internet access.

Brain fog is not classed as a medical condition in itself, but a series of symptoms. It is, however, frequently associated with a number of illnesses: sufferers of ME, fibromyalgia, lupus, and chronic migraine may be aware of the feeling. I have to be honest and say this is the kind of condition I would previously have treated with scepticism. It sounds too loose, too nebulous to grasp – until it happens to you. At that point it becomes alarmingly real. These conditions are sometimes called 'invisible illnesses', but in my case it was perfectly visible. You saw it in my face, in my manner. I was irritable, I was angry.

I think I found it particularly difficult, as previously I'd always prided myself on being quick. I don't mean physically – on one school sports day, my class entered my jiggling teenage form into the 100 metres 'as a joke'. Mentally, however, I've always been sharpish – maybe like one of those big knives old people use to open letters. You know, not sharp enough to cut an apple, but sharp enough that they probably wouldn't let you take it on a plane. Alacrity of thought was, in essence, my trade. Overnight, I lost half a step mentally. I felt like I went from class clown to class dunce.

I did wonder if I'd ever be funny again. Whatever happened on that boat robbed me of many things – my balance, sure, but also my sense of humour and, with that, my identity. Just as I could no longer see the beauty in the dappled light of sunset, so too could I no longer find the humour in the simplest things, such as an old man unabashedly farting.

Brain fog mimics exhaustion, and it is in itself exhausting. We've blasted through the first few rounds of this book. In boxing terms, now is the point where stamina becomes every bit as important as strength; where lungs and heart are as integral as hands and fists. But the brain matters too. The ability

The Champ and The Chump, back in 1986

The Champ, The Chump (*right*) and the boy who put a banana
into a video machine, my brother Charlie (*left*)

A man in uniform: Terry in the US Marines

Terry (*bottom left*) and his Marine boxing squad at the Golden Gloves tournament

Me (*right*) making the best of it at the special forces boot camp

The relentless marching beginning to take its toll

My grandma Barbara watches one of Terry's fights from the crowd

Terry and Barbara celebrate their wedding in 1958

Grandma and Pop, the newly-weds

Camille and I getting married at Islington Town Hall in 2017

Barbara with Camille and me on our wedding day

Me at Higher Tregerest, the farm Terry was evacuated to during WW2

Arguably the closest I've come to elite sporting competition, performing in
sketch show *Mr Edinburgh 2016* with Owen Roberts (*centre*) and
Ciarán Dowd (*right*) of BEASTS

Terry celebrates claiming the
iconic Lonsdale Belt

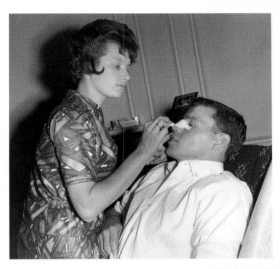

Barb applies 'lotion' to Terry's
vulnerable nose in the build-up
to his Wembley world title fight

Terry (*right*) in the process of
defeating Paul Pender for the
world middleweight crown,
11 July 1961

Terry celebrates his world title win with wife Barbara (*left*)
and mum Hilda (*centre*)

A cut and bruised Terry holds the world title aloft in 1961

to make those instant micro-calculations, to spot opportunity and avoid danger.

Writing requires a similar combination of reflex and endurance. You need to be instinctive in the moment and show the patience and persistence to chisel away until you have a finished product. That's hard when you can't seem to concentrate for more than a few minutes without succumbing to migraine or meandering thoughts. It's difficult to focus when you can't, well, focus. Returning to writing took time. Just as I was learning to put one foot in front of the other, I slowly started to put one word after the other too.

Perhaps in an attempt to speed my return to productivity, on hearing about my plight several people (doctors included) suggested that it might be a good idea to stop drinking. It makes sense: we all know it's bad for us. To the contrary, I found that having at least one drink a day eased my symptoms. It somehow quelled the waves, dampened down my misfiring nervous system. The sensation of the world moving around you is somehow less alien with a bit of alcohol in your system. You don't feel broken, you feel like a cheap date. I kidded myself I was Samuel Coleridge. As Byron had used opiates, I used Kopparbergs.

Of course, this was a dangerous habit to acquire for the child of two alcoholics. In the space of a few weeks I went from an 'occasional drinker' to nightly nightcaps. Not exactly dependency, but not exactly independence either.

Round Five

MARINES

'You've got sixty seconds to get your gear together and get on the move!'

Move? Moving seems impossible. I can barely complete the latest command of thirty press-ups, my arms quivering and crumbling under the weight of my bloated body.

Exhausted, aching, and unsure if I'm about to cry or be sick, I reach into my bag for a snack. It probably demonstrates my naivety about what I was getting into that I've deemed it appropriate to bring a 200g bar of Dairy Milk with me. This after all, is a special forces-style training boot camp. A chance for me to see if I can follow in my grandfather's marching footsteps. A weekend where competitive spirits gather to push themselves to their very limits. None of the other cadets have brought Cadburys.

Desperate to replenish my ailing sugar levels, I quickly stuff a few squares into my mouth. However, before I can swallow them, there are more orders. We're unceremoniously told to hit the deck and produce another thirty press-ups. As my aching arms heave me up and down, the Dairy Milk starts spilling out of my mouth, brown-stained saliva dripping down my chin as the drill sergeant looks on in horror.

They've never seen anything quite like this. It's special, alright: a chocolatey mockery of military might. Later that weekend, they'll teach me survival techniques, but it will be far too late. I'm already way beyond saving.

The next chapter in Terry's life began when his YMCA boxing team faced their US Marine equivalents at the military camp in Quantico, Virginia. Terry actually lost his bout, but his friend Elwood 'Country' Myers,* won his in style. After the fights, the pair were approached by a Marine major to ask if they'd be interested in signing up. The pitch was appealing: once the gruelling initial training was over, they were promised they'd be transferred to the relatively local camp at Quantico, and given weekend passes back to Baltimore whenever they wanted. 'Life is luxury in the Marines when you're on the boxing squad,' they were assured.

Another factor in Terry's decision was the looming prospect of conscription via the US Service draft. He knew that call would most likely come in his early twenties, exactly when he hoped to be boxing professionally. If he joined the Marines at seventeen, he could do the required three years' service and be out of there before turning twenty-one – and all with his mate 'Country' along for the ride.

---

* There are few things less imaginative than the male nicknaming process. 'Country' was so called because he lived just outside Baltimore rather than within the city.

Or so he thought. By the time he resolved to sign up, Myers' draft for December 1953 was already full, so Terry was allocated to the January 1954 set. He would be undertaking this journey alone. He was told he'd be dispatched to a training camp at Parris Island, South Carolina. Well to Terry, that sounded like a tropical paradise, like Margate with palm trees. He pictured girls in coconut bras and hula skirts feeding him coconut water and Hula Hoops. To top it off, they offered him six weeks' wages up front. All he needed to do was get through the intensive twelve-week training period. How bad could it be?

Turns out, pretty bad. 'You couldn't make a film out of it and make it look bad enough to be true,' Terry once told an interviewer. He might be right, but if anyone has come close it's Stanley Kubrick. His 1987 movie, *Full Metal Jacket*, is partially set at the Parris Island camp and does provide a flavour of the abusive nature of the drill instructors. The casting assistant, Leon Vitali, provides some insight as to what those actors were put through to try and emulate the disciplinarian regime they would have encountered in the Marines. 'We found the extras in the Territorial Army,' Vitali told *The Guardian*. 'I auditioned them first, then had them come to Beckton. I'd ask them a few basic questions, but what can you tell from that? So actor Lee Ermey – who had been a former drill instructor – and I decided we would line them up, just as if they'd got off the bus at the training camp, and then Lee would go down, one by one, and just decimate them. It was astonishing.'

I have to say, I don't think that sounds like an acting role I'm particularly cut out for. I once walked out of a dance rehearsal for children's TV series *Horrible Histories* because I thought the choreographer was being too critical of my hip-hop moves.

When Terry and the rest of the hundred or so sign-ups

from Baltimore stepped off the bus, the abuse hit them like a wall of heat, drenching them in disdain. It's psychologically bruising, and fighting back only results in more punishment. Being a Brit – 'a limey' – meant Terry was singled out for worse treatment than most.

Upon arrival at the camp, you underwent the weighty symbolism of being stripped of your civilian clothes, which were posted back to your home address. Heads were shaved, skin disinfected, uniforms applied. The classic fatigue hat was pulled down over your eyes to force you to keep your head up. Of course, the upshot was that if a sergeant aimed a whack at you, you wouldn't see it coming. The physical abuse was relentless. 'It's a hell hole,' Terry said later. 'It's worse than any prison could be.'

'It was awful', confirms my grandma. 'Pop used to tell me that if you didn't shave well enough, they'd put a bucket over your head and make you shave in there, while they whacked it with batons. People would come out cut to pieces.'

Initially, there was no real combat training, just mental conditioning. 'You was just dirt until they drilled you long enough to be called a Marine', said Terry. This was a period of intense exertion, exhaustive psychological profiling. It's essentially brainwashing, shaping you into a potential super soldier. Terry, previously quick to talk or punch back, had to learn to bite his tongue, the scar he acquired as a teenager in Taunton a permanent reminder of the price of insubordination.

At Parris Island, around a dozen of Terry's platoon dropped out. Maybe they were the lucky ones. In the course of the initial training, two people committed suicide. An advance of six weeks' wages doesn't feel like much against months of torture. Terry was put on a night sentry duty, meaning it was his job to go round waking the recruits whose nerves were so frayed that they had begun wetting the bed.

Escape is impossible: the entire camp is surrounded by alligator-infested swampland.* Two years after Terry's boot camp in 1956, a drunken drill instructor ill-advisedly took his assigned platoon on a punitive night-time march into Ribbon Creek, a marshy tidal bog. Six recruits died, drowned in the swamp.

The incident led to changes to drill-instructor training and recruitment − but it came too late for Terry. In his time at Parris Island, there was a degree of depravity, of institutionalised abuse, to some of the punishments inflicted. One story tells of a young recruit being put in the clothes dryer as 'part of the training'.†

Eventually, somehow, Terry made it through. Towards the end of his boot camp, he wrote to the major who'd initially approached him, saying he was almost done with training and ready to cash in that promise to join the boxing squad at Quantico. A reply came back saying that the major had been posted to Korea. 'Crikey,' thought Terry. 'Must have been a big envelope.'

*   *   *

---

* Alongside my issues with monkeys, I did once encounter an eight-foot alligator during a family holiday to Florida, when I was about nine years old. It had wandered on to a golf course at the resort we were staying in. Because they look all sleepy and slow, I thought it would be a good idea to go and poke this alligator with a stick. Somehow, I survived. I remember a man shouting at us to move away, and he later told us gators were as fast as a horse. If that's true, I insist we enter one into the Grand National or something. Imagine the spectacle.

† It's not clear from reports whether or not he came out shrunk.

When I told people that I was doing a full special forces-style boot camp led by genuine ex-SAS staff, they looked at me like I was mad. Many were legitimately worried for me, like this might be indicative of some latent intent to destroy myself, a voluntary suicide mission. For some reason, the fear never quite sank in with me. I would just shrug that it was fine, that I was doing it 'for a book' and query how bad it could really be.*

In advance of the trip, we were sent a list of essential kit. Some seemed obvious: waterproof jacket, ankle-supporting boots, tent. Some items were a little more specific: a 'Silva' compass, glow sticks, a small notebook with four fifty pence pieces taped to the inside cover.† Frankly, it was all the same to me: I didn't have any of this stuff. I've lived in London for fifteen years: the only hike I'm bothered about is the recent increase in the congestion charge. By the time I'd assembled the necessary kit I'd spent more than double the total cost of the course.

One of the things about these training camps is that they like to continually move the goalposts, to keep itineraries and plans secret and surprising. The idea is to put you in a state of continual confusion, to see how you can handle the amplified stress. This process actually began about two weeks out, when the course location was moved from Essex to the Brecon Beacons over 200 miles away.

I'll be honest, that's when I began to worry. There had been something comforting about the fact that the course was relatively nearby, within my relative comfort zone of the Home Counties. I guess I had the security of knowing that, if it all

_____

* Answer: Very bad.

† Never found out what that last one was for.

went really wrong, I could always fall back on the same tactic I regularly deployed in my school days: tearfully calling my mum and asking her to come and get me.

I travelled to Wales the night before, turning my rucksack inside out to make sure I had all the compulsory kit. From the little I knew of special forces discipline, any omissions were certain to be punished. As I rifled through, disaster struck: I realised I had forgotten my gloves. What's more, it was 9pm, and what few shops there were locally were almost all closed. It was also May – warm gloves were technically out of season. In a state of panic, I sprinted into an Aldi and bought a pair of fluorescent pink gardening gloves. I hoped that, at the very least, the SAS guys would appreciate my resourcefulness.

One upside of the switch in location is that, unlike Parris Island, the Brecon Beacons are legitimately beautiful. As I pull into the campsite at 6.30am, the scenery takes my breath away. Unfortunately, I never get it back.

The first sign of trouble comes when I ask the bloke setting up camp next to me what brings him here. It turns out he's ex-military and is here for a taste of the old days and to test himself against special forces standards. And he's not alone: quite a few of the thirty or so participants have served in some fashion. The rest are grizzled Tough Mudder types, the sort of people whose social media profile pictures show them posing at the top of a mountain. I hadn't anticipated this – I thought the relationship between this weekend course and full military service would be akin to that between Hackney Marshes and the Premier League. I'd expected a few mad Gareth Keenan types, a couple of stag dos, but basically a load of people a bit like me. Let me be clear: there is nobody here like me.

My confidence is dealt another blow by the fact people keep

asking me how long I've trained for the event. The answer is approximately twenty minutes – the length of time it took me to jog round my local park at the start of the week. It turns out some people have spent months running up and down mountains with their 'bergens' (or backpacks) on their back. I only bought mine the day before. I haven't even watched an episode of *SAS: Who Dares Wins*. I'm reminded of the old saying: 'Fail to prepare; you're absolutely fucked.'

We've been told that we must put up our tents and register before 8am. However, at 7.15am, the drill sergeant calls us all in and announces we're starting right now. Anyone who points out the discrepancy is accused of insubordination, and subjected to a dizzying cocktail of press-ups, sit-ups and burpees. They call this exhausting form of punishment 'beasting'. Before long, we're all being beasted into submission. Scores of press-ups are handed out for the most minor indiscretion: it might be a blank look, a frown or even a smile. There's no pleasing these guys.

I don't know quite what I expected from the drill sergeant: I thought he'd be firm but fair, like Paxman or something, but this guy is all stick and no carrot. In fairness, the drill sergeant (or 'DS') isn't half as bad as his hype men – half a dozen brutes who stalk around the group looking for stuff to shout about. This is obviously a bit of a laugh to them: they palpably enjoy dishing out a slither of what they've had to endure. They're like private school prefects – or worse, PE teachers. In some respects, it's fair enough: people have paid for a realistic experience, and these guys certainly play the part well. One of them, who looks a bit like J from nineties boyband 5ive if he fell into the transformative super-slime from the Teenage Mutant Ninja Turtles, singles me out early on. 'Watch it, you,' he says. 'You're catching my eye for all the wrong reasons.'

I haven't told anyone what I do, or why I'm there. I don't want special treatment, but I get it anyway. The sergeants suggest that the optimum special forces candidate is one who flies below the radar, who senior staff almost never notice – a 'grey man'. Bad news for me: I've spent my whole life trying to be noticed, and I'm not exactly grey – in fact, I'm wearing a fluorescent-blue raincoat with rainbow trim. I have at least made the sensible decision not to wear glasses, hoping that'll somehow disguise my frailty. Contact lenses are my camouflage. And yet, those eagle-eyed military men spot me right away.

I stand out like a sore thumb. The upshot of the early start is that I am not ready. My kit isn't properly organised, the guide ropes on my tent are flailing in the wind, and crucially I have not had breakfast. There is no mercy: we're all immediately handed an armband with a number – I'm number 73 – and told to crawl from one end of a muddy field to the other and back. And 'crawl' isn't quite right: with the drill sergeant's backing dancers yelling about the dangers of hypothetical shots flying overhead, we're told to drag ourselves, flat on the ground, face to the floor. I know they say an army marches on its stomach, but this is ridiculous.

Two bad things happen as a consequence of this miserable mud crawl. The first is my first dose of public humiliation. Once the group have gathered again, punished with more press-ups for leaving a few stragglers behind,* the DS calls us to attention.

'We've got a problem,' he says. 'Somebody's left "sign".'

This, it's explained, is when a piece of equipment or rations is left behind. It offers the enemy intelligence on your position, your supplies, your movements.

---

* Was I among said stragglers? No comment.

'So,' he continues, 'who is responsible for this?'

And with that, he holds up a little yellow packet of Soreen, the sweet malt loaf I had intended to be my breakfast. In my first few minutes in the military, I've given away our position by dropping what is essentially a lump of cake.

'Who eats this shit?'

Sheepishly, I raise my hand. 'I knew it'd be you, 73.'

'Leaving sign' is a crime, you'll be shocked to hear, punishable by press-ups. Already nauseous from the exercise and the embarrassment, I solemnly hit the deck and endure my sentence, J from 5ive shouting 'encouragement' in my ear throughout. It is not a good start.

The second bad thing is that, just a few minutes later, I realise that somewhere in the surrounding fields, my car key has fallen out of my pocket. I was in such a hurry, I forgot to tuck it safely away. I've left another 'sign' – sooner or later our imaginary enemy are going to find out that Britain's finest are about to arrive in a Vauxhall Corsa.

The Welsh countryside is thankfully free of alligators, but that's now my primary route of escape off limits. I'm stuck here.

Can I just shock you? I've never wanted to be in the Special Forces.

In fact, being in any form of military is pretty much my idea of hell. Nothing about it appeals: the uniform looks uncomfortable, the activities look dangerous and as far as I can tell there is very limited opportunity to engender laughter and applause.*

When I reached the sixth form at my school, we were given

---

* In fact, if that happens, you're almost certainly doing it wrong.

the opportunity to join the CCF – not the Communist Chinese Forces, that would be weird – the Combined Cadet Force. It's a Ministry of Defence-sponsored scheme that runs in almost 500 schools across the UK, granting young people between the ages of twelve and eighteen the opportunity to play at soldiers.

We were offered the chance to join a mini version of either the British Army, Royal Navy or Royal Air Force. From my point of view, the navy was discarded straightaway – under the lore of the playground, the navy had been determined to be 'gay' and at my school that was pretty much the worst thing you could be. There are few places more homophobic than a boys' school, it's almost a reaction to the inevitable homoerotic tension created by having hundreds of hormonal teenage lads on the same campus. Anyway, the widespread belief was that this particular branch of the military was in fact nothing more than a cover-up for a non-stop twenty-four-hour gay sex party – and, for some reason, this was determined to be a bad thing. As far as I recall, there was no logical basis for this assumption about naval practice, other than some obscure myth that 'they share beds'.*

The air force option was out of the question too. Their prime selling point was that at some point during the two-year course you are handed the controls to a plane. On that basis, I was immediately out. I'm not someone who should be trusted with the controls to any vehicle, let alone one that operates in three dimensions. It was around this time I turned seventeen and began driving lessons. Naturally, I was excited about the possibility of driving and the added freedom that might grant

---

* Once again, the Village People presumably have something to answer for here, on account of their 1978 hit *In the Navy*.

me. There wasn't even a bus stop in Letchmore Heath, so a car opened up all kinds of possibilities. After one particularly satisfying lesson, I felt I had the driving bug. 'I know,' I thought. 'I'll just go out and start the car in the front drive, reverse it back a bit, and then park it again. Just for a bit of practice.'

Of course, that isn't what happened. I somehow got my pedals mixed up, and instead of braking managed to accelerate backwards through the garage doors, tearing them off their hinges. These doors were electric, and apparently the cost of replacing them spiralled into four figures. I didn't drive again for a decade.

It would be another twelve years before I passed my test. In my first attempt, I failed in the most ridiculous fashion imaginable: for speeding. The instructor had to terminate the test as I had casually cruised up to 50mph in a 30mph zone.

Which is all to say: I knew even as a teenager that I should not be allowed to fly a plane.

That left me with the army. As far as I could tell that meant marching about while you were bawled at by a teacher masquerading as a drill sergeant. As a rule, being shouted at by teachers did not appeal to me – volunteering myself into a situation where that was effectively guaranteed seemed unreasonably masochistic. You did get to hold a gun, but given my general cack-handedness, I suspected this wasn't a good idea either.

And so, like Muhammad Ali before me, I became a conscientious objector.* The school made arrangements for those

---

* Despite being a military man himself, Terry actually launched a campaign supporting Ali's bid to box again after he was banned for refusing to be inducted in the armed forces in 1967.

who would not sign up for CCF on account of a) ethics or b) cowardice, setting up a range of volunteering schemes. I chose to do gardening in the school grounds, which was largely enjoyable apart from an incident where I was swinging around a pair of shears like a scythe to cut some long grass, accidentally let go and watched them fly within a yard of a boy called Mark Lobatto's head. Ironic really that despite making a pacifistic choice, I very nearly killed a man.*

If the Combined Cadets Force isn't ringing any bells with you, do not be alarmed. The CCF is principally the preserve of fee-paying schools, the elitist institutions attended by just six-and-a-half per cent of the population. Yes, in my own way, I was brainwashed and institutionalised: I went to private school. As I always say: 'As a wealthy six year old, what else was I going to spend my money on?'

Joking aside, the fact that I attended a private school remains a considerable source of unease, even guilt. That might seem absurd, because it wasn't my choice, but nevertheless it's true. I've always been flattered when people have suggested that I 'don't seem like' I went to private school. That's because, however vague that statement might seem, I know precisely what they mean. They mean that I don't seem like a cunt. I recognise that when someone who's been educated in a state school imagines a public schoolboy they basically envisage Boris Johnson. They assume it's a bunch of blond, blue-eyed bigots departing from Platform Nine and Three-Quarters to go and fuck pig skulls. While that wasn't my experience (some of

---

* I also did a stint volunteering at a local old people's home. At no point did I mention my distaste for life in the armed forces. It seemed a bit disrespectful as they love all that.

the boys had brown eyes), I understand why it's become the stereotype.

Consequently, I've probably actively cultivated the idea that I didn't benefit from such ludicrous privilege. I've chiselled a few consonants away from my cut-glass accent, no doubt. I've never talked about attending a private school on stage, for fear that the audience suddenly turn on me, and start throwing olives and heckling me with Karl Marx quotes. I confess that while I've had no issue talking about accidentally defecating in an art lesson, talking about school in general makes me feel uneasy. For all my many flaws, it's the fact I went to private school that instils in me a panic that you'll no longer like me.*

It is uncomfortable. I am proud of my working-class roots, but roots are all they are. The trunk, the branches, the leaves all stretch out into the middle classes, and there is no more powerful symbol of that than my pricey education. And I'm embarrassed about it.

I'll tell you who wasn't embarrassed about it: Terry. He sent all four of his children to fee-paying schools. I know for a fact that being able to do so is something he was incredibly proud of. Yes, it was arguably a means to cement the family's social ascent, but it was also simply a case of a father trying to do the best for his kids.

His three sons, my uncles, all attended Haberdashers' Aske's Boys School in Elstree. It's there they befriended my dad, Barry. Through them, he met my mum. And it is there that, decades later, I would be enrolled as a seven year old.

---

* Perhaps that's why it's taken me the better part of 150 pages to get round to talking about it properly.

The school was founded in 1690 by a Royal Charter granted to the Worshipful Company of Haberdashers. Having originated in Hoxton in London, the school moved to Hertfordshire in 1903 to occupy its current 104-acre plot. To attend Haberdashers' – known more commonly as Habs – currently costs an eye-watering £7,053 per term, approximately double what it did in my day. That's over £21,000 per school year. To put that in context, my fee for this book will not pay back a single year of my education. It's difficult to mount an argument that it was money well spent.*

My parents funnelled a huge percentage of their income into our education, placing them and their relationship under considerable strain. There were other boys at the school whose families were even more stretched – a high proportion of the students were from second-generation immigrant families, who must have made enormous sacrifices for their kids. Habs lacks the pretention and pageantry associated with some private schools – there are no boarders, no boaters. There was a real emphasis on academia – in 2014, *The Telegraph* placed the school at eighth in the country for A Levels, with 80.87% of students achieving the A*–A grades. For Terry, sending his kids must have seemed a way of getting a firm foothold on the social ladder.

The thing is, with an education like that, you're supposed to get a proper job. Approximately twenty per cent of Habs students go on to study at Oxford or Cambridge. All being well, there should be some kind of guaranteed return on the huge layout, a career in the back end.

---

* Conveniently, I am able to comfortably assert that I won't send my children to private school on ethical grounds, all the while safe in the knowledge that I'll never be able to afford it.

The trouble is that while you can buy an education, you can't really buy class. You can't buy values. Of the four children Terry put through private school, only one – my uncle Richard – went to university. My dad went, but chose the niche subject of Ancient Oriental Art at SOAS, the School of Oriental and African Studies. He dropped out after a term to pursue a career in the music industry, without telling his parents. Neither my mum nor my dad have ever admitted to me what grades they left their expensive education with. I'd venture that both families understood the price of education, but not necessarily the value.

I called my mum up to ask, one final time, how she did at school. 'Honestly? I never went,' she says. 'If a report came back and it was bad, Grandma just used to hide it and tell Pop there wasn't a report that term. And he didn't know any better.' In some respects, for Terry's family the pressure was off. The fact their kids went to private school was already the achievement. That was enough in itself.

My mum, however, says she learned from the mistakes of her generation. 'I knew that we'd squandered it a bit, and I knew how not to make that mistake with you.'

Unfortunately, I wasn't someone inclined to take advantage of all the opportunities made available to me. I remember that at the start of sixth form, there was a big meeting one lunchtime which we were encouraged to attend if we were considering applying for Oxbridge. After encouragement from a couple of teachers, I decided to go along. I remember an opening address in which a member of staff explained that if we didn't really want it, if it wasn't what we desired above anything else, we shouldn't be there. I immediately got up and left. Looking back, part of it was a kind of inverted snobbery, part of it was laziness. I didn't want to do the work. To be presented with such an opportunity, and turn your nose up at it, reeks of entitlement. It didn't feel like it at the time though. It felt like rebellion.

Around the same time at school we went through an aptitude test – a series of exams which formed a statistical profile of our strengths and weaknesses, and recommended jobs accordingly. I remember that bizarrely my score for 'spatial awareness' was by far my highest, which led to the somewhat niche suggestion that I become an 'art gallery director'. I was just relieved it didn't say 'lawyer', the role that my teachers seemed to have earmarked for me.

The bulk of pupils that leave Habs seem to go into one of three jobs: doctor, banker or lawyer. The boys who excel in science study medicine, and the boys who excel in maths enter the city. I was part of the third group, the type who excelled in fluffier subjects like 'English' and 'Art'. Becoming a lawyer was the optimum outcome for our particular sector.

But I didn't want that. From a young age I remember being determined to do something creative, to follow a career path that took me off the beaten track. In an environment packed with high-achievers, an artistic route does become an act of mutiny. There's a bit of a history of that at Habs, which has spawned comics like David Baddiel, Sacha Baron Cohen and Matt Lucas. My own dad left school with aspirations of a career in the music industry. He was the peroxide-quiffed front-man for a New Romantic band called Vibroge. It was only my birth, when he was twenty-three, that forced him to enter his dad's building business, McNicholas Construction, in search of a more stable living. I've always carried some guilt over that – and it's no coincidence that at thirty-five I still haven't had children. I didn't want anything taking me off my path, like I took him off his. Dick Downes would doubtless approve.

My performative streak really began to emerge at around sixteen. I guess for a chubby kid in specs being on stage presented a rare opportunity to be the centre of attention. I did go to university, in theory to study English Literature. I sat through the seminars and flicked through the books, but most of my time was spent working on my acting – either in the university's drama society, or in tutorials pretending to have read the relevant text. Throughout this period, I think my parents probably harboured hopes that I would eventually correct course with a much-vaunted 'law conversion', a kind of plea bargain made by remorseful arts students when they realise the true horror of their career prospects.

After university, however, I spent a year at drama school, which is probably the closest I got to any sort of boot camp. They didn't make me shave my head, but they did make me cut my Mick Hucknall-esque locks shorter in order to open up more casting opportunities.*

Drama school is nonetheless an intense environment. I saw people break, I saw people cry, I saw a man wiggling around pretending to be a snake. Don't think I haven't lived because I have.

Conventionally, actor training courses take three years. It's a slow, steady process, in which your bad habits are gradually worn away and replaced with technique. The course I attended, at the Central School of Speech & Drama lasted less than ten months.† It was just enough time to expose your flaws, make

---

* It didn't.

† The school has recently been renamed as The 'Royal' Central School of Speech & Drama, a change entirely meaningless to me but which delighted those more aspirational elements of my family. I've basically put this in for my grandma.

you acutely aware of your shortcomings, and then fling you out into the industry.

The course I did was entitled 'Classical Acting', which meant it had a focus on heavyweight historical texts, from Ancient Greece through to Elizabethan-Jacobean England. Nothing prepares you for a career in the modern media like studying plays written hundreds of years ago. You do get shouted at, but usually by other actors rather than drill sergeants. They scream Shakespeare monologues into your face, hoping against hope that by turning up the volume they'll somehow amplify the feeling.

It is training though, and it is useful. There are vocal exercises, movement exercises, you learn techniques to connect to emotion. You learn that the appearance of spontaneity is often underpinned by technique – something which is equally true in sport. Is it strictly necessary? No. A Marine *has* to learn how to fire that gun. It's a non-negotiable. If an actor doesn't do a term on Sanford Meisner's Repetition Technique, they can probably still do the job. Loads of actors that have never set foot in a drama school become stars. It's probably rare you get a guy coming into the army like Rambo without a single day's training.

On the day I graduated drama school, they awarded comedian Jo Brand an honorary degree. The fact that she didn't have any kind of performing qualification hadn't seemed to hold her back until then. She actually did a joint social science degree with a registered mental nurse qualification at Brunel University. That's proper. That's impressive. That's an education. But had she ever seen a man wiggling around pretending to be a snake? Had she fuck.

*   *   *

I quit the boot camp at approximately 9.30 a.m. Or at least, I try to. We're on what's known as a 'TAB' – tactical advance to battle – essentially a quick-paced march across the Welsh countryside, wearing our backpacks loaded with kit. Except my carefully packed bag is haemorrhaging equipment at a dangerous pace. Desperate to avoid a repeat of my Soreen shame, I've got a sleeping bag tucked under one arm, an inflatable mattress under the other, and a tub of hypoallergenic shower gel between my teeth. It's less brigadier, more Buckaroo.

How has it come to this? Well one of the many baffling exercises we'd been asked to perform on this exhausting morning was to empty out the contents of our backpacks for inspection. And when I say empty out, I mean it: even the sleeping bag was unfurled onto the still-wet grass. Once we'd proven we had the requisite gear, we were given 120 seconds to get everything back into the bag.

Now anyone who has tried to put a sleeping bag back in its bag knows that alone takes a good deal more than two minutes. I had spent hours meticulously packing my bergen, using every inch of available space to cram it with medical supplies and malt loaf. When I hurriedly attempted to shove it all in, there simply wasn't room.*

And so here I am, running uphill, quite literally trying to hold it all together. When I drop my sleeping bag in a puddle, I give in to my heavy heart and heavier legs, gasping for breath, and slow to a stop. Just a couple of hours into the training, I have absolutely made my mind up to quit.

---

* Apart from physical fitness, it seems the main attribute required for a life in the military is the ability to pack a bag quickly. On that basis, I'm thinking of sending my wife.

Apparently, however, that isn't an option. One of the staff informs me that actually I won't be quitting. Not only that, I'll be catching up with the rest of the group, who are pulling away. I buy into the idea. A comeback story? Picking myself up off the canvas and fighting back? I like the sound of that.

'Think of your family,' screams one of the staff.

He's right. What would Terry think? We fight on.

Approximately five seconds later, I am heaving again, just wishing desperately for it all to be over. We can't all be heroes.

It becomes very clear, as the day wears on, that I am incredibly under-prepared and entirely ill-suited to the demands of the course. The boot-camp process, I'm told, has two primary purposes: to improve your fitness, and to separate the mentally strong from the mentally weak. The hazing, the insults, the seemingly inane orders – it's all intended to turn you into an action hero automaton. They break you down and build you up. It's drama school all over again.

The exhaustion and the monotony of the drills combined with the officious, aggressive staff gives me flashbacks to school PE lessons and the annual horror of the 'Bleep Test' (sometimes called 'Beep Test') where children are asked to run back and forth across a sports hall at ever decreasing intervals until they are eliminated. It's survival of the fittest, and a slaughtering of the fattest.

There are bits of the training I can tolerate. A lesson on map-reading provides me with some precious recovery time. The first-aid session, led by a couple of paramedics, is genuinely useful for someone as injury-prone as me. We're taught how to hold and carry weapons – and let me tell you, it turns out that nothing grips a rifle like a pair of Aldi gardening gloves. But other than that, the constant attempts to bamboozle you are just maddening. Join the SAS and it seems you have to leave your logic at the door. You can't reason with anyone because the process is, by its nature, unreasonable. At one point, J from 5ive demands that I run to the end of a far field and tell him 'what colour that bush is'.

I dutifully stumble down to the bush in question and return to inform him, 'It's green.'

'No, no it's not,' he says. 'It's blue. Run down there and check it again, and I think you'll find it's blue.'

I can't decide if he's a cunt or he's colour-blind.

There are other incidents that defy rationality, such as when the DS announces we'll soon be embarking on another morale-sapping march. Before that, he undertakes an inspection of our water supplies. I've recently had a drink, so my bottle is only about eighty-per cent full. In response to this perceived misconduct, the DS promptly empties the remainder over my head. It doesn't strike me as the best use of precious supplies.

Even some of the anecdotes about serving in the front line are pretty weird. When one of our group asks if they can leave their sleeping bag in their tent, a seemingly sensible question, one of the SAS guys embarks on a dramatic monologue about a tour to Afghanistan. 'Me and two other guys ended up having to sleep out in the middle of nowhere overnight,' he explains. 'We had one emergency blanket between the three of us. We had to lie there, huddled together and shivering, with a desert storm blowing against us. There was only one way we could keep warm: farting on each other.'

Talk about a windbreaker.

I manage to stifle a laugh and bite my tongue. I try to keep a low profile. The problem is, I don't need to speak to give away how out of my depth I am. I'm not just a fish out of a water, I'm a fish in a deep fat fryer.

As the day wears on, my departure begins to feel like an inevitability. It's a case of when not if. The course is designed to break you, and I am breaking badly. The final straw comes when my own incompetence begins to impact on others. The drill sergeants have a neat trick of punishing everyone else for your mistakes. After I put my bag down without permission, the rest of the platoon are made to perform thirty press-ups, shouting 'Thank you, number 73!' between each one. My job is simply to stand in front of them, shouting back, 'You're welcome'. Grateful though I am for the rest, the shame and the guilt is intolerable. It's enough for me. I hand over my armband. This time, there's no going back.

Why do I quit? It's psychological, but physical too. I'm certainly unfit and the dizziness hasn't helped. Hungry, dehydrated and exhausted, that never-ending rocking has been wilder than ever. But I don't want to offer any excuses.

'Are you injured?' asks the medic.

'No.'

What else can I say? 'Not exactly. But I got on a boat a couple of years ago and frankly I'm still recovering.'

All the talk has been about separating the wheat from the chaff, the mentally strong from the mentally weak. I guess, then, this makes me weak. As I trudge back to my tent, I certainly feel it. I feel embarrassed, I feel ashamed – perhaps even a little regretful. I could have carried on. I just didn't want to. I'm a deserter.

In that moment, I feel entirely alone. Usually, when comedians are put through this kind of nightmare, there's a camera crew there compelling them to continue. I don't even have a friend accompanying me, someone to urge me to keep going. I suddenly understood Terry's disappointment at being separated from his pal, Country Myers. The presence of a familiar face would have offered encouragement, but also potential embarrassment. Without that, quitting became too easy.

There was more to it than simply taking the easy option, though. From the moment I arrived, the whole experience was anathema to me. I felt so wrong, so out of place. It was such a visceral feeling, like an allergic reaction. I felt as if I had to get out of there.*

I hated the feeling of being quite so bad at something, but more than that I hated the idea that I was letting other people down. I accept that in quitting I was letting them down in another fashion, but it certainly felt like the lesser of two evils. I found it impossible to shed myself of my pride, my ego, to submit to the baiting and the beasting. I imagine it was much the same for jack-the-lad† Terry, but he found a way to overcome. All in all, he lasted three years. I couldn't last a day.

There are a few consoling words from one of the drill sergeants.

'Maybe you're just not cut out for a career in the military,' says one.

---

* I've felt that dawning realisation of my unsuitability for something before. In the build-up to my wedding, I signed up for some personal training sessions. Part way through, with the trainer laying into me in the name of motivation, I looked in the gym mirror and just thought, 'You're a writer. What are you doing here?' Suddenly I saw the absurdity in trying to be something I patently was not. I never saw the trainer again.

† Interestingly, 'a Jack' is military speak for a slacker. They keep shouting at me, 'Don't be a Jack!' I decide not to tell them that I nearly chose 'Jack Downes' as my stage name.

The thirty-five-year-old comedian picks his jaw up from the floor at this epiphanic revelation.

'Ultimately, maybe you've learned that you're just mentally weak,' adds J from 5ive.

Yeah, maybe, cheers for that. Now you get back to following those orders, mate – crack on, I'm going for a pint.

While I dismantle my flapping tent, I reflect on whether he's right. Maybe it's more pride, more ego, but I'm not sure that I entirely agree. I don't consider this failure especially indicative of weakness. I came into their world and struggled. If they came into mine, they probably would too. Granted, I made for a disastrous soldier, but equally I wouldn't stick any of these special forces lads on at the Soho Theatre – that material about a bush being blue is definitely going to split a room.

There is certainly huge mental strength required to unquestioningly follow orders, however senseless, however absurd – but I'm not sure it's a kind of strength I aspire to. Guys 'just following orders' have made for some of the greatest heroes in history, but also quite a few exploitable accomplices.

As I pack my things away – slowly, unhurried and defiant – I am admittedly quiet, introspective. I pass rapidly through the first four of the five stages of grief – denial, anger, bargaining, depression. The fifth stage, acceptance, remains out of reach. Maybe I did let my band of brothers down? I spend most of my life working alone; I have always felt an outsider. I don't find it easy to subsume into the hive. Maybe I came to this too late, the idiosyncrasies of my personality now too rigid to be sufficiently flexible. Maybe I'm too old to learn, too stubborn to change. I'll never make a military man, and I am grateful for the privilege that means I most likely won't have to. You better hope there's no third world war. If I'm ever conscripted this country is in big, big trouble.

I guess what made Terry extraordinary is that he could have it both ways. He was a showman in an individualistic sport, who had the fortitude to swallow his pride and stand in rank and file. He let men he knew he could knock out treat him like dirt. Maybe it was the knowing that enabled him to do it.

I crawl through one of the surrounding fields again, this time desperately searching for my car keys. It takes me forty-five minutes to find them – an agonising, long goodbye.

As I pack my things away into the boot, I talk soberly with another participant who has also handed over the armband. He's being attended to by paramedics for an Achilles injury. I ask him what he does in 'real life': he's a former military man, who now works as a professional boxing trainer.

'Oh, my grandad . . .' I begin. But I stop myself. This man has just seen me throw in the towel. I don't want to embarrass Terry or myself.

I come away from the experience humbled. I've always known there were things I just couldn't do. Now there are forty lads in a field in Wales who know too.

On the way home, I call my grandma. 'Don't worry,' she says. 'The important thing is that you tried. Pop would have been so proud of you.'

'Thanks Grandma,' I say. But this time, deep down, I don't believe her.

With his hopes of an easy life at Quantico dashed, Terry was instead posted to Camp Lejeune, another North Carolina base. At enrolment, a sergeant called for the 'Jockstrappers' to line up – Marine slang for athletes. Sports were read out in a roll call, and one by one football players, basketball players and others squatted to signal their specialism. Terry was left standing alone.

'What in the hell are you?'

Terry explained that he was a boxer, but the first hint of an unusual accent prompted the sergeant to ask where he was from. 'Baltimore' didn't cut it. When Terry revealed he was in fact a Brit, he opened himself up to a barrage of abuse, punctuated with a dig in the ribs with a parade-stick. Caught off-guard, and with a line troops on their haunches behind him, Terry stumbled back and fell to the ground.

Then something caught light in him. Suddenly he wasn't Private T R Downes; he was two-fisted Terry Downes, the wise-cracking, jaw-shattering boxer.

'If you want to fight there's a ring over there. Put 'em up or shut up.'

The sergeant accepted the offer of a fight but elected a champion to participate on his behalf – a heavyweight, a good few stone heavier than the spindle-limbed Terry. What Terry gave away in weight, however, he made up for in smarts. With a crowd of soldiers watching on, Terry let the big slugger punch himself out, before cutting him down with a body shot to the stomach.

In that moment, Terry won more than the fight; he won respect – even from the snarky sergeant. Before long, he found another way to curry favour. At Camp Lejeune, sweets and chocolate were in short supply. A bar of chocolate could fetch up to a dollar on the black market. With a nose for opportunity, Terry set up a trade in what Marines call 'Pogey bait' – illicit candy. Having served an apprenticeship wheeler-dealing in

London's wartime blackout, for Terry this endeavour was a piece of contraband cake.

It wasn't without its challenges. Stowing the snacks away was difficult, especially when inspection time came. You couldn't just tuck your tuck away under the bedding: the sergeants would drop a silver dollar on the mattress, to ensure the sheets were pulled tight. If it didn't bounce, you were for it.

Marine camps also have a habit of putting grunts on constant patrol, 'guarding nothing from nobody,' as Terry once eloquently put it. He regularly had to sneak past his fellow Marines to stock up on supplies, grabbing some of the popular American snacks of the 1950s: no Soreen or Dairy Milk, but Turkish Taffy, Marshmallow Peeps and 1954's exciting new release, Peanut M&Ms. What would Terry have thought if he'd known that half a century later, there would be a three-storey shop in his native London dedicated exclusively to M&Ms? That's progress for you.

Aside from sweets, Terry's other big problem was snakes. Like Indiana Jones, Matt Damon and Eve (from the Bible, not the rapper), Terry was no great fan of these slithering reptiles.* At Camp Lejeune, they were everywhere. When the troops were out on exercises, Terry would regularly be punished for being last to 'hit the dirt', simply because he insisted on checking he was in a snake-free zone.

Eventually, Terry earned his first trip back to Baltimore – and from there, he was finally posted to Quantico, just eighty miles from home. This was what he'd signed up for. There was, however, one small catch: with the major who'd convinced him to join now posted abroad, there was no boxing team to

---

* It's a good job he didn't attend my drama school.

speak of. It was fully nine months before an ad appeared in the camp paper about tryouts for a new boxing team. Initially, 200 plucky volunteers came to the trials, presumably partly just to get the afternoon off their usual duties. Slowly, they were weeded out, leaving a team of around twenty. Terry was part of the squad, as was his old pal 'Country' Myers. When the Marine Corps championships rolled around, Terry and team were flown down to Miami, where he faced defending Marine champion Randy Horne and won. Finally, he was getting a taste of glory – the only catch being that, as an amateur fighter, Terry was forced to wear a headguard which rendered the new champ unrecognisable around camp. What's the value of success, without recognition?

It was while in Miami that Terry had a fateful encounter. The referee for that bout with Horne was one Willie Pastrano, himself a promising professional from New Orleans. Terry was desperate to impress, and he did – with Pastrano and trainer Angelo Dundee hailing him as the tournament's outstanding prospect. They weren't alone in that assertion. The *Miami Herald* called him 'Classy Terry Downes, a leather-throwing example of the fighting Leathernecks'. For the young Terry, this endorsement provided huge encouragement. Little did he know then that Pastrano would one day bring the curtain down on his professional career.

As Terry's reputation grew, his friends in the Baltimore press were building up the hype. 'He's gotta go the route,' local trainer Mack Lewis told *The Evening Sun*. 'He's the future champion of the world. I have never in my life seen the likes of Downes. He's just too much.'

Terry went on to win several more Marine contests and become a champion in the prestigious American amateur

Golden Gloves competition, defeating the well-regarded Rudy Sawyer along the way. Reporter Dick Slay wrote: 'Only mad dogs and Englishmen go out in the midday sun, says the ditty, and only Terry Downes, the transplanted Englishman, could end the string of Rudy Sawyer's sixteen consecutive victories in the Golden Gloves.'

At the 1956 inter-services championships, Terry secured the trophy for the Marines by beating Pearce Lane. He was, by this measure at least, the best fighter in his weight category in the entire US military.

This period, Terry would always insist, was the making of him. Eight months of the year were spent focussed on boxing. He fought more times in the Marines than many do in an entire professional career, winning 63 of his 67 fights. It meant that by the time he turned pro, he was already a hardened fighter. He had left school at sixteen, but this was his university. It's no coincidence that for the remainder of his career he wore red trunks and gown with gold trim – the US Marine colours.

His spell boxing for the military was almost crowned by an even greater glory. Terry's success in the Marines earned him a shot in the trials for the 1956 Melbourne Olympics. 'A Cockney wearing the American Olympic vest sounds a little crazy to me, but Terry's in the Olympic reckoning right enough,' wrote *Boxing News*. He was one of seven Marines among 100 triallists in New York. Like a family at Christmas, he fought four times in twenty-four hours, coming through unscathed to be hailed as a star prospect. It looked for all the world like Corporal Downes was headed Down Under.

But then, a hitch: the small issue of his nationality. He'd served three years in the Marines, but that wasn't enough for citizenship – he needed an extra year. Newspapers campaigned for him, but like someone trying to eat a Babybel in a hurry, there was just too much red tape. When the last stage of the trials was announced he'd beaten three of the four finalists – including Pearce Lane, who would ultimately represent the US in Melbourne.

Terry was devastated: 'I was all right to be in the bloody Marine Corps, catching bullets in the frontline, but with boxing gloves they said no, you can't represent us.'

He felt that his service meant nothing – that America were happy for him to fight for them, but not *fight* for them. The boy who'd wanted a medal more than anything saw his dream of Olympic gold dashed by bureaucracy.

And so, he went home – to his real home. Back to Blighty, back to the smoke, and back to boxing. He left the Marines, but decided to earn his stripes in another fashion: by turning pro.

IN MY CORNER

There are facets of the English language that seem to suggest a correlation between our balance and our sanity. We know the importance of being 'level-headed', of 'keeping our feet on the ground'. Bereft of balance, I became emotionally unstable. While on the one hand I knew the room wasn't really moving, on the other I knew I was definitely spiralling.

The rocking and swaying was intolerable, and caused my self-esteem and self-confidence to plummet. I felt I was being failed by my faculties.

My desperation to find a medical fix played into my psychological problems – it was obsessive, all-encompassing. I found myself endlessly googling variants on the same set of symptoms, trawling internet forums and Facebook groups. I still get junk emails from the website CruiseCritic.com, as their message board was frequented by people who suffered the same kind of enduring land-sickness. Most, I noticed, were middle-aged women, some of whom simply made their peace with it and endeavoured to spend as much time as possible aboard cruise ships, where they experienced something like normality.

The Facebook groups were more depressing. People like me, searching for answers, hoping for a cure. It was particularly disheartening to read of people who'd been suffering similar symptoms for years, in some cases decades. This seemed un-imaginable and unbearable, a fate that in my darkest moments I genuinely considered might be worse than death – being cast adrift at sea forever. One woman with almost identical symptoms to me believed her best shot at a cure was forcing her brain into a hard reset, so she travelled round the globe riding the world's most turbulent rollercoasters in the hope that one day she'd step off with her balance restored.

I quickly learned these webpages could be a source of despair as well as hope. The people who frequented them, invariably, were still suffering. Those who found a cure, or at least a way of coping, typically moved on. These were dark places, full of lost souls still adrift in that endless ocean.

For Camille, this must have been a draining period. I've always been someone prone to bouts of anger and frustration – I'm not a prolific puncher of people, but I have been an occasional puncher of walls. The rage is reflexive, it's not directed at anyone else – but it's still unpleasant to be around. As that toxicity began to erupt to the surface more frequently, Camille implored me to seek professional help.

I'm a little ashamed now to admit I was resistant. I'd love to say I was afraid to show vulnerability, but the reality was worse than that. I struggled with what I perceived as an admission of being somehow defective, of being broken. I had a kind of emotional snobbery about it all.

I also didn't have sufficient respect for the practitioner's expertise. There was an arrogance in me, a foolhardy determination to solve this crisis on my own. I think I actively resented the idea that my problems might be fixed by something learned in a textbook; I hated the idea that this could all be worked through by a flow-chart. I imagined myself saying in one of my first sessions, 'Actually, both my parents were alcoholics' – and facing a barrage of questions about their addiction, enduring a catalogue of clichés which felt utterly irrelevant to my own plight.

Above and beyond all else: I didn't think I was depressed. I was sad, angry, perhaps even hopeless – but to my mind I wasn't depressed, I was just ill. How else did people expect me to feel? The way I saw it, I couldn't feel better until I *got* better, and I resented the idea that improving my psychological state might improve my physical symptoms. That, to me, was tantamount to telling me it was 'all in my head'.

In the end, Camille gave me an ultimatum. Things got bad enough that if I wanted to save my marriage, I had to commit to counselling. This was my rock bottom. Like a fighter who'd walked straight onto a firm right hand, I was on the canvas. The question now was whether I could get back up.

Round Six

BARB

I have always had a very glamorous grandma. She wouldn't want me to tell you her exact age, so let's just say she is more than eighty-one and less than eighty-three. She has survived cancer, severe pancreatitis and sixty-odd years married to Terry Downes – and all without a hair out of place.

If Terry is working-class spirit made flesh, Barbara Alice Clarke is simply class personified. She grew up a stone's throw away from Terry in Paddington, but Grandma has always been keen to establish some distance between their upbringings. 'My family were quite posh,' she tells me. 'We had our own toilet.'

When she met Terry, she was only seventeen. I asked her if she could recall the very first thing she noticed about the man she would be with for the next six decades of her life. 'Of course,' she says. 'He had a black eye.'

Terry had returned from Baltimore with his dad, heartbroken at never stepping inside an Olympic ring. From the ashes of that disappointment, his return to London provided two fresh pathways that would come to define his life: with professional boxing, and perhaps more importantly, with Barbara.

They met, she tells me, at 'a local club'. She says that it wasn't a nightclub, but nor was it a youth club. It was simply a place where young people could have a drink and a dance. So a nightclub, then? 'No, not a nightclub.' Why, was it in the daytime? 'No, it was night. It was just a club at night.' I give up.

A bit of online detective work tells me it was at Beauchamp Lodge – a regency building on the bank of the Grand Union Canal in Little Venice. It has had some illustrious residents in its time, including the writer Katherine Mansfield and the first French President Napoleon III. For me, however, its greatest significance will always be the meeting of these two young lovers. According to his own account, Terry stood on the sidelines, as having only just returned from America he was out of step with London's dance scene. Much like me in my aforementioned period dance exam, he simply couldn't jive.

'I was with my friend Sonya,' Barbara recalls. 'I spotted his black eye and said, "Look at that Teddy Boy over there."'

For the uninitiated, Wikipedia has Teddy Boys as 'male youths in delinquent gangs who had adopted Edwardian-era fashion' – in short, anachronistic anarchists. I imagine it was a bit like how all the lads fighting outside pubs nowadays look like something out of *Peaky Blinders*. They were the original British subculture. The look might have had its roots in Edwardian tropes, but it also took cues from rock and roll and American gangster movies. It was a culture of violence too, hence my grandma's suspicions.

Fortunately, someone pointed out that Terry's black eye had not been acquired in some gangland scrap, but in a boxing ring. 'He came over and he started chatting to me,' says Barbara.

'He had a bit of an American accent. He had a car, even then, which was very flash, and he gave me a lift home. I can remember the numberplate even now. MMX 445 – a Hillman.'

Having spent the last three years in America, Terry was a complete stranger to Barbara – and she had no knowledge of his family either. The mythical reputation of the Downes clan had somehow not reached her. 'I'd never met a Downes in my life,' she says. 'Never heard of them. But then you have to remember I was quite posh. Did I tell you we had our own toilet?'*

What was the distinction between the Downeses and the Clarkes? 'Well, most of the Downeses were scoundrels, and none of my family had anything to do with anything like that. Most of my dad's family fought in the war, my mum's youngest brother Dennis died in Palestine. When one of the Downes uncles went off to war the whole family were there to wave him off – only he done a runner and got back home before they did.'

There was definitely a distinction between Grandma and Pop – he was unapologetic about being a bit of rough, coarse until the last. He clung to his roots. There's something slightly more socially aspirational about my grandma. Even today, you have to listen carefully to hear her real accent peeping out from behind her perfectly honed telephone voice. The impression I have is that it was her who dragged my family up into the middle classes.

---

* Another great example of my grandma's aspirational tendencies arrived in the making of this book. When I went to her house to pick out the photographs that adorn some of these pages, she asked more than once for me to use the photograph of Terry with the late Prince Philip. I politely declined.

When Terry dropped Barbara off after that first meeting, he mentioned he had a fight coming up in a few weeks' time – his first professional bout, no less. The date was to be 9 April 1957, the venue: the Harringay Arena – at the time as good a place to watch boxing as any in the country, with a raucous crowd and a capacity of over 10,000. Sadly, it closed a year or so later. It's been replaced with a shopping park now. These days, on the site of the old arena stands a Sainsbury's Superstore – but if you go down there about 5pm, when the yellow stickers come out, you get some idea of what the atmosphere used to be like.

Barbara decided to take Terry up on the offer of a couple of free tickets to the fight. 'I wasn't really interested in him, but when I found out he was a boxer I thought, "Oh that'd be quite a nice thing to go and see",' says my grandma. If, that is, they could see anything at all: Terry didn't exactly provide her with ringside seats. 'If there were 10,000 people there, there must've been 9,999 with a better view than me,' she says, still sounding a bit aggrieved. 'I'm not exaggerating – we were in the second row from the back.'

Terry was paired with a journeyman fighter from Covent Garden by the name of Peter Longo. Top of the bill was a British lightweight championship fight between Joe Lucy and Dave Charnley, but boxing connoisseurs were there to witness the debuts of two Terrys: Downes and the equally promising Terry Spinks. Pop would've been particularly motivated to out-shine Spinks – representing Britain in the flyweight division, he'd returned from Melbourne the previous summer with an Olympic gold medal.

Terry snuck out before the fight to see Barbara in boots and wraps, earning a first peck on the cheek in the process, before disappearing back to the changing rooms. The young lovers weren't kept apart long: the fight was over inside the first round. 'The man behind me had a pair of binoculars, he kindly lent them to me for the start,' says Barbara. 'Well, the fight was over in a minute and a half. Poor bloke didn't see a bit of it.'

Terry floored Longo three times before the referee made the merciful count of ten. Of the fight's ninety seconds, Longo spent twenty-six on the canvas. Terry's devastating display was an effective riposte to the crowd, who had turned on him in distaste at his pre-fight bravado. They didn't take kindly to Terry's ostentatious white boots, scarlet shorts, red-and-gold gown and unrestrained showmanship.

Tom Phillips of the *Daily Herald* was there that night, and reported: 'If [Downes] has a concrete chin, then there is nothing to bar him from reaching the top of the middleweight heap. He's going to be a rich, lucky, famous young man – yet won't be popular! I smelt that at Harringay, where that tough crowd had never seen a debutant so cocky. Sudden fame has its penalties and my advice to Downes if the cheers turn to boos is, "Don't worry". He won't be the first to attract crowds to see him licked.'

In his column for *The People*, Ernie Jarvis took a different view: 'How little some fight patrons know the business! I'm referring to those who took exception to the showy and colourful entry into the ring of Terry Downes. He was full of bravado and confidence – the only way a fighter should climb into the ring. No one gave Sugar Ray Robinson "the bird" when he went into his act . . . Terry's one-round win was a fillip for British boxing.'

It's funny to think how big a part of the spectacle of boxing those ring walks have now become. For an old-timer, Terry never turned up his nose at those sort of antics. He knew even back then it was part of the game, part of the entertainment. As it was, his all-action style quickly won round the dissenters.

Terry earned a purse of £100 for that first fight. While he had already spent some of it hiring professional sparring partners in preparation for his debut bout, that was still a substantial return – the equivalent of several thousand pounds in today's money. Barbara was therefore decidedly unimpressed when the post-match meal he treated her to was fish and chips, served in newspaper.

Any disgruntlement at that first-date dinner soon dissipated. From that point on Terry had Barb in his corner. Within a few months he was buying her a ring of her own – square-cut, of course. Terry would return to America on boxing business, but from now on his life was in London.

It's a good thing the Longo fight ended as quickly as it did. Had Barb had to endure watching Terry in more gruelling contests, she might have thought twice about 'going steady' with a boxer.

'I never liked the fights,' she tells me. 'I used to have a programme, and I would read it from front to back. By the end of the night I could tell you every word of every advert. After that first fight, I never ever watched. It was too nerve-wracking. You want to be there in case something happens, but you also don't want to be there. And you're looking through your hands and then you hear someone say "Oh, he's cut" . . . It's awful.'

I can't imagine what it's like watching someone you love go through that. I suppose my wife has had to endure the indignity of watching me have a bad gig, but at least (in most cases) I wasn't bleeding heavily throughout.*

Being married to a boxer feels like a very particular way of life, with its own fears, its own rhythms, its own difficulties. I stumbled across an interview with my grandma which provides some insight. The version I found appeared in the *Liverpool Echo*, although Grandma is quick to point out that it was circulated nationally. It was published on Monday 10 July 1961: the eve of Terry's fateful contest with champion Paul Pender for the world middleweight title.

The story sits on the *Echo* Women's Forum page, surrounded by some charmingly period advertising. In the top-left corner of the page, an ad for Shubette's 'little black dress . . . for the girl who likes to create a stir at parties', all for just fourteen guineas. And there, on the right, is a picture of my grandparents, cradling a two-year-old Wendy – my mum.

The piece is written under the headline 'Life With Terry'. 'Do you fancy whipping up a couple of raw eggs in a glass of fruit juice at 6 a.m., feeding the ducks in Hyde Park at six-thirty? It's not a routine to appeal to most women. But it's the

---

* There was a notable exception to this. I was performing at a night in Peckham and decided to finish my set with a 'magic trick' in which I put an entire jar of jam into a saucepan and pulled out a perfectly formed jam donut. I'd love to say this routine was better in the flesh than it sounds, but it wasn't. Anyway, in doing so I somehow managed to smash the jam jar inside the pan. I pulled out the donut and bit into it, to bewildered and halting applause, before realising the glistening crystals on its surface were not grains of sugar but shards of glass. I ended up spending half the night in A&E waiting to discover if I'd slashed my oesophagus to pieces. Camille was at the gig, and much like my grandma at ringside, she was indeed watching through her hands.

regular one for twenty-one-year-old Barbara Downes, wife of British middleweight champion boxer Terry Downes.'

It's an endearing portrait of their young life together, albeit one clearly defined by Terry's career. In the build-up to a fight, they lived by a strict regime. They would rise at six so Terry could depart for his morning run. If the weather was good, they might drive from their home in Willesden Green, north London, to Hyde Park. 'Terry does his running there,' my grandma told the paper. 'Wendy and I feed the ducks and watch the horses being exercised.'

They'd return to have breakfast at 9.30 a.m. – one of Terry's two meals a day. Typically he'd have a combination of bacon, eggs, grapefruit and toast, before heading off to look after his business interests, which included a car dealership and later his betting shops.

Terry would come home again at lunchtime, perhaps even have a nap, before an afternoon in the gym. 'Sometimes he'll sneak an hour to play with the baby in the garden,' said 1961 Barbara. In the evening, there was sometimes another workout for Terry. If not, they might find time to watch home movies on their projector – assuming Terry hadn't commandeered it to study tapes of old fights.

The most inflexible element was a strict militarian policy of lights out at 9 p.m. – a fact that clearly affected Grandma's social life. 'The worst part is going to bed so early each night,' she said. 'It means turning off the set in the middle of that play you were watching. You're not able to go out to friends – you arrive just in time to leave – or have friends round here. Most of them don't understand about leaving at nine.'

In the interview, Grandma talked of losing touch with some people since her marriage to Terry. 'It's just that your life becomes completely different from theirs and you haven't got a point of contact'. Boxing provided them with everything they wished for, but the price went beyond the physical one paid in the ring.

The fear of harm coming to her husband was naturally, however, never far away. Grandma admitted to feeling 'a bit depressed' in the build-up to a big fight, and that the tension could make Terry a little 'edgy'. When I ask her about that, she says she doesn't recognise feeling depressed – but time has a way of dampening emotions, applying a sepia glaze to the past. It is her nature to emphasise the positive. Sometimes it feels like her memory is selective, like she chooses to remember the good times over the troublesome. Writing it out, you wonder why anyone would ever consider that a bad thing.

She remains something of a traditionalist. Back in 1961, Grandma told the newspaper that she thought 'the right place for a woman is at home'. Although Terry and Barbara had the wealth to provide them with nannies, cleaners and other hired help, she was still a dedicated housewife, diligently ensuring his boxing gear was fresh and pressed every morning.

That's not to say she didn't have aspirations of her own. In the very next line, the journalist Emma Powell describes Grandma as having a 'flair for fashion', and even ambitions of a career in that world. 'Barbara herself hopes that one day Terry will buy her a small fashion boutique,' she writes. As it happened, that never came to pass. There doesn't appear to be any real disappointment on my grandma's part. 'It would have been impossible,' she suggests. 'I had four children!' After my mum, she had three sons: Terry Junior, Paul, and Richard. She lost another baby at birth, something which remains a scar on her heart.

She has found an outlet for that passion for fashion. My mum now has her own clothes' shop, and Barbara makes a habit of popping in there to help out several times a week. She has no need to do that: she is in her eighties. Even in the grip of the pandemic, she'd willingly pop on a mask and sit there behind a perspex screen, processing payments and chatting away to customers. She doesn't mind a bit of hard graft.

Something I keep returning to – perhaps the most startling aspect of her appearance in that newspaper article – is how very young she was. She was just twenty-one, with one child already, and mourning a stillborn second. My generation and lifestyle has been one of prolonged adolescence; hers one where youngsters play at being grown-ups.

She might not have chosen to marry a fighter, but, ultimately, she felt she had no choice. 'I loved him and he loved me, and that was the end of it,' she tells me. 'If he'd been a cat burglar I still would've married him. When you know, you know.'

Being a performer is, in its own way, a very particular lifestyle. I'm lucky in that I married someone who understood that implicitly: she does precisely the same thing.

I met Camille at the Edinburgh Fringe in 2013. We were performing in back-to-back shows, her with her sketch group Birthday Girls, me with my friends Owen Roberts and Ciarán Dowd, better known as BEASTS.* I fondly remember the premise of Birthday Girls' show was that it was set fifty years in the future – only they'd done the maths wrong and called it '2053', a mere forty years on.

---

* Although still, it's worth making clear, not particularly well-known.

It was not, I'll admit, love at first sight. In fact, the thing Camille remembers most about me that hot summer is that I 'always had food stuck in [my] teeth'.

'Also you had so many props in your show. It used to really piss me off as it took you so long to get out of the theatre.'

Charming. Anything else? 'I do remember thinking you were the tall one in the group,' she says. Okay, more promising. So was that a positive? 'Erm,' she thinks. 'It's hard to say because I was completely indifferent.

'You had your funny outfits, your curly hair, your glasses. I thought you were just kind of sweet and a bit geeky.' And funny? 'Oh, yeah, funny too I guess. Sorry, I forgot to say that.'

Our romance, then, was a slow burn – from both sides, actually. We had other partners at the time and were professional contemporaries. More than that, we were friends.

The upshot of that is that Camille saw me at my very worst – and I don't just mean 'performing sketch comedy', surely as unattractive a pursuit as there can be. She saw me after bad gigs and bad reviews. She saw me be a bad boyfriend. That we are now together, in spite of all that, feels miraculous. It is such a privilege to be married to your best friend; to be accepted for who you are rather than striving for who you might be.

Camille and I are different, however. She takes me out of my comfort zone, particularly socially: she's very outgoing, whereas I don't like going out. People call her 'the life and soul', whereas I've been accused of having neither of those things. While in one sense I have been unexpectedly robbed of balance, in another she has provided a steady supply of it.

She makes my life better, and easier. I'm grateful for that;

I know it takes work. Being married is a bit like curling: furiously sweeping away at the ice to ensure a seemingly smooth journey.

Like Terry and Barbara, we married soon after getting together. In fact, we decided to get engaged just eight weeks into our relationship. Camille had originally intended to propose on Leap Year Day 2016.

'I actually had the idea a couple of months before on New Years' Eve, before we were even properly together,' she says. 'I just had a feeling I was going to marry you. Everyone said, "That's mad, you're not even going out with him!" I kind of said it as a joke, but something inside me felt it was true.'

She bottled it, but when she later admitted her plan, I told her I would've said yes. That was that. Like my grandma says, 'When you know, you know'.

As a child, I spent every possible weekend at my grandparents' house. Barbara had spent so long living by Terry's watch that the discipline had become habit, and her own time was now governed by strict routines. Every Saturday morning, we'd get up before seven to head to Watford's Harlequin shopping centre. Every Saturday morning, we'd go to Ponti's for a bacon sandwich – always 'extra crispy'. Every Saturday morning, we were outside Marks & Spencer before it opened at 8am 'to beat the rush' (there was never any rush).

Perhaps the real reason we went so early was that it meant we were usually home by about ten o'clock, just in time to make Terry his breakfast. Even in retirement, he was still setting the clock. I loved those weekends with my grandparents. Once he was up, Terry would bark instructions at me while I mowed the lawn or repainted a fence. Then we'd come back inside and Grandma would bring in some tea and biscuits. She showed interest in anything I did, whether it was schoolwork or acting or collecting Pogs. Terry did too.

While other teenagers were drinking alcopops and snogging at house parties, I was drinking tea and watching *Coronation Street*. It was a time of simple pleasures. Grandma and Pop's pace of life had slowed so dramatically that I found it incredibly peaceful, a sharp contrast to the drama that sometimes enveloped my home life with my parents. I remember that sometimes on Friday after school I'd be surprised that instead of my mum waiting to pick me up, it was one of my grandparents. I later found out that tended to mean one of my parents had been drinking – sending me to Terry and Barbara's was a way of trying to grant me some solace, some sanctuary.

What my grandma offered me is presumably what she offered Terry for so many years. She offered some refuge, some stability – and she still does, whether it be from unexplained assaults, mental exhaustion, broken bones or just bad auditions. She has been the perfect cornerwoman – she still is. We speak almost daily and she never fails to make me feel better. I think it's because she gives so much and asks for so little in return. When I think of my childhood, I don't think of my parents' drinking. I think of my grandma bringing me hot tea and crumpets. What a gift that is.

I will always remember when Terry died in 2017, and she asked me to do the eulogy at his funeral. It was one of the most difficult things I have ever done. People often make the mistake of thinking an actor is ideally suited to speaking on such occasions. Not in my case: the entirety of my drama school training was about helping me emotionally connect to a script. At a funeral, that's a recipe for a blubbering disaster. Give it to a dead-eyed uncle, for God's sake.

Inevitably, the build-up of the pressure and the words and the occasion and the emotion led to me breaking down in tears. And every time I glanced up, I saw that reflected among the congregation. Until, that is, my eyes settled on my grandma in the front row. She was looking up at me, eyes admittedly misty, but smiling. Really smiling. The same smile I'd seen at countless school plays and average gigs.

It took me a split-second to register it, to understand why. In the darkest of moments, she was still proud of me. Her pride outweighed her grief. I finished the eulogy.

The life of the comedian and the life of the boxer both come with their temptations on the road. That's the beauty of marrying someone already embedded in that world.

Separate worlds, separate lives, can lead to issues, principally infidelity. I make no excuses for it, but that's certainly something I fell foul of in previous relationships. I doubt Terry was much different. In fact, we know as much. As happy as he and Barbara were in later life – and they truly were – things weren't always rosy for the young couple. I always remember a passage from the final chapter of Terry's book, in which he says, 'I've done everything in life, from birds to booze'. It struck me that those didn't seem like the words of a man who got married at twenty-one.

His wandering ways became all the more apparent a few summers ago. I was at the Edinburgh Fringe when I received a phone call from my mum. 'I've just had a Facebook message from my sister,' she said. 'You haven't got a sister,' I replied naively. But, of course, she had.

My mum had received contact from Melanie Cook – a woman ten years her junior, whose father was also Terry Downes. The product of an extramarital affair, her existence had been kept quiet for almost forty years.

Quiet yes, but not a secret. Terry had embarked on a relationship with Melanie's mother Gay, who in typically inexplicable fashion, he had insisted upon calling 'Liz'.* It was an open affair. My mum knew, and my grandma certainly knew. This was a relationship that stretched into years, one that saw Terry bounce back-and-forth between households. Melanie (known as 'Min'), tells a story about the time Terry said he was nipping out for a pint of milk, but instead disappeared with Liz to the Mexico Olympics. My mum remembers being taken to an unfamiliar flat and introduced to baby Melanie. It was unconventional, even in the liberal late Sixties. I've always been somewhat envious of my mum because her parents stayed together. Navigating this situation, however, seems substantially more complex and confusing for a child than any divorce.

When Min was two years old, the affair ended. Liz moved away, and soon married. By the time I was born, it was no longer talked about. 'My mum always said, "If you want to get in contact, you can", but I thought it might be a bit disrespectful to my stepfather,' says Min. 'When I got to twelve or thirteen I said, "I'd just like to see his face," but my mum

---

* I wonder if his macho persona might have struggled with the idea of having a partner who was, quite literally, Gay. But then I remember he called a sheep Poofy.

didn't know anyone who could put us in contact. As I got older, it was always there in the back of my mind.

'I knew he chaired social meetings for the Home Counties Ex-Boxers Association. I said to my husband Jules that all I wanted to do was turn up and see him through the window or from the corner of a pub. Just so I could see what he looks like. I didn't want to go piling into a family, putting noses out of joint.

'Eventually I decided to make a bit more of a concerted effort, so I decided to try via Facebook.* That's how I found your mum and sent her a message saying, "I think I might be your sister."'

My mum, who had spent a lifetime wondering what had become of baby Melanie, was delighted. She met Min independently, before a few weeks later she was introduced to the wider family – including Terry and Barbara.

'He and I just sat there holding hands the whole time, grinning at each other,' says Min. 'And then he just said, "Where've you been?"'

It was an extraordinary thing for the family to go through – the revelation of Min's existence, the reopening of old wounds, and the reclamation of a long-lost sibling. And through it all, my grandma could not have been more positive. She welcomed Min with open arms, showering her with love and affection as if she was her own. It was an astonishing display of selflessness; of putting her family first. 'The first thing Barbara said to me was, "How's your mum?"' says Min. 'She's so, so kind.'

It doesn't surprise me that Barbara and Min's mum have a

---

* Facebook to the rescue *again*. Love that Zuckerburg – as far as I'm concerned he's welcome to my data.

kind of distant camaraderie. They both know what each other put up with; that Terry was a brilliant man but a difficult one to live with. All that testosterone comes at a price.

There is a paradox in my grandma, one that is probably not atypical in her generation: that of being someone seemingly subservient, but undeniably strong. The girl who believed women belonged at home, but who built that figurative home with her own bare hands. The strength she showed was not in asserting her independence, but in managing to keep her relationship going.

For all the difficulties they endured, my grandparents were ultimately happy when I knew them. Much of that depended on my grandma's capacity to forgive. Something that's sometimes a little absent in our society is that forgiveness, that selflessness, that willingness to suffer for something bigger. I'm not saying what she did was right, but I respect it.

Terry was very clear that he fought for his family, but it was Barbara who had to keep it together.

That was her fight. And in her own way, she too was a champion.

IN MY CORNER

It was British sportswriter Pierce Egan who first referred to boxing as 'The Sweet Science', as far back as 1813. Egan, a devoted follower of bare-knuckle fighting, saw the strategising behind the violence. He recognised a boxer depended on his capacity to calculate, as well as his clout. He knew that winning a fight required a combination of cognitive, perceptual and motor skills – the very skills I felt I was losing. Before fighters fully knew the risks for their brain in any given fight, they understood the organ's importance.

Boxing has been compared to the ultimate cerebral sport, chess – every punch combination represents an intricate series of possible moves. Grandmaster Jonathan Rowson is a subscriber to the belief that boxing is the sport that most closely resembles his own. 'In part it's the purity of the competition,' he says. 'There is virtually nothing to mediate the one-to-one combat. Boxing has gloves, but there are no balls, no goalposts, no clubs or racquets. The emotional impulse behind chess, and the pain it inflicts, is comparable – but just takes a different form.' In chess, the bruising is just as bad, but it's sustained by the ego. The vernacular language around the board game is peppered with references to 'crushing', 'destroying' or 'smashing' the opponents. Russian world champion Garry Kasparov described chess as 'the most violent sport there is'.

Former world heavyweight champion Lennox Lewis credits his passion for chess with keeping him out of trouble during his East London adolescence. It helped his boxing too: he could never match the explosive violence of Mike Tyson, but he could divide the ring into 64 squares and engineer a way to dominate the centre – a Queen's Gambit to help him become King of the Ring. Now Lewis employs a chess master to help train a new generation of fighters. 'In my camp I'm bringing in a chess instructor because it creates discipline, patience and strategy,' he explained. 'All the skills needed in the ring. I still play all the time on my phone when I'm travelling or in a hotel. It's my new goal to create a champion from my foundation and the mindset that chess teaches is a part of that, not only for boxing, but for life skills. Why not? It worked for me.'

In 2003, Dutch performance artist Iepe Rubingh developed the concept of 'chessboxing' – a physically and mentally demanding sport that sees combatants alternate between rounds of boxing and turns of chess. In recent years, this new sport has emerged as a professional pursuit.

I played a bit of chess in my youth, which helped keep me out of trouble in leafy Hertfordshire. Admittedly, when it came to strategy I was more focused on Dungeons & Dragons-style fantasy games than chess. Why move a bishop when I could mount a dragon?

Science, however, has never been a strong suit. You are dealing with a man who once got thirteen per cent on a mock

GCSE chemistry test. Biology made me blush, and the laws of physics were to me as baffling and pointless as the laws of cricket. But when my brain started playing up, I suddenly found myself having to dust off my textbooks and come to grips with science once again.

Long before Rowan ever began teaching me the vocabulary of fighting, explaining the nuanced difference between a slip and a feint, I had to expand my scientific glossary. It started when I was referred to a neuro-otologist. Neuro-otolgy is, I now know, the investigation of the neuroscience and clinical disorders of the balance system. Although 'otology' literally means ear science, neuro-otology also considers other inputs, such as the visual and proprioceptive systems, as well as assessing the central integration process taking place in the brain. I had to learn about the vestibulo-ocular reflex – the automatic system which stabilises the gaze during head movement. If you think about it, your head is constantly moving – left, right, up, down. When you're walking it bobs along like a buoy on the water's surface – and yet you're never conscious of that motion. It's your vestibulo-ocular reflex that acts as a kind of visual suspension system, making constant adjustments to give you the perception of a smooth ride – and mine, it seemed, was well and truly banjaxed.

For a man with a permanent headache, some of these long words were pretty taxing. Suddenly, in my thirties, I had to go back to school. I didn't know or understand what had got me into this mess – but I knew that science was my best chance of getting out of it. Things were desperate, but I had faith in the doctors. It was check, but not checkmate. And so it was that I began a journey of understanding the science of the brain that has quite literally opened my mind.

Round Seven
THE RISE

For Terry, romance and his career seemed to be blossoming in tandem. After dispatching Longo, his second fight saw him shoot to the top of the bill – above even his rival Spinks.*

'There'll be crowds hoping for a miracle outside Manor Place Baths, Walworth, tonight – the miracle of a spare ticket,' Tom Philipps wrote in the *Daily Herald*. 'A ticket to get into a show "sold out" weeks ago . . . a show featuring two fighters each having his *second* professional fight. The pair with this terrific drawing power? The whiz kids of British Boxing, Terry Downes and Terry Spinks.'

Terry's opponent, Jimmy Lynas, was a tough nut who'd never been stopped. As the fight began, Terry noticed Lynas was front-footed, leading with his face. While others might have

---

* On the night of Terry's debut, Spinks had defeated Jim Loughrey by knockout. He would go on to reign as British featherweight champion from 1960 to 1961 – but in this tale of two Terrys, it was Downes who came out on top.

been intimidated, Terry took it as a bluff – Lynas was trying to avoid getting hit in the body. A sharp left-hook to the ribs in the third round put an end to the fight.

'Whisper it amongst yourselves, not too loudly – just yet,' the write-up in *Boxing News* read. 'Britain has found another crashing, bashing, dashing kid . . . Downes is the name, or Terry the Terrible.* Headlining Jack Solomons' annual charity promotion at Manor Place Baths, Downes simply demolished Jimmy Lynas inside three rounds and Lynas hasn't had that happen to him in almost five years of fighting . . . He didn't give a fig for the other man's intentions, or punches. Aggression and yet more aggression. To hell with anything but quick victory, that's Terry's motto, and British rings have been crying out for a fighter like it for years.'

Six days after Terry turned twenty-one, he faced his third fight: a contest at Shoreditch Town Hall against Nigerian Dick Tiger. Tiger had fought eleven times in England, losing five – including a defeat to Lynas, who Terry had dispatched so effortlessly in Walworth.

But there was more to this opponent than met the eye. Although Tiger had fought less than a dozen times in Britain, he had already amassed at least as many professional fights in his native Nigeria. Even in the world of boxing, where the fairytale can become quotidian, Tiger's remarkable back story

---

* That 'crashing, bashing, dashing kid' moniker would follow Terry throughout his career – surprising really as 'Terry the Terrible' is decidedly snappier, albeit with the potential risk of an alternate meaning. He was most frequently called 'The Paddington Express' – a trailblazer in that respect, as the high-speed Express line between Paddington and Heathrow wasn't even opened until 1998.

reads like an outlandish tale from some slightly racist comic book. Born Richard Ihetu, he is said to have built his formidable work ethic tilling the land on his father's farm in Amaigbo, a village in the East of Nigeria. When his father died, he and his mother moved to Aba, where Tiger took up the job of scavenging for empty bottles and selling them to local warehouses. He came to the sport rather late, at nineteen. As with Terry, boxing proved a natural sidestep for a teenager with a reputation for street-fighting and a hunger for a different life.

His first bouts were inter-club contests arranged by British military officers at a barracks on the outskirts of town. It was there his tenacity and power earned him the soubriquet 'Tiger'. It appears that in the Nigerian boxing scene of the 1950s, there was a real flair for names: Tiger's domestic contests saw him overcome the likes of Easy Dynamite, Mighty Joe and Super Human Power.

In 1955, Tiger had set sail for Liverpool on a mailboat, a pugilist stowed among the post. Once on Merseyside, he'd begun work in a paint factory, and set about adapting his style to the British fight scene – with decidedly mixed results. And so to Shoreditch, where the eye of this Tiger was fixed firmly on Terry. Matchmaker Mickey Duff explained his thinking thus: 'I'd seen Tiger lose to a nobody in Liverpool, and thought he was a perfect opponent – one who would make a show, but wouldn't be good enough to win.'

The first sign of trouble came at the weigh-in, with a six-pound advantage in Tiger's favour. For a middleweight, he was a hulking presence – thick thighs, and arms that rippled and flexed like two over-full hoover bags. The exoticism of Tiger's origins led to some loaded language in the papers of the time. The journalist A.J. Liebling once described Tiger as having 'a chest like an old-fashioned black office safe'.

He looked even bigger, Terry admitted to reporters after the fight, when you were lying flat on your back. After Tiger caught Terry with a peach of a left hook in the opening exchanges, he was laid out on the canvas. It was only the second time in Terry's fighting life he'd been off his feet.

At least he was conscious. Terry used to tell me that getting knocked out was a reflex – some people had a good chin, some didn't. To an extent, science appears to back that up – genetics certainly play their part. As far as I can make out, loss of consciousness is basically your body's equivalent of turning a device off and on again in the hope it'll iron out any kinks. When a head injury is sustained, the membrane of nerve cells is disturbed, meaning calcium flows into the cells causing swelling and damage. The nerve cell has the ability to pump the calcium out and restore balance – but in order to do so it has to divert a huge amount of energy away from other functions. And so: lights out.

Certain things can mitigate the risk: strong neck muscles can help fighters withstand the whiplash effect of taking a punch. Ultimately, however, a blow to the face forces the cranium back into the frontal lobes of the brain. Each individual brain has a different threshold and tolerance for damage before it shuts off. Contrary to popular commentary, determination, guts and mental strength play no part in it. It's mechanical. Maybe Pop was right to call it a 'reflex'.

Fortunately for Terry, he was blessed with a high resistance to getting knocked out – although in the long-term, that can be a curse too. Staying conscious can mean taking more punishment for longer. Against Tiger, Terry's mistake was getting up too quickly. In America, he was accustomed to referees giving fighters a mandatory eight count to catch their breath before resuming, even if they were already back on their feet. On this occasion, he sprung up after three, but was shocked to be underway and ducking blows again after four.

Terry's vision was blurry, his legs unsteady. Much like me in my first few training sessions with Rowan, everything was wobbly. Another whack swiftly put him back on the floor. This time, at least, he had enough sense to stay down until seven.

When the bell tolled for the end of the first round, Terry must have felt like a beaten man. His face hurt, but not half as much as his pride. The jack the lad in the scarlet shorts had been shown up, and the Shoreditch crowd weren't shy in letting him know about it. The much-fancied prospect didn't look so fancy now. In an intimate venue like that, you see every face, you hear every jibe. It's not unlike a comedy gig – if you show weakness, they'll eat you alive. The words of Terry's cornermen were drowned out as his head buzzed with the devastating impact of that opening three minutes.

From somewhere, Terry found the will to go on. Perhaps it was as simple as pride: he wasn't prepared to accept defeat, not in front of a paying public. His capacity to continue was not, after all, down to some supernatural pain threshold. 'I remember asking my dad, "Does it hurt when you get hit?"' says my mum. 'I thought he was going to say, "No, the adrenaline takes over, you don't feel it." But he said, "Yes, of course it bloody does. It hurts every bloody time."' Somehow, I suppose, that's even braver.

At the start of the second round The Paddington Express steamed into Tiger, only to be met with another thumping right hand. Down went Downes again, the Shoreditch patrons leaning in to hammer the ring apron in delight or fury, depending on where they'd laid their money.

Tiger must have hoped for a case of third time lucky. However, somehow – whether thanks to neck muscles, nerve cells, or just plain old reflex – Terry stayed in the contest. He hauled himself up on the count of eight and began turning the match into a fight. His only option was to box his way out of the corner, each hook and jab and uppercut helping to redress the balance.

It was ultimately an insurmountable task. Terry's right eye was closing up – Frank McGhee in the *Daily Mirror* wrote that Terry had 'a bruise the size of a pigeon's egg'. It's a questionable analogy – never seen a pigeon's egg, doubt many of Frank's readers had either – but it doesn't sound good. In the sixth round, another clawing forehand from Tiger opened a cut over Terry's left. Fighting Tiger was hard enough when you could see him; doing so with impaired vision was just plain dangerous. Cuts would go on to be the bane of Terry's career; he had skin that tore like perforated toilet paper.*

At the end of the sixth round, Terry's cornermen decided this was damage they couldn't repair. They threw the towel in for him, thank goodness. Even half-blind, Terry might not have had the good sense to quit himself.

'His right eye was badly swollen,' wrote Jack Wilson of *Boxing News*. 'He had a jagged tear across the bridge of the nose near the other eye, he had been down for three counts, taken considerable punishment and was never at any time in control against this ebony-skinned puncher from Nigeria.'

Terry lost the fight, but not his sense of humour. When reporters asked him after the fight who he wanted to fight next, he looked over at a cowering Mickey Duff and said, 'The bastard who made that match.'

---

* Ultimately, facial cuts would be the cause of five of Terry's nine career defeats.

Although he had suffered his first defeat, in box-office terms Terry was a huge success. The Tiger fight was one of the first to benefit from the lifting of the Entertainment Tax that had forced boxing into an industry-wide recession. Every ticket for Shoreditch Town Hall had been sold – and Terry's display of courage ensured people would pay to watch him fight again. 'Downes came out of the defeat with reputation enriched after six rounds of terrific punching and some clever manoeuvring,' said Lainson Wood in *The Daily Telegraph*. 'He has established himself as a money-spinner and his future seems assured.'

People watch boxing for the drama, and Terry's fights had plenty of that. While it can be enthralling to watch a maestro dominate a one-sided contest, the greatest fights have more back and forth, more story, more uncertainty. That means close contests – and sometimes, it means losing. That's show-business.

Of Terry's forty-four career fights, he lost nine. These days boxers are protective of an unblemished record – that '0' in the L column can begin to feel like a yoke round their neck. It brings pressure; it brings fear. Terry is maybe fortunate his disappeared so early; it meant he could attack fights with less to lose. But there's also some poetry to the occasional loss. A perfect record is impressive, but also somehow unromantic. There can be glory in defeat. With defeat comes the prospect of retribution, of revenge, of the rally. Defeat can be what propels you forward, what makes you come back stronger.

The important thing is that, like Terry after those nightmare opening rounds, you get back up. In his eighteen-year pro-fessional career, Tiger himself would suffer seventeen losses. There is no shame in that. Fighting is partly about your response to pain, how you counter when on the back foot. Within four years of this fight, both Tiger and Terry would be world champions.

I know how it feels to suffer an early setback – and I'm not referring to being kidnapped by a monkey as an infant. Flush with the excitement of my first few sessions with Rowan, and inspired by my grandfather's endurance and ability, I embarked on what was by my standards a pretty rigorous training schedule. This included some jogging, a decision to only drink at the weekend, and an absolute blanket ban on profiteroles.

I don't mind suffering for my art. There's something in me that's always known my life was a bit too 'easy' – I like the idea of having to sweat or having earned something. This manifests in curious ways. When I performed regularly with sketch group BEASTS, I'd frequently propose ideas for skits that involved me suffering some sort of physical discomfort. It could be eating or drinking something unpleasant, or being hit over the head with a metal tray (as you can no doubt tell, we were a pretty subtle, high-brow act). It never required a great deal of athleticism, but it did at least make me feel like I'd actually exerted myself – like I was working. In one sketch, I was tied to a chair and had an entire yum-yum donut forcibly pushed down my throat. That was my Everest. That was my world title.

So in some ways, I relished this new opportunity to push myself. However, just like when I drove a car through my garage doors, I let my excitement get the better of me. The force of my enthusiasm was too great to be sustained by my ailing body. What began as a health kick felt more like a kicking. After just a few weeks of jogging, my back completely packed in. Humiliatingly, this came to light as I was sat on the toilet, leading me to call for my wife's help, only to remember I'd locked the door, leaving me tortured and trapped like a hostage in one of the *Saw* movies.

I toppled over on to the bathroom floor, bum as yet unwiped, as I screamed my symptoms through the door to a non-plussed Camille. To me it felt like someone was playing my spinal discs like a big bony accordion. I'm no orthopedist, but I knew it wasn't good.

Once I made good my escape, with lasting damage to both my back and my dignity, I sought out a physio. They cited it as a case of 'running before I can walk' – or in more literal terms, 'running before I can run'. The likelihood was that I'd been lumbered with a lumbar disc problem. It was essential that I rested. The advice was that, as in Terry's case when confronted with Tiger, getting up too quickly would be a mistake. My best course was to take the count and stay down – for a minimum of eight weeks.

This was a significant setback. I had envisioned a Rocky-esque training montage, only set exclusively in the suburbs of north London. I imagined me running through the streets of Muswell Hill, high-fiving bemused passersby, before tri-umphantly charging up the steps of Alexandra Palace. Those dreams were now in tatters.

This put me into something of a quandary. How to emulate my grandfather's training regimen when I am not allowed to train? And then, like the grandparent-slash-guardian-angel she is, in steps Barbara.

'There's loads of other mad stuff he used to do,' she suggests down the phone.

'Like what?' I ask.

'Well, he'd run backwards.'

'Sorry, what?'

'He'd run backwards, round Hyde Park. I remember one time he called round and told me he'd run into a tree.'

I don't know what's stupider: skiing into a tree or running backwards into one. I guess at least Terry has the defence that he couldn't see where he was going.

Apparently he thought it improved his balance and co-ordination. It's pointless me doing that: I have none to improve. Given that I've managed to injure myself running forwards, this seems unwise.

'He'd do a lot of training with his dog,' Barbara continues. She doesn't mean for Crufts, I should point out. Terry would go on long runs with his boxer dog, called Champ. I have a French bulldog, called Belle – a substantially less athletic breed. The idea of getting her to run is preposterous – most days I can't get her to walk. There has been some progress on that front of late: she is now prepared to walk round the park, but only if she is carried all the way there in a bespoke backpack.

Was there anything else?

'Well, he had "The Pendulum".'

In my head, I'm picturing some sort of Gladiator-style assault course.

'What's "The Pendulum"?'

'Well, he'd take a fifteen-pound weight and tie it to a sling attached to his head, to strengthen his neck and jaw.'

I'm not doing this. I have enough headaches as it is.

'Then there's all the eggs he used to eat . . .'

Jackpot. I might not be able to train, but if there's one thing I can do, it's eating. But just how many eggs are we talking?

'An egg is a man's best friend,' read the headline on the

Mirror's interview with Terry in October 1960. 'The milkman delivers a daily dozen to the Downes household, and Terry eats most of them.' If this sounds like an absurd amount of eggs, remember this is the Sixties: before either veganism or cholesterol were invented.

Terry's eating habits call to mind the boasts of Gaston in Disney's *Beauty and the Beast*: 'When I was a lad I ate four dozen eggs every morning to help me get large; but now I am grown I eat five dozen eggs so I'm roughly the size of a barge.' Until this point I had dismissed these lyrics as being underpinned more by rhyming structure than nutritional science, but maybe Gaston was right. Maybe consuming the product of a hen's ovaries really can make you as physically intimidating as a flat-bottomed canal vehicle.

'It is nothing unusual for Terry to demolish six eggs for breakfast,' continues the report. 'Although not in the accepted form, but raw, in orange juice.'

'I eats them that way,' says Terry, sounding like a cockney Gollum, 'Because they ain't so hard to get down. There's a limit to the number you can actually enjoy.'

Well, that sounds to me like a challenge.

Terry didn't stew on the Tiger defeat for long. Less than a month later, he was fighting again. He lost to Tiger on the 14 May 1957 – by the end of June he'd got three victories under his belt. All in all, he'd fought six good fights in the space of two months.

He began making small tweaks to his setup to improve his chances. Terry ditched his fantastically-named trainer Snowy Buckingham and began working with Tom Ryder in a dingy basement off Warren Street. At this point he was soaking up knowledge, honing his style. When he returned to Shoreditch Town Hall for a fight with Derek Liversidge, he received a valuable piece of advice. American boxer Jimmy Carter, former world lightweight champion, was in the crowd that night. He advised Terry to shorten his stride and shorten his punches. Terry's style had been to fight with legs spread, to generate greater punching power. He did not entirely abandon his walk-in style, but adapted his approach a little to make himself a more compact, technical fighter. Ryder even had Terry train with a piece of elastic tied between his ankles, to help adjust his stance.

Terry's progress was almost derailed when he was ordered to join up with the British army for national service – fortunately, having served in the US Marines, they determined he could be discharged after just twenty-four hours – which is still longer than I managed on the special forces training camp.

Until now, Terry had been lodging with an aunt, earning a bit of extra cash working in an East London factory. With his professional career starting to take off, his circumstances changed. He was able to buy his first property – a house in Harlesden – after just eight fights. He put down a deposit of £700 against the price of £2,000. The return to England, and the pursuit of a professional career, must have felt vindicated at that point. 'It makes me laugh when people say boxing is a mug's game,' he said years later. 'Where else could a bloke like me have copped that kind of money without thieving?'

The most important piece of matchmaking of his life had already happened with his engagement to Barbara, but it's fair to say Terry's dad didn't initially see it that way – even when Dick and Hilda travelled from Baltimore to meet their prospective daughter-in-law. 'I remember his dad said something about me,'

Barbara tells me. 'He said to Pop, "I don't know what you're doing messing about with girls". We weren't "messing about", we were engaged! Well, I thought Pop was going to hit his dad. He wouldn't have anyone say anything about me – *he* could say what he liked, but nobody else could. Not even his dad.'

After a fight with Les Allen in November 1957, Terry might have grudgingly wondered whether his dad had a point. The match was due to take place on the Tuesday night, but on the preceding Sunday, Terry and Barbara had spent the day with family. Terry must have partaken in one too many sandwiches, because when he weighed in the day before the fight he came in at 11st 10lb – the highest he'd ever scaled.

Trainer Ryder was not best pleased, and instructed Terry to shift as much weight as possible by the following day. Terry sweated out some of the excess weight, and consciously dehydrated himself to try and lighten the load. When he stepped on the scales the following day, he was shocked to discover he'd shifted six pounds overnight. The rapid weight loss left Terry far from his best. After eight exhausting rounds, Allen was given the decision.

I've never had to 'make weight' per se, but I do approach costume fittings for acting jobs with a similar degree of trepidation. When an actor signs with an agent, they typically make them fill in a form with their sizes: chest, waist, collar, etc. Of course, with the passage of time, bodies change – but in my experience actors aren't quick to volunteer that information. Thus, every time I land an acting job, I turn up to the fitting to try and squeeze into a pair of trousers about three sizes too small. It would be so much more practical to just hand over updated measurements – but that, of course, would be a tacit admission that I'll never be slim again.

Full of regret over excessive consumption of cake and sand-wiches – a feeling I know all too well – Terry decided it was time to set his priorities in order. He and Barbara were engaged, but Terry dutifully explained to her that there would be no wedding until he was British middleweight champion.

I drank the eggs. While Terry had Barbara whisk his up in a pint glass, I took a modern approach, deploying a Nutribullet: a weapons-grade smoothie maker designed for destroying fruit.

Camille had insisted the eggs we used were free range, which made it quite an expensive endeavour. All that was left was to select the orange juice. For a touch of class, I opted for Tropicana Smooth.

So how was it? Honestly, it was like swallowing a load from the Tango man. It was like someone had dug up a bottle of Sunny Delight, that had spent the last twenty-three years since the product's UK launch fermenting in a nuclear test site. I knew Terry was brave, but not this brave.

Downing orangey ovums wasn't the weirdest thing Terry did. There was, it transpired, plenty more where that came from. I rang my grandma to explain my experience of drinking a pint which had both the look and texture of blended goldfish, when she revealed another peculiar quirk.

'Of course, he pickled his hands . . .'

Sorry, what now?

It seems Terry placed some faith in the old wives' tale that the hands could be hardened if soaked sufficiently in a kind of witch's brew. I find it incredible that a world-class sportsman was basically adopting tactics I would later see applied to conkers.

It's a tradition that dates back to the bareknuckle fighters of the 1800s. Nat Langham was a fierce middleweight who hardened his hands with a concoction of horseradish, whisky and hedgehog fat.* Langham's protégé, Jem Mace, used a mixture of gunpowder, green vitriol, and whisky – later fighters used turpentine. The legend goes that the great twentieth-century American boxer, Jack Dempsey, washed his face with vinegar and soaked his fists in horse urine in order to toughen his hide. Imagine being hit in the face by Dempsey: not only would it hurt, but it would stink to high heaven.

Fortunately, my attempts to replicate my grandfather's methods will not force me to extract the fat from a hedgehog or the piss from a horse. His own recipe was comprised of 'raw lemons, spices and brine' – all significantly more readily available.

'He used to do it after training, for about half an hour,' says Barbara. 'I wouldn't let him do it in the house, it would stink too much!'

She should count herself lucky. He could have been sat there with his hands in a bucket of roadkill and animal urine.

The recipe was unhelpfully vague. It's lovely that it specifies 'raw lemons'. I'm forever cooking lemons, boiling them, broiling them. Then it just says 'spices' – that's pretty broad. It could be as humdrum as black pepper. It could be as exotic as Chinese five spice. I don't think you can buy brine. I know this because I walked into a supermarket and said, 'Hello,

---

* It begs the question: where was he getting all that hedgehog fat? I reckon I've seen an unsquashed hedgehog maybe twice in my life? Maybe before the advent of the motor car, the English countryside was awash with hedgehogs. Maybe millions of them swarmed across the countryside, a prickly plague laying waste to the soles of unsuspecting feet.

have you got any brine?' Apparently brine is just a saltwater solution. I could have made my own – instead, I bought a tin of olives and poured the liquid out into a bowl.

Here's a little tip: if you've started your day glugging down orange juice and raw eggs, don't follow that up by eating 14 olives. It's a bit much. Already feeling somewhat nauseous, I then sat for half an hour marinating my mitts in lemony brine. I smelt like a sink full of washing up in a Greek restaurant.

But were my hands stronger, tougher, more ready to win me a world title?

Absolutely not. They just stank.

Terry had first seen Pat McAteer fight during his time in the US Marines. In front of a crackling television set, Terry had watched the Birkenhead-born fighter face off against the American 'Spider' Webb. A patriotic Terry was the only soldier in the camp backing the Brit.

There was plenty for a young Terry to admire in McAteer. He cut a dashing figure, with dark wavy hair and a face that suggested he knew how to slip a punch. His record backed that up: the veteran had once enjoyed a run of forty fights without defeat.

Now Terry's eye was on McAteer again, only this time with a very different intent. Training schedules and opponents were selected with McAteer in mind. In preparation for facing the champion of Britain, Terry began taking on international-calibre fighters. He beat the Tunisian Hamouda Bouraoui – 'I had more trouble saying his name than fighting him' – and the Frenchman Serge Leveque, who went down four times in four rounds. A fight with Welshman Freddie Cross had high stakes attached – a win would put him in line to face McAteer – but it wasn't to be. A clash of heads saw the familiar sight of Terry's face awash with a crimson mask. The cut was bad enough for the referee to stop the fight. Terry had lost a pint of blood, and seemingly his shot at McAteer.

However, a couple of wins over Dennis Booty and Salah Ben Farhat thrust Terry into contention again. His management were able to agree a fight with McAteer at Harringay Arena, but yet again the opportunity was whipped away from him. This time, McAteer was unable to compete due to injuries sustained in his previous outing – against a familiar foe, one Dick Tiger.

Instead, Terry fought and beat the Costa Rican Tuzo 'Kid' Portuguez. The victory meant he had earned £4,000 from seventeen fights in twelve months – the best part of £100,000 in today's terms. Terry looked to make the money work for him, speculating to accumulate. He bought and opened a second-hand car dealership with his cousin Pat at Stonebridge, named 'Speedway Motors'. Business was booming.

The real jackpot was struck when a date was finally set for Terry to face McAteer: 3 June 1958 – a non-title match, but with the understanding that a win for Terry would see him granted an opportunity to face the champion again for the belt. It was to be an outdoor affair at London's White City stadium. Terry loved this venue; it had a long walk to ringside building tension and drama, and the open-air setting added to the ambiance.*

As he skipped out to face McAteer, Terry attacked his pre-match shadow boxing routine with even more gusto than

---

* I've had some tense walks around White City myself. What once was the stadium is now the site of the BBC's Media Village. It's there I've trudged for fruitless auditions, lukewarm meetings and cold coffees.

usual – a reporter even joked that one of these days he was going to knock himself out.

Terry dominated the ageing champ; the points decision was a formality. In *Boxing News*, Jack Wilson wrote: 'He took the fight to Pat Mac, used both hands with impertinence and impatience and disdained completely the best punches that came his way from the champion's fists.'

After the fight, Terry got changed and rushed out to watch the remainder of the bill. No sooner had he taken a seat at ringside than the MC announced to the crowd that McAteer had retired. He stood to make thousands from a title fight with Terry, but professional pride had prevailed – he knew he was done. Terry stood at ringside, politely joining in the applause, aching inside as he saw the title fight slip away from him. The only person more disappointed might have been my grandma – with the British title still eluding Terry, the wedding was on ice again.

Good management, however, goes a long way. With the British title vacant after McAteer's retirement, promoter Jack Solomons paired Terry with Phil Edwards of Cardiff on 30 September 1958 – and then lobbied the board for it to be recognised for the vacant title. They consented, meaning Terry had done it – within twenty fights, he would fight for the British championship. Edwards was the overwhelming favourite, an experienced pro with fifty-one fights over five years. By contrast, Terry had been a pro for just fifteen months.

There was a familiar face in attendance that night. The fight at the top of the bill saw Willie Pastrano, the New Orleans fighter who'd refereed Terry during his stint in the Marines, coming to the UK to fight Brian London. This time Terry and the American shared a dressing room, granting both men an opportunity to reflect on their previous encounter in Miami.

Pastrano was a star of international calibre now, the sort Terry knew he could one day become. They were destined to meet again, of course, in the closing act of Terry's career.

Scores of Edwards fans arrived in London via that familiar railway line into West London, many anticipating victory. Gron Williams of the *Birmingham Daily Post* wrote: 'Today's Cardiff to Paddington trains will have aboard a strong contingent of those lusty-lunged Welshmen who have for years greeted with rousing song the emergence of one of their compatriots as champion. Tonight the 'boys bach'* will hope to do the same for Phil Edwards, who comes from one end of that railway line. Cardiff. His opponent, Terry Downes, was born at the other end: Paddington . . . Downes is a rip-roaring, wild fighter, mad to get at his opponent from the opening bell. He has been very effective against men without the punching power to take advantage of his almost complete lack of defence . . . The Welsh boxer should deal like a successful matador with the bull-like rushes of Downes and I expect to hear the Welsh supporters making lovely music indeed along the tiered hillside of Llanfair-Pwll-Harringay tonight.'

Those sentiments were echoed by *Boxing News*: 'Colourful Downes will no doubt force himself into the favourite's position on the night of the fight. The Downes personality is from another generation, the generation of the sword rather than the pen. Downes will supply the colour, from the moment he leaves the dressing rooms.

'But fights and titles are won with boxing skill, with brain and brawn. Edwards will not be one to be subjected by Downes' personality or his spectacular ring capers.'

---

* This is apparently a Welsh equivalent to 'lads'.

For Terry, the contest against Edwards would be his first fifteen-round fight. Until this point he'd only fought eight-rounders, and some pundits expressed their concerns that he wouldn't last the pace. They hadn't reckoned on the Marine training, The Pendulum or the backwards running. Terry dominated the fight, delivering a vicious beating until it was stopped in the thirteenth round.

Peter Wilson wrote from ringside that Terry tore into Edwards 'like a circular saw . . . he offset his opponent's greater skill by sheer non-stop aggression and the rugged type of fighting that has made boxing almost a lost art'. Edwards managed to avoid going down under the barrage, but he might have been well advised to. As his arm was held aloft, Terry gave an earful to the journalists at ringside who'd questioned his capabilities.

What a feeling that must be. Every comic has had the odd bad review – or, somehow even worse, an average review. If a critic gives you a one- or two-star write-up, you can console yourself that they're simply someone of poor taste, or perhaps suffering with some kind of mental illness that makes them impervious to comedy. But a three-star – a rating that essentially says 'yeah, I guess it's fine' – is unforgivingly brutal.

But it's rare you get that gratifying opportunity to say you've definitively proved them incorrect. Success in comedy is defined by taste rather than titles. How sweet it must be to look your detractors in the eye and say, 'You were wrong,' – presumably with, in Terry's case, the addition of several expletives.

The primary accusation Terry seemed to face from his detractors was that he was all guts, no guile. He would have vehemently disputed that, but ultimately his career may owe more to his competitive spirit than his technique. If so, I think that makes his achievements all the more remarkable.

In his television interview afterwards, Terry said it had been a good contest but that Edwards 'looked like a steamroller had gone over him . . . the bumps and bruises will go down in a few days, but the referee couldn't wait that long.'

He was right: Edwards was given such a severe beating that he didn't fight again for four months. Despite the battering, he and Terry somehow remained on good terms – the former even opened a cafe in Cardiff with a cardboard cut-out of Terry stood in the doorway, a freeze-frame reminder of that cold September night at White City. There are few people as forgiving as a fellow fighter.

Terry and company celebrated at Jack O'Clubs in Brewer Street, Soho. On the way home, he made sure to buy the morning's papers, enjoying a string of rave reviews, including this from the *Daily Mail*: 'Terry Downes, the Paddington boy who learned to fight the tough American way in the US Marines, is the new British middleweight champion . . . Edwards had his face cut and carved into a grotesque mask. Both his eyes had great bruises around them. His nose was squashed, his mouth agape and bleeding. It was the most thorough beating a man can take without going down.'

The following day, it was Barbara who made the morning papers, snapped posing with the new champion on the bonnet of a car on Terry's forecourt. It was three months later, however, that her true moment in the spotlight would arrive. British title secured, a date was set for 21 December 1958. Barbara and Terry were to be married at St Saviour's Church, Warwick Avenue, Paddington.

*   *   *

Eventually, my spinal column realigned sufficiently for me to return to training with Rowan. Progress was good. My strengths and weaknesses were, frankly, predictable: I had retained some of the punching power that so dramatically floored Dean Jacobs in third form Chemistry. My footwork, however, left much to be desired, with Rowan pleading with me to 'get those hips moving', like an exasperated judge assessing an overweight politician on *Strictly Come Dancing*.

At one stage we hit a clear wall in my development. In order to fix some fundamental errors in my technique, Rowan asked me to punch with almost no power. And yet, I couldn't do it. Even when I consciously tried to hit the bag as lightly as possible, there was still palpable force behind it.

This, Rowan explained, was not unusual. Although I eventually managed to pull the power from my punches, many male students never do. 'It's ego,' Rowan explains. 'It's the guys who come in here thinking they know what they're doing, the "Wetherspoons Sluggers". They want to show me how hard they can hit; they want to be a tough guy. To take all that away and just focus on the technique requires some humility. You have to admit you don't know what you're doing.' Unsurprisingly, that was something I could just about manage. I know I'm not a great fighter, so I'm comparatively unencumbered by that masculine need to demonstrate aggression. I'm a model beta boxer. Maybe my wokeness could fix my weakness, after all.

I like Rowan. We are different, but given that I already feel wildly different from members of my own family, that doesn't seem especially problematic. When we train I'm reminded of those weird videos from the internet about two animals that become unlikely friends, like a wolf and a duck that inexplicably hang out. I'm fascinated by a man for whom violence is commonplace, quotidian. Over the course of our time together, I set about discovering where that comes from.

The most straightforward answer is 'South Africa'. It is a country where the threat of violence is so much more prominent, more palpable. Between April 2019 and March 2020, 21,325 murders were recorded in South Africa. That's fifty-eight murders per day. In the same period in the UK, there were 695.*

'There's a total lack of respect for life,' says Rowan bluntly. 'People die of so many things – from hunger to AIDS. And there is a lot of violent crime. There is a plethora of threats, continually, every single day.

'One of my earliest memories is that a family in my area had a home invasion. They were all put it one room, doused with petrol, and set alight. That was when I was like six or seven, and it happened in one of the houses down the road. I was a perceptive kid. And when you realise that as a kid, you're like, "Wait – what happened?" The stakes are high. The amount of murders that would happen in our area is unbelievable – and this wasn't a gang area. This is in the suburbs.'

But the reason that little boy learned to fight was much more personal. 'I got into combat sports as a necessity,' he explains. 'I was probably seven or eight, this kid in the playground – Dylan – punched me in the face. I can't remember why.

'I'd never been punched. I came from a good family, and I was soft. I just remember being punched in the nose and running and hiding in this big concrete tube in the playground,

---

* According to the latest population estimates, that's about 35.8 murders per 100,000 people in South Africa. In the UK, murder rates are consistently around one per 100,000 people.

and just bawling my eyes out. And I remember thinking, "Okay, this can never happen again". I knew what I needed to do.'

Rowan, who was a fan of the karate movies of the 1990s, headed to a local dojo. He progressed quickly – before long he was competing regionally, then nationally. But that wasn't the only extra-curricular fighting he was doing. 'I was the nicest kid in school, teachers used to love me,' he says. 'I wasn't loud, wasn't a little shit. But I used to fight in the playground all the time. I enjoyed it.'

It was those playground scraps that pushed him to expand his skill set. 'I remember I lost a fight one time,' he says. 'When you lose a fight at school, it's humiliating. There's a whole big circle of people, they're all watching. It feels shitty.'

Karate is based on the principal of controlled contact. Rowan wanted something with more immediacy, something more carnal to satisfy his newfound love of fighting. 'I was very young in karate terms,' he says. 'At that age it's like you step in and they block – it's almost like a dance. But I wouldn't do it like that. I would look at them and step forward as fast as I could; I'd hit them straight in the face and say, "Block if you can." What happens then is they make you go and sit in the corner while the judges decide if it was controlled – if it's not controlled, you're disqualified.

'I felt it was controlled, but then you'd have these kids crying with split lips. I remember once my mother coming to me in the tournament and begging me to go soft. She literally came over and said I was embarrassing her. All the other mothers were like, "What's wrong with your child?". She cost me a gold medal doing that. I said, "I'll never forgive you for that."'

And so, one afternoon, a fourteen-year-old Rowan stepped into a local boxing gym. 'I told them, "I'm a black belt in karate, I'll be okay". But the first time I stepped in the ring, I got my ass handed to me.

'From then on, I was done with karate – I respected it as a martial art, but I just wanted to fight. That's all I cared about. And in boxing, that's literally all you do. You punch the bags, you work the pads, maybe you skip – you fight.'

As Rowan threw himself into a new sport, fighting outside of the gym began to escalate. 'That's when things changed,' he says. 'I became a teenager, so that's when things intensified with school fights changing to street fights. When you're kids, you're only going to take it so far – there's authority, there's the fear of getting expelled or whatever. But at high school it's different – and my high school was like *Dangerous Minds* or something. You're teenagers, and you start going out at night. And then you are literally on the streets. And that's different, right? Especially in South Africa.'

Street fighting is different – you're not bound by the same rules you are in the ring. I ask Rowan if, in that context, there's anything he wouldn't do to win. 'That depends,' he says. 'Because I'm also not like a violent crazy idiot, so I'm not going to rip someone's eye out over nothing. But if you to mean to survive? Absolutely not. Of course, nothing. I'll eat you to survive.'

Rowan's prowess in the streets saw him pick up work as a bouncer, then eventually in private security. His fearlessness in the ring owes something to the brutality he has witnessed outside of it. 'I've been stabbed four times,' he says matter-of-factly. 'The worst one was bouncing – I was just having a quiet drink at one of the clubs where I worked. I walked out the door and accidentally bumped this guy's shoulder. So he turned around like, "What the fuck?" I can't remember who threw the first punch. Whoever it was, there was four of them and we climbed into each other.

'Back then I wasn't averse to fighting with a group of guys, but usually the rule is that when they attack you, or when it's a mutual thing, you've got way less of a chance. If you make the first move you can knock three or four guys down like bowling pins – but you need that element of surprise.

'I was kind of getting pulled around, but I remember laughing because I knew my security were going to see what was happening and intervene. They came over – and the next thing I remember is one of my guys coming to me and being like, "Boss, boss, boss – your back! Your back!" And then I just went into the bathroom, lifted my shirt, and I could see my spine. It was hectic back there. It was just a big, mangled cut, and I could see the bone. It was the worst moment of my life. I thought I was going to die right there, I was texting my mom. It was crazy.'

The blade missed his lung by a centimetre. He called for an ambulance, but it never arrived. 'Welcome to South Africa on a Friday night.'

In the end he went to hospital via taxi, ending up in an argument with the driver who complained about the blood spilt over his back seat. All in all, the cut required forty-eight stitches inside and out.

Just three weeks before that, Rowan had eleven teeth knocked out after being hit in the face with a brick. 'I was blindsided,' he says. 'The guy hit me from behind.' It certainly places my Hampstead humiliation in context. I mention that I've damaged my teeth in a similar incident, feeling like a fraud even as I speak.

I tell him that Terry was my grandfather. Rowan is a student of boxing and he says the name 'rings a bell', presumably no pun intended. I should feel proud, but the revelation makes me vulnerable. It feels like admitting to being a disappointment. I still avoid talking about the dizziness. I might feel sorry for myself, but I don't want anyone else's pity.

Rowan's story is a world away from my own. I guess, to someone like me, it is shocking. But I can't stress enough: he doesn't seem crazy, he doesn't seem dangerous. If you had to label him as anything you'd say he was cynical – that he has a pessimistic view of people and society, and that he sees violence as a necessary guard against others.

As he regales me with tales of his fighting exploits inside and outside the ring, I can't help but think back to that little boy, weeping in the playground after a punch to the nose. I wonder if there was a moment in Terry's life that made him similarly determined to defend himself, whatever the physical cost.

I have one final question: 'Is there anything I could have done? To prevent being blind-sided?'

'Not really,' says Rowan. 'Sometimes you're just unlucky. But at least now you know a bit about how to handle yourself. You can be unlucky, but fortune seems to favour the prepared.'

While Barbara set about making wedding plans, Terry kept up the fighting. First he dispatched Mohammed Ben Taibi of Morocco in typical all-action style. 'What a strange mixture this Downes is,' wrote Tommy Farr in the *Sunday Pictorial*. 'He doesn't claim to be an intellectual, but he studies his boxing like an eager undergraduate. Terry is aware that lovers of orthodox boxing accuse him of taking two punches to land one. He shrugs that off with, "I'm in the ring to entertain. If I wanted to do a slow foxtrot I'd go to the dancehall."'

And then, on 9 December – just twelve days before the wedding – Terry was paired with the American, 'Spider' Webb. It was another of those moments of remarkable synchronicity – Webb was the fighter Terry had watched take on McAteer during his stint in the Marines a few years before.

Now, I hate to be the bearer of bad news but 'Spider Webb' was not his real name. His real name was Ellsworth. He had a measly two legs, and he couldn't even shoot sticky stuff out of his wrists. But boy could he fight. This was a step up for Terry – Webb was ranked number three in the world. Again the press thought Downes might be out of his depth, and early on it looked as if they might be right. A first-round knockdown had Terry reeling.

However, he gritted his teeth and fought his way back into the contest. Both men gave everything. Terry was bleeding badly, Webb was exhausted. At the end of the eighth round, the referee decided Terry's cuts were bad enough to stop the fight.

And to be visible in the wedding photos. If Terry was heartbroken to lose a fight he felt he was winning, a knees-up at the wedding was a welcome consolation. The write-ups helped too, with the *Daily Mirror* full of praise for Terry, even in defeat: 'Bring out the medals! Hang out the flags! Sound the trumpets and proclaim the courage of cockney whizz-kid Terry Downes – Britain's middleweight champion, and a throwback to the days when raw-fisted Britons fought until they could not see, and then boxed on by braille . . . I hope that once again we have not crushed a bright star so rapidly that he will burn out like a meteor.'*

---

* A good example here of how boxing can produce particularly imaginative writing. It's a product of necessity, I suspect, as the sport requires reporters to find an infinite amount of ways to say 'one guy punched the other guy'.

I loved every minute of my own wedding day. I had breakfast with my groomsmen at home in Highbury, then we were married at Islington Town Hall. The party took place at the Yard Theatre in Hackney, where we had friends performing comedy and music. To top it all off, a certain 'DJ Maj-ik'* took to the decks and infuriated the older generation by insisting on a playlist comprised exclusively of UK Garage. Camille and I were literally the last people on the dance floor at 3 a.m. The show was stolen by the speech from the father of the bride, Sait Ucan, a man whose story is every bit as preposterous as Terry's and has some notable parallels with Rowan's. He arrived in this country as an immigrant from Turkey in 1989, marrying Sharon Clapson and assuming responsibility for an infant Camille. He spent twenty-five years working nights as a kebab man to support his family. His passion, however, had always been karate – he had previously competed for the Turkish national team, and continued to train in his spare time, attending seminars and competitions. Once retired from the doner kebab game, he was able to focus more on his martial arts. In the build-up to the postponed 2020 Olympics, this culminated in Sait being appointed as head coach for the Team GB Karate squad. I was very proud to have the kebab van serving guests at our wedding; a fitting homage to his remarkable tale.

Grandma and Pop's big day had a personal touch too. They had a page boy decked out in Terry's trademark red and gold gown, and posed for photographs under an arch made up of boxing gloves. At the reception, Jack Solomons read out a telegram from world champion Sugar Ray Robinson, saying he was waiting to fight Terry as soon as the honeymoon was

---

* Real name: Majid.

over. That was to be in France, with Barbara taking her first-ever flight. She was nervous, and a mischievous Terry was in no mood to set her mind at ease. In fact, he told her that when she walked down the aisle to go to the toilet, it was imperative she remained in the very middle, otherwise the plane would tip up. Little did he know it, but honeymoon imbalance would become a running theme in our family.

IN MY CORNER

Long before I could learn to box, I had to try and remember how to walk. I sought out Nicola Harris, a physiotherapist who specialises in vestibular rehabilitation. Typically she works with patients suffering from vertigo, dizziness, nausea and loss of balance, teaching them exercises that help the brain compensate for a balance disorder.

Still yearning for a clear diagnosis, I stumbled across Nicola's website. The blurb was uncanny: 'Do you feel unsteady on your feet? Do you feel drunk when you haven't had a drink? Perhaps you feel like you are on a boat? Sometimes the way you feel will make it difficult for you to spend time in crowded places such as shopping centres. It may even stop you going out altogether.'

Nicola offered something I was prepared to pay any price for: hope. 'You don't have to accept that this is the way it is,' she wrote. 'What you must never do is just accept that this is the way things are. Regardless of your age or lifestyle, there are ways to improve your quality of life and reduce – or in many cases eliminate – your symptoms.'

I read through the testimonials on the site. One in particular struck a chord: 'My speech, my cognitive processing power, my vision, my memory, my executive thinking, control of my moods and my awareness was downgraded to dodgy dial-up internet compared to my usual superfast fibre-optic speed.* When I first came to Nicola, I was freaked out. I didn't know if I would ever get better. She instantly helped me understand that my recovery was going to be a balancing act between exercise, adaptations and the medication. In getting all elements of my condition, such as migraines, fatigue and balance, under control you are able to then progress.' The prospect of progress, perhaps even something approaching normality, was impossibly alluring.

At our first session, Nicola made me walk back and forth across the room, and stared into my eyes, like a referee checking a boxer over after a knockdown. Through her I began to understand the complexities of the vestibular system. It turns out the delicate nature of our balance depends on, well, a delicate balance. In order for us to stay upright, as well as relying on sensory information from the balance organs in our inner ears, we also depend on our vision, the sensors on the soles of our feet and our joints. These multiple inputs feed complementary information about where our head and body are in space to the balance centres in the brain. If the information from either our balance organs or the brain's coordinating pathways is faulty, then the result can be dizziness, nausea, vomiting and imbalance.

She asked me to interrogate the circumstances in the build-up to this neurological storm. I told her about the stress of preparing for the wedding, the turbulence of the Indian Ocean, the pain of Terry's passing. I told her that I was short-sighted,

---

* Almost as if, you might say, her brain had moved over to Virgin Broadband.

that I'd suffered a few bangs on the head. I told her about being assaulted, about skiing into a tree.

Nicola explained that she sees the brain like a jug, with a fixed capacity. Each of these precipitating factors – a faulty vestibular input, a previous head trauma, a fresh emotional trauma – cause that jug to fill up a little. Fill up too much, and it overflows. It was an image that resonated with me, someone who felt permanently and perennially awash.

But there was hope, there was a way forward. My vestibular system may have been misfiring, but it could be recalibrated. The way Nicola described it, for almost all of us balance is an unconscious process, akin to driving a car on automatic. Now I needed to learn to drive on manual. As someone who had desperately struggled to learn to drive on either, that sounded suitably daunting.

I had initially been wary about undertaking physiotherapy – since the onset of my symptoms, the gym had been an intolerable environment. The loud music, the illusory elliptical movement of the running machine, the head-pounding exertion of weight-lifting, simply did not agree with me.

But Nicola knew to start small. We started with baby steps, exercises as straightforward as drawing a cross on the wall and fixing my gaze on it, trying to keep it in one place. She encouraged me to walk while turning my head from side to side, scanning for objects and attempting to rebuild my understanding of movement in space. The ultimate goal was to stabilise my horizon and stop the gruelling perception of movement.

And so, I committed to it. Over a period of months, on a daily basis, with a dogged discipline that Terry might even had admired: I trained.

Round Eight

WINNING THE TITLE

In 1992, the then mainstay of the British high street, WH Smith, held its thirty-fourth annual British Young Writers' Competition. The contest led to sixty-eight aspiring authors having their work published in an anthology, entitled 'S is An Anaconda' – the panel chaired by one of the giants of twentieth century poetry, Ted Hughes. A dozen or so of the hopeful children were picked out as award winners – and there, in the under-eights category, a prodigiously gifted five year old by the name of James McNicholas was selected for special commendation for his epic 200-word tale, The Mouse's Pet:

James McNicholas (5)

Once upon a time there was a mouse who didn't have any friends. He was very sad but one day his uncle sent him a letter. Inside was 50p. He wanted to spend the 50p so he put on his coat and went for a walk. He came to a pet shop – it said mammoth sale. The mouse went in.

Inside there was a cat, a snake, an owl, a parrot. The man came up to him.

'Now what can I do for you?'

The mouse said, 'I want one of these.'

'Are you sure?' said the man.

'Yes, I am sure,' said the mouse. He chose a cat. He had it in a big bag. He thought to himself how am I supposed to carry it.

The man came up to him and said, 'What can I do for you?'

'I can't carry my cat,' said the mouse.

The man said, 'I will carry it for you.'

When he got home the cat chased him round the living room. The mouse scrambled into his mouse hole. The cat put his paw inside his enemy's home but when he tried to pull it out again it was all red. He danced away screaming.

Look, it's not perfect. The dialogue could be more imaginative. 'The man' who works in the shop initially appears only capable of repeating the phrase 'What can I do for you?' as if the relentless grind of his pet-shop-based career has worn him down into a mindless automaton. Yes, the mouse is perhaps unrealistically encumbered by the tragic flaw of his hubris, believing somehow that he'll be able to master a predatory pet. It requires a substantial leap of the imagination.

But let's be frank: there's a lot to admire here. There's the opening passage about the mouse's loneliness, an overture dripping in pathos. Lest we forget, he 'didn't have any friends'. There's the bait and switch with 'mammoth sale' seemingly leading you towards the purchase of a giant elephant, and the mouse then acquiring a cat. There's the violence and beauty

Terry celebrates the world title win
with Barbara and my infant mum, Wendy

Terry with my mum aboard the
RMS Queen Elizabeth, returning to
America as world champion

Terry sparring at home with his father, Dick Downes

Pop with his boxing idol: the inimitable Sugar Ray Robinson

And here growling with 'The Greatest', Muhammad Ali

A flamboyantly dressed Terry outside one of his empire of betting shops

Terry embracing the culture at the 1968 Mexico Olympics

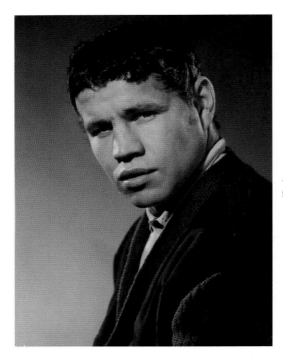

A Terry Downes acting headshot from the 1970s . . .

. . . and, to my utter shame, a James McNicholas acting headshot from my early twenties: I look like a combination of Michael Bolton and the scary painting from *Ghostbusters 2*

Pop treading the boards
in policeman's uniform

Another subtle,
naturalistic acting
performance from Terry

Terry (*back row, centre*) with
'The Group: a memorable
assembly of England's
contemporary luminaries'
(*Status* magazine, 1966)

A seasick Camille during our whale watching
expedition in Sri Lanka, 2018

The best photograph I managed to take on that fateful whale watching trip –
there's a whale in there somewhere, I promise

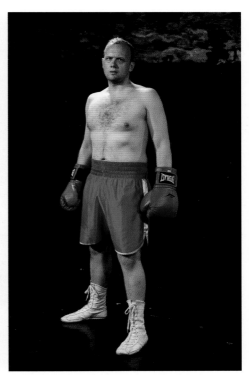

Top left: Terry is consoled by Barbara after his final fight against Willie Pastrano in 1964

Top right and below: Performing my one-man show based on Terry's life, *The Boxer* (2019)

Terry in his office with his beloved Lonsdale Belt, circa 1980

The Champ and The Chump, pictured in 2017

of the haunting final phrase: 'He danced away screaming.' There's not much length to it, but then as Cicero said, brevity is a great charm of eloquence.

I was five and I was a champion. Have I won anything since then? Admittedly, no. I've been deservedly resting on my laurels. And what laurels: I had my picture taken with the chairman of WH Smith. I don't remember his name but I'm going to go with 'Mr WH Smith'.* As far as I'm concerned, Ted Hughes had endorsed me as his spiritual successor, the voice of my generation. To reiterate: A *mouse* bought a *cat* as his pet. Feel the dramatic irony burning through you. It's Chekhov's gun, only instead of a gun it is very much a cat.

I've been associated with other victories. Arseblog, the site for whom I co-present an Arsenal podcast, has been recognised multiple times by the Football Supporters' Federation for the quality of its output. *Horrible Histories*, a show for which I've written and performed, has won multiple BAFTAs. But the WH Smith Award – that was all me. What a coup, what a triumph, what a start.

But where to go from there? The life of a professional athlete can be hard. They're often retired by their mid-thirties, faced with the feeling that their standing is now in perpetual decline, a long, drawn-out diminuendo through middle age. They find themselves chasing old highs and plumbing new lows.

But that's nothing. Imagine that the high point of your achievement, the very peak of your performance in your chosen field, occurred when you were five. What next? What do you do when you've reached the summit of the mountain, ascended

* It transpires that WH Smith formerly owned Headline, who have published this book. I've simply come full circle; the prodigal son hath returned.

into the heavens of achievement and realised enlightenment still eludes you? Are all my accidents really accidents? Or are they just an attempt to feel something again – to once more experience the kind of adrenaline rush you can only get when meeting the chairman of a major high street retail chain.

It has been, since then, a life of conspicuous underachievement. I swiftly went from child prodigy to podgy child, and it's been downhill ever since. I guess I did okay academically, but without achieving anything particularly outstanding. In the context of my highly competitive school, I was pretty average. My parents had wanted me to be a barrister; I once failed to get a job as a Costa barista.

The tangible nature of Terry's achievements has always hung over me. I remember his office as a child, shelves lined with trophies and title belts. I remember marvelling at the spoils of his victories, imagining a time when I'd have a wall like that in my own house. And yet, the McNicholas trophy cabinet stands empty. To be honest I shouldn't have bought one, I'm shy on space in the flat as it is.

Being British champion suited Terry. To him, it was always a formality, an inevitability – as this passage from an *Evening Standard* interview makes clear:

'The car-dealer executive propped his feet on the office desk, tilted his cloth cap rakishly over one eye and pondered my leading question. "What," I had asked, "is it really like to be Britain's middleweight champion?" Terry Downes, one of our brightest contenders for world title honours, and certainly the most colourful personality in the thick-ear trade, thought hard. Grinning toothily, he said, "You know, I thought I'd be champ one day. A lot of people were surprised when I won the title, but I had to work hard for it; took a lot of hard punches too."'

The British title provided Terry with some of the star status he craved – and brought with it some other unexpected perks. 'It's funny how your private world suddenly changes when you are a somebody,' Terry continued in the interview. 'Even the family are affected. Say my mum gets some rough meat from the butcher, immediately the butcher says she should have told him it was for Terry Downes. "Say it's for Terry and you'll get the best."'

While British champion, Terry engaged in a tug of war over the title with John 'Cowboy' McCormack. McCormack was straight out of the wild, wild west (of Glasgow), and earned his nickname due to his bow-legged stance. What's more, he had something in common with Jack the Ripper, Julius Caesar and Napoleon Bonaparte: he was left-handed, a southpaw – a trait which makes any opponent tricky to fight, even if they do struggle to use conventional scissors.

McCormack and Terry fought for the British title twice in two months. Over the course of these contests, a proper rivalry developed. If the Scotsman was the Cowboy, then the cockney was the Indian. For all the people Terry had fought profession-ally, this was the first time there was a personal enmity.

The hostility was born out of the conclusion of the first fight. McCormack won the title after Terry was disqualified for a hotly-debated 'low blow' – this despite knocking his opponent down ten times in just eight rounds. Nine of those knockdowns were the consequence of body blows, so Terry inevitably focused on his opponent's midriff. One mistimed shot too many, however, saw the referee step in. In 1999, the fight was named by *The Mirror* as one of the seven most farcical boxing results in history. 'John "Cowboy" McCormack is the new British middleweight champion,' the same paper wrote some forty years earlier, 'but none of the 10,000 crowd who were at Wembley last night will believe he is the best 11st 6lbs man in Britain until he meets Terry Downes again.'

McCormack, for his part, was embarrassed by the manner of the victory. His manager didn't step into the ring to celebrate with him as champion, and that night he didn't even take the belt home. Terry was so angered by the result, he threatened to never fight for the British title again unless the rule permitting the title to change on a disqualification was abolished. A £100 fine from the Board of Control did little to calm him down.

But the lure of the belt was too strong. Seven weeks later, the pair met again at the Empire Pool, Wembley. It was a very different fight – eager to prove he was a fighting champion, McCormack came out of the blocks flying. That suited Terry, who knew the Scot could not sustain the opening flurry of punches. Steadily, he took control of the fight – until cuts threatened to derail him once again. His left eye swelled almost to closing, and his nose split in a crude V-shape. McCormack was blood-spattered too; partly by a graze over his eye, partly by Terry's spurting blood spilling on to him. It was a gruesome spectacle, as ex-boxer Ernie Jarvis of *The People* attested:

'I've seen some tough fights in my lifetime. I've also been in plenty. But never have I seen anything so brutal and barbaric as last week's middleweight championship bout between Terry Downes and John McCormack. For the first time in my life I was shocked and sickened by the sight of blood. And, coming from an old-timer like myself, that's really saying something. I was even more shocked the following night when the fight was shown on television. It was horrifying. I thought of the thousands of kids all over the country who would be watching it. I'm convinced that the televising of this fight has done more harm to boxing than any of Dr Edith Summerskill's campaigns.* And If we see any more like it on our screens I forecast that boxing will be buried alongside the old sport of cock-fighting.'

Terry was bleeding like a haemophiliac who'd headbutted a helicopter rotor-blade. He'd lost so much blood he feared the fight would be stopped. Every time he knocked his opponent to the ground, he turned away from the referee to hide how badly he was cut. In the eighth round, Terry delivered the decisive blow, a right hand delivered with such ferocity it sent the exhausted McCormack toppling over the top rope, like a WWE superstar in their annual Royal Rumble. Shaine 'The Ultimate Ego' Downes would be proud.

Terry had his title again – and with the score settled, Downes and McCormack parted on good terms, as the *Evening Courier* reported: 'Anyone who has the impression that boxing is bad for the character should have been in the dressing rooms at the Empire Pool, Wembley, last Tuesday, after the damaging middleweight title battle between Terry Downes and John McCormack. Before the fight no one bothered to hide the fact that Downes and McCormack had no great regard for

---

* Summerskill was a physician and politician who campaigned to ban boxing. In 1956, she wrote a paper entitled 'The Ignoble Art', denouncing the sport on medical grounds. Speaking in 1960, she said: 'Can anybody sensibly suggest that the screaming crowd round a boxing ring is having implanted in it the fine qualities of pluck, endurance and restraint? We are told by those in this business that the sole object in view is to give the spectators a display of a sport regulated by rules calculated to ensure the maximum enjoyment of boxing techniques. If that is so, why are these bouts accompanied in the newspapers and on the radio by a commentary deliberately phrased to emphasise the brutal element?'

each other . . . Half an hour after it was all over, McCormack walked into the champion's dressing-room. Downes' with his cut nose stitched, peered at him out of his one good eye. Said McCormack, "You are the gamest so-and-so I have ever met." Downes smiled a grotesque smile and replied, "What about yourself? You were great tonight." "What about a drop of that tea?" said McCormack, and Downes handed over his cup.'

A cup of tea for McCormack, but the title was Terry's. What they shared, however, was a friendship. Years later, Terry would be in McCormack's corner as his second for a fight against American George Benton.

You don't get into comedy to win prizes. Which is a good job, because I haven't even come close.

My friend John Kearns has won things. The biggest prize in British live comedy is the Edinburgh Comedy Award, formerly and famously 'The Perrier'. John won the best newcomer gong in 2013, before returning to take the main prize the following year. He always aspired to be in contention for awards, simply because so many of the comics he admired had been recognised before.

'I was working full time when I won and wasn't really paid to perform stand-up,' he tells me. 'I knew an award with a cheque, a theatre run and possibly a trip to Australia could set me up to making a career for at least a year! It could be something I could show my parents as well, making it tangible.'

Jordan Brookes won the Edinburgh Comedy Award in 2019. Ordinarily, award winners are not eligible to enter the competition again, meaning they hold their title for just twelve months. Coronavirus and the subsequent cancellation of the

2020 Edinburgh Fringe means he's now the longest reigning winner in history. Of course, a bit like being a world champion, winning this award is something which stays with you for life. It's a permanent mark of commendation on your CV. 'I think the award represents something concrete,' Jordan says. 'Particularly in an industry where any feeling of success constantly feels elusive and illusory. It's no wonder that people place a lot of value in it.'

Interestingly, unbeknown to each other, both John and Jordan used the same phrase for describing what winning comedy's top prize felt like: 'It felt like a full stop.'

'There is a feeling of completion, which makes you look back at what you've done,' explains John. 'Is that healthy? You look back with pride but also at what you sacrificed. Was it worth it? In that moment, yes – but the problem with a full stop is that eventually you have to continue. Knowing how hard it is to create a show, it can be daunting when faced with another blank page.'

There's elation, too. Winning feels good. But reaching the end of the rainbow isn't uncomplicated. 'I've worked hard over the years to build an act I liked and was excited by, so having a sort of tangible acknowledgment of that is nice and cool, but it does also feel a bit hollow,' says Jordan. 'It's like, you spend your career running towards a succession of mirages, each one promising you contentment and satisfaction, but as soon as you get it you don't feel that thing you thought you might feel.'

And what happens next? When you get to the top of the mountain? 'I learned a life lesson,' says John. 'It turns out you always have to go again.'

*   *   *

British title regained, Terry set his sights higher still. Terry Downes, champion of Britain, sounded good. Terry Downes, champion of the world? Even better.

His next couple of fights had a suitably international flavour. He battered the Belgian waffler, Carlos Vanneste. Then he took on Orlando DePietro, leaving London to fight at the old Liverpool Stadium on St Paul's Square, where The Beatles performed in their second-ever gig. Victory came at a cost – another cut to that increasingly infamous nose leaving Terry with what he described as 'a hooter that looked like a crossword puzzle'. Terry's post-fight quips to the press covered up deeper concerns: he knew that a boxing career was unsustainable if his skin kept tearing like tissue paper. After the DePietro fight, he seriously considered the possibility of having to retire.

I know how he must have felt. I've certainly considered having to leave my own profession on account of my face. I remember a conversation with a former agent who said to me directly, 'You don't see lots of people on television who look like you.' She can't have meant 'white guys with glasses' – frankly, we're everywhere – so it can only have been a comment on my idiosyncratic features. I'm the kind of bloke who gets told his best asset is his shoulders, which to me just sounds like they've looked at my face, thought, 'Well, it's definitely not that', and picked the nearest thing. It's a joint, it's not a bit. It's like saying someone's got nice elbows – it's not a thing. It's like reading this book and then telling me you liked how it was bound.

Terry had to take steps to amend the situation, and unlike me, he had the requisite funds to pursue plastic surgery. He worked closely with the legendary surgeon Percy Jayes of the London Clinic. Jayes had previously served at the East Grinstead

Hospital, stitching up the disfigured features of injured RAF servicemen. Not even Terry's scar-tracked face could scare him, and Pop consequently became one of his best and most loyal customers – Terry used to say it was between him and Elizabeth Taylor, and, curse his luck that he never caught sight of her in the waiting room. In the course of his career, he had 373 stitches. They were done so expertly that the only lasting scar he took into retirement was the one he owed to a teacher in Taunton.

I've never really considered anything cosmetic. I don't even wear moisturiser. Looking at my weather-beaten face, I suppose that's obvious. It has been suggested to me fairly recently that my acting career would benefit substantially if I were prepared to undergo a hair transplant. At drama school they made me cut off my hair to open up casting opportunities, now the industry wants it back!

I've been losing my hair since the age of twenty-three. I say 'losing it'; it's not like I've misplaced it – it appears to be departing of its own volition. It started at the crown and is steadily emanating out. I often think my head is like an allegory for global warming: the ice caps have melted and soon I'm going to get really badly sunburnt. If I had to describe my current hairstyle, I'd say it looks a bit like when you open a box of eggs and one has a little bit of feather stuck to the top. Maybe a transplant would get me work, but here's the thing: 1) I'm a comedian, I'm not a romantic lead; 2) Should a man with chronic headaches really be undergoing an operation where they effectively drill new hair follicles into your skull? Probably not.*

Speaking of headaches, the other thing Terry did to protect

---

* All that said, if anyone wants to offer me one for free, please contact me immediately.

himself was have a special headguard made in America. It had a protective bar that came down to shield that vulnerable nose, meaning that Terry turned up for training looking like a Norman warrior.

He faced another Belgian, Richard Bouchez, before a fight on the home front. This was a defence of his British title – a rematch with Phil Edwards. The stakes were high: winning the title and defending it twice meant being able to keep the revered Lonsdale belt. Just as importantly, there was to be a guest of honour at the Empire Pool that night. The American fighter Paul Pender – the new world middleweight champion, no less – was to be in attendance. Pender was an ex-firefighter who'd realised there was more money fighting fellas than fighting fires, and he was renowned as the only man to have beaten the great Sugar Ray Robinson twice, both times for the title.

Terry was determined to impress and did. Edwards was beaten over a bruising twelve rounds, and Terry celebrated with his customary post-match clinch with Barbara, an embrace that made the front page of the following day's papers.

Accosted by the press at ringside, Pender quipped that Terry might make a good opponent for a heavyweight. The world champion clearly wasn't exactly itching to face this plucky Londoner. But it put Terry on Pender's radar. The wheels were set in motion.

Before facing Pender, Terry needed to prove himself against another American. The defeat to 'Spider' Webb had damaged his credibility on the other side of the Atlantic – but now Terry was determined to spin a new story.

The chosen opponent was Joey Giardello. The Brooklyn-born fighter had served underage in the Second World War, and had subsequently built up a reputation as an old-school middleweight with relentless energy and a good chin.* The critics once again had the temerity to suggest Terry would be out of his depth – and once again, they were wrong. Giardello was dispatched relatively comfortably. 'The Yank Is Crushed', read the triumphant headline in *The Daily Herald*.

And so a date was set for Terry to face Pender for the world middleweight title. This was Terry's shot at the summit: a chance to fulfil his dream and declare himself the best in the world. After months of haggling, the deal was eventually hammered out in a three-minute phone call. It begs the question: how were they doing the haggling prior? By post? Pick up the phone, for Christ's sake.

Pender was one of the Boston Irish, an ethnic group with the accent that so entertainingly bamboozled Martin Sheen in Martin Scorsese's *Departed*. His family hailed from Killarney in County Kerry – a town that I used to visit regularly on holiday with my dad's family.

I did, of course, have two grandfathers. My paternal grandad, Tommy McNicholas, was born in Yorkshire but considered himself a proud Irishman.† He was, in his own way, an extraordinarily high achiever – in the no less macho world of the construction industry. Tommy took over his own father's company, McNicholas Construction, and turned it into a mul-

---

* Giardello's name may be familiar to movie fans: it is his fight with Rubin 'Hurricane' Carter that is the climax of the Denzel Washington Rubin Carter biopic, *The Hurricane*.

† Infuriatingly, his birthplace means that no degree of pride is sufficient to help his grandson qualify for an Irish passport.

ti-million-pound, international business. Both branches of the family tree see me overlooked by overtly masculine, hugely successful men. Tommy and Terry got on like a house on fire, the flames often amplified by a healthy dousing of booze.

Tommy had a house in Kerry, and we'd visit regularly as children. My most fertile memories of those trips are of the neighbouring town of Killorglin and 'Puck Fair', an annual festival that takes place in August. If I told you what happens at Puck Fair you wouldn't believe me, so here is an extract from the Wikipedia page, verbatim:

'Every year a group of people go up into the mountains and catch a wild goat. The goat is brought back to the town and the "Queen of Puck", traditionally a young schoolgirl from one of the local primary schools, crowns the goat "King Puck".

'The goat is then put into a small cage on a high stand for three days, and on the third day of the fair, he is brought down to be led back to the mountains. In the middle of the town square, he is crowned and this signifies that the festivities may begin.'

Looking back at that, it raises some pretty serious concerns, not only for the sanity of Killorglin's inhabitants, but also the safety of the goat. Poor old goat, stuck up there fifty-odd feet in the air for days on end. At least David Blaine was getting paid for that sort of shit.

On the subject of animal cruelty, Pender had a reputation for 'rabbit punching'. Although this may sound like an entertaining fairground game, the terminology actually refers to the practice of illicit punches to the back of the head. He was also an infamous grappler – journalist Harold Mayes said he knew 'more holds than any wrestler'.

Experience made him a canny operator, one who relied on brains more than brawn. In some respects, he was the anti-Terry:

a cerebral fighter, intelligent in and out of the ring, well-read and capable of reciting passages of Shakespeare at the drop of a hat. He was very much a forerunner of the Lennox Lewis 'chess grandmaster' school of boxing.

At thirty, Pender was the older man by six years. He had already retired more than once, citing brittle hands. The fool: didn't he know about soaking them in horse piss?

Pender was no entertainer – but Terry believed that made him dangerous. 'He is an underrated fighter,' he told the media during the build-up. 'He is not interesting to watch, but he is intelligent.' Like David Dimbleby, I guess.

'It will be an easy fight mentally,' Pender told a press conference. 'What can Downes show me after I've been in with Robinson for thirty rounds? It's like going from calculus to short division.' Zing!

Terry's preparation was struck by misfortune and misery. A month before the fight, my grandma lost what would have been their second child – a son, stillborn.

'The terrible part about it is that it was ten days before Christmas,' says Grandma. 'That was awful. The baby arrived on its due date. He'd stopped moving just before the birth, but I was told that was normal.

'I had that baby at home in Brondesbury Park. I had a private doctor and a midwife. When I had the baby, the midwife just said, "Oh my god" – and I thought, "Oh my god, what's wrong?" Pop wasn't even there, he was out with his cousin Pat.

'The doctor said he must have died about two days before he was delivered. He looked exactly like Pop, he had black curly hair.

'It was terrible for your mum. All the while I was telling her, "We're getting a new baby, you're getting a new brother or sister." She was only little, but she must have been wondering, "Where's the baby?"'

As ever, she is astonishingly stoic: 'Really and truly, it wasn't so bad for me. I hadn't been due to go with Terry to America, but then I did. I'd never been there before, and I went to New York, Baltimore and Boston. I spent time with Pop's family. It took my mind off it. The way I look at it now is that if I'd had that baby and it'd been alright – and who knows if that baby would've been alright anyway – I wouldn't have had my Richard.

'For Pop it was hard. When you're preparing for a fight, you've really just got to get on with it. He almost had to try and block it out. You can't think about things like that.'

But of course, he was only human. The trauma must have weighed on him throughout that training camp. Even if he'd wanted to talk about it, there was no time. Perhaps the distraction of a world title fight was, in fact, precisely what he needed.

The drama did not, however, end there. A few days before the fight, his manager Sam Burns suffered a heart attack. In the gym, there was growing friction between Terry and trainer Tom Ryder.

The fight did provide an opportunity to stop over in Baltimore and visit the YMCA gym where he had started out. He was welcomed as a wandering son returned. But ahead of his first fight outside the UK, there was also a degree of caginess. Terry felt the Americans would do anything to hold on to the title, and suspected a fix. He insisted on bringing his own doctor, and even carried empty gin bottles so that he could bring his own water into the fight.

With Pender's personality lacking in pizzazz, it was down to Terry to drum up media interest for the fight – not an easy job, given that he was competing for space on the front pages with JFK, the politician named after an airport, who was in town vote-collecting for the forthcoming presidential election.

As always, Terry talked a good fight. In a column for *Boxing News*, he wrote: 'Paul Pender is going to have to put up the fight of his life if he hopes to stand a chance of beating me. I'm going to get a few thousand pounds for this contest, but I'm so keen to get my hands on that world title, that I would box Pender for a nickel. I know the setup in the States. They want to lose one of their titles like they want to be second in the race to get a man on the moon. Well, they're going to be disappointed.'

Unfortunately, Terry was wrong on both counts. After years of waiting for the opportunity, it was almost over before it started. He was knocked down in the first round, and badly cut in the second. Blood cascaded from his lacerated nose, with the *Daily Mirror* reporting: 'In a matter of seconds his face had turned to some strange barbaric flag.' As always with Terry, you were more likely to see that crimson flag than a white one. He did not know the meaning of the word capitulation (literally). 'I wasn't in trouble,' he told *Boxing News* later. 'I got my senses back at four, was cursing myself at five, and was on my feet at seven.' Terry fought back, striking Pender with such force it knocked his gumshield from his mouth in the fourth. As the bell rang to sound the end of each round, doctors and officials descended on Terry, asking whether he could continue, pressuring a decision. After fifty-seven seconds of the seventh round, the ref had seen enough. Pender won by a nose.

'Bravo, Terry Downes!' hailed *Boxing News*. 'Terry failed, but what a gallant failure! The Cockney Courageous was still on his feet at the finish. In fact, he was fighting like a tiger when the battle ended in the seventh round. His wonderful bid was ended by referee Bill Connelly, who considered that cuts

on Terry's eye and nose were too much of a handicap for him
to carry on. Terry is now a greater hero than before the battle
of Boston. He thrilled the world.'

Arguments over who would have emerged victorious but
for the cuts continued long into the Boston night. Many in
attendance felt Terry might have come away with the title –
his dad, interestingly, thought otherwise, and wasn't shy in
letting the press pack know about it. He believed Terry simply
'wasn't himself'. Back home, *The Daily Herald* went with the
cruel headline 'Kiss For a Loser', accompanied by a picture
of Barbara planting a smacker on Terry's bloody cheek. Scant
consolation for a dream shattered.

But not dead. Terry's management began negotiations
for a rematch – this time, in London. Pender was made an
astounding offer: a guaranteed $84,000, plus commission. There
was more: although the British Board of Control did not permit
rematch clauses, Pender was offered another $35,000, held in
an American bank in London, as a deposit on a potential third
match. If Terry took the title, he and Pender would meet again
in a final, decisive fight.

Terry's date with destiny would be 11 July 1961, at the
Empire Pool, Wembley. Embracing his military background, he
held his training camp at the Parachute Regiment Territorial
Army gym at White City. All was progressing well, but on
the final day of sparring, Terry suffered a cut to the nose in
a clinch with sparring partner Wally Swift. While this clearly
had physical implications for the fight, Terry's camp also feared
the psychological impact. They didn't want Pender getting a
sniff of Terry's dodgy nose. When photographers caught sight
of Terry wearing a plaster, Terry's management claimed the
dressing was simply used to aid the application of a special

lotion he'd acquired from Harley Street to harden the skin. They even went through the charade of having a press photographer come out to take a photograph of Barbara applying the fake lotion. 'I can't remember what we used,' she laughs. 'Probably just a bit of yoghurt or something.'

In the build-up, Pender once again refused to play up for the cameras. While Terry had the air of a gladiator, Pender behaved like a statesman. 'What am I supposed to do?' he asked reporters at a London press conference. 'Growl at Downes? Boxing is an athletic event like any other sport. Footballers aren't expected to go around growling at people to show they mean business. I'm not going to provide any sensation stories while I'm here. All I'll promise is that on the night of the fight I shall try my hardest.'

The usually pugnacious Terry played along. 'I've growled at a few people in my time,' he admitted. 'But only when it has become necessary. To growl at someone who is not growling at you only makes you look like a real idiot. Let everything be sweet until the fireworks start at Wembley.'

Heading into the fight, Pender was 7/4 favourite – fair enough really, given that he hadn't lost a fight in nine years. Terry, however, was convinced this would be his moment. Like Michael Jackson, the only thing Terry truly feared was his own nose. Sure enough, after a cagey opening round, it split open in the second. 'It's just a scratch,' said Terry's cornerman, inadvertently paraphrasing Mercutio.*

Champion and challenger traded blows in the centre of the ring. Terry fought for that belt desperately, as if he was headed

---

* William Shakespeare's *Romeo and Juliet*, Act III Scene I. (Paul Pender presumably already knew that.)

into a very important business meeting, wearing trousers that were seven sizes too big for him. Terry's left eye was closing, but Pender had a cut to his right. As Pender's eye swelled so did Terry's courage. Pender had always been someone who fought in bursts, but they were becoming fewer and further between. Terry could sense he was flagging.

The giveaway came in the ninth round, when Pender came out of the blocks flying. He was giving everything he had for one last push – by that stage, it was win or bust. After all he had been through with his dad, Terry knew a gambler when he saw one.

At the end of the round, Terry laughed in Pender's face: 'Is that all you got?' Pender's answer was, seemingly, 'yes'. After nine rounds, he told the referee he couldn't go on. He was slumped on his stool like a boy who'd shit himself in an art class and was blaming it on his pencil case. Terry always suspected that Pender simply didn't 'love the job' – and to be fair, when the job involves getting repeatedly hit in the face, I can quite understand.

The film footage of the fight was believed lost for decades, but by some miracle of the internet it reappeared on YouTube during the research for this book. The decisive moment is somewhat anticlimactic. Terry returns to his corner to prepare for the tenth round, only for the referee to come over and raise his fist aloft. Why did Pender quit? Was the punishment too great to sustain? Could his pride not handle going out on his back? Did he resign knowing he had the comfort of a possible return fight, back on home turf?

Whenever we spoke about it, I sensed it always rankled with Terry that Pender quit. When you imagine winning a world title, you dream of delivering that knockout blow. You dream of an instant in which your life, your legacy changes. In some respects, Pender's abdication snatched that moment away from him. The champion quitting was such a story in itself that it cast a slight shadow over Terry's achievements.

'I was robbed,' Terry told reporters after the fight. 'He didn't let me finish my work. I was going to knock him out and he knew it. That's why he quit and he took all the glory away from what should have been my biggest win. Yeah, he quit. And I got embarrassed. What a helluva thing to happen to anybody. He went out like a quitter instead of how a champion is supposed to go out.'

Later, he mellowed somewhat – the balm of victory providing a soothing effect. 'The fight was not going Pender's way, and he wasn't daft,' he told the *Daily Mail* in 2011. 'He jacked it in because he knew he had a return fight in Boston. He was getting beat and did not want to take a battering. So, he quits on his stool.

'If he'd got the guts to carry it through, it was a smart move. He knew that in Boston he could get everything he wanted: a home fight, a referee and maybe his title back.'

Any sense of anticlimax about the manner of the win was surely overcome by the tidal wave of validation – that feeling of arriving at the top of the ladder, the end of the rainbow. This was before the vast proliferation of belts across the divisions: in Pender, Terry beat the man who beat the man. He was the true, lineal champion. He was the best, and he had the belt to prove it – just the third British man to win the world middleweight title.

My grandma had been in the crowd, watching from behind her programme in customary fashion. 'I had to manoeuvre up the ring steps in high heels to see him,' she recalls. 'I got up there and gave him a kiss. Do you know what he said to me? "Don't make a fuss, I knew I was going to win." I said, "I wish you'd told me!"'

Terry and company held a celebratory party that night in Piccadilly's Pigalle nightclub – having been tipped off by Terry's mum Hilda, the Downes family were out in force, a who's who of hooligans mingling with London's finest. They hoped, I imagine, Terry would be there to pick up the bill. In fact, he snuck out after half an hour, preferring to savour the victory alone with Barbara.

They drove from Piccadilly to their home in the suburbs of north-west London. I ask my grandma what those moments were like – how did he handle the enormity of realising a lifelong dream?

'It wasn't his dream,' she rebuts. 'I said, "Oh my god, what do you feel like?" He said, "I don't feel any different. I knew I'd do it." He wasn't flash. He just had supreme confidence. He knew that if he'd trained the hardest, worked the hardest, done all the right sparring, then only a cut could stop him. And sometimes, not even a cut.'

She doesn't remember the route they took home that night. In my mind I like to imagine they drove west – past the old Pembroke boxing club and up through Paddington. Past the railway station, the school where he had his first fights, the house on Westbourne Terrace where he grew up. When they got home, they found a photographer waiting on their doorstep. The front page beckoned.

The only blot on this momentous night was Terry's interaction with his father. 'His dad turned round and said to him, "You should've stopped him before then,"' recalls my grandma. 'He couldn't even say, "Well done," not even when he won the world title . . . I'll never forget that.'

I doubt Terry did either.

That's so typical of those older generations. Even if he'd wanted to, Dick didn't have it in him to throw his arms around Terry, to tell him how proud he'd made him. He didn't have the emotional facility. If there is something absent in this world of manly men, it's surely that: openness, tenderness, affection. So much goes unspoken. These men are hard, but they're stiff too.

Such things are hereditary. I know that Terry found it hard to praise his own sons, that his first instinct was to criticise, particularly when it came to their sporting endeavours.* Tommy was the same with my dad, and he in turn has never been particularly affectionate with me.

It's something I railed against, even as a youngster. I intuitively took against it. I remember as my brother and I turned from boys to teenagers, family members like Terry and my dad would subtly transition from offering hugs and kisses to handshakes. I resisted. I may not be especially tough, but I'm stubborn: I kissed Terry every time I saw him until he died. In its own way, I guess, it's as transgressive or intrusive as a jolting jab. There's some strength in that willingness to be vulnerable. To this day, I insist on kissing my dad goodbye. I don't know whether Terry or Dad liked or like it. I expect that even if they did, they couldn't say.

Age has a habit of softening hard edges, though. I feel so lucky, so grateful, that for all his experiences with his father, Terry found it in himself to be proud of me, and to tell me so. To come to school plays, to average comedy gigs, and laugh and clap and cheer. That this elite sportsman would come to watch a chubby boy play rugby or trundle down the track at sports day. That he managed even to be proud of a frankly

---

* One story tells of Terry turning up to watch one of his sons play cricket at school. When they were dismissed, he turned on his heels and left, without so much as a word of consolation. He expected as much of them as he had of himself.

ridiculous story about a mouse having a cat for a pet. That for this champion of the world, it was enough to see me try.

The day after his title win, Terry held a celebratory press conference at the car showroom he owned in Paddington. A young female journalist from London's *Evening News* asked: 'Mr Downes' I understand some boxers look at their opponent's eyes and others look at their gloves. What do you do?'

'I always look at their gloves darlin',' said Terry. 'I ain't been hit by an eye yet.'

Terry's study is almost untouched since he died in 2017, a shrine to his successes. My grandma is protective of it, she doesn't like people going in and out. I visited it recently, turning the key in the lock for the first time in weeks. Dust hangs in the air like memories, the reflective brass of trophies and medals giving a sepia tone to the whole room. On one wall hangs a poster advertising that glorious night at Wembley: Pender vs. Downes – 'only 10,000 seats available for the contest ten million want to see'. There is a framed letter, dated 2011, from the WBC congratulating Terry on the fiftieth anniversary of his world-title win. There are photographs with royalty and celebrities, with Princess Diana and with Elton John. There is a handwritten note from his final opponent, Willie Pastrano; the Golden Gloves he won in the US Marines; and in a felt-lined wooden case, his precious Lonsdale belt. Tucked away in a corner, porcelain dulled by dust and time, sits a seemingly inconsequential teapot. And on a central shelf, in pride of place, a picture of his father Dick Downes. The man he wanted to impress more than any other; the gambler he always hoped would bet on him.

IN MY CORNER

I didn't find it easy to talk about what was happening to me. I think that's partly because as a newlywed, particularly one that's recently returned from an exotic honeymoon, there is an assumption that you're experiencing bliss. I didn't want to disturb the notional fairytale. I was ashamed to shatter the illusion, afraid to reveal how broken I felt. I hid.

Occasionally though, I would confide in people. Sometimes it would be out of necessity – to excuse why I suddenly drank more often or to explain why I'd started wearing ear plugs in public. I'd tell them the story outlined in the prologue: that I stepped onto a boat and then back onto land forever altered, ground that undulated and bobbed like the surface of the water. I told them how it had changed me and changed my life, and how I wasn't sure I'd ever be fixed. And almost always they'd ask the same question: 'Do you regret going on that boat?'

I wanted to scream at them: 'OF COURSE I REGRET GOING ON THE BOAT. IT RUINED MY FUCKING LIFE.'

What did they expect me to say? 'Nah, actually this is what

I wanted to happen. I consider this outcome ideal.' Or perhaps, 'I reckon it's a fair exchange. Ultimately, having had the
opportunity to see a whale in the wild, it strikes me as only
reasonable that I should spend eternity strapped to the prow
of an imaginary ship.'

There were other motifs that would recur in conversation.
People regularly put forward suggested diagnoses or possible
treatments, as if they just happened to do a spot of neuro-otology
in their spare time. They'd tell me their cousin had something
similar, which sounded from where I was stood to be altogether
different, usually because it was missing the crucial component
of 'magical boat curse'. Sometimes, I strongly suspect, they just
didn't believe me. I didn't really blame them for that: it still
seemed utterly implausible to me too, and I was living it. Often
people would look at me like I was mad. Sometimes I thought
they might be right.

My family knew, but it wasn't something we talked about all
the time. I sensed they wanted to look at wedding photos and
honeymoon snaps unencumbered by the reality of my illness
and my depression. In truth, I was also somewhat embarrassed
about the ridiculous nature of my condition: when other family
members had been battling cancer, when Terry had passed away
just a few months prior, my complaints felt absurd.

After all, I knew it wasn't going to kill me. I had the cursory
scans for brain tumours, so I knew I wasn't exactly dying – but
equally, I wasn't exactly living either.

And so I made light of it in conversations with friends and
family. I didn't feel able to tell them how bad things were, to
show them how hard it was to even get out of bed. It was only
Camille who bore that; who saw me at my lowest ebb.

But, at her behest, I had begun counselling. In my first session

I had to sit there and tell my therapist, Alicia, that I always felt like I was on a boat and it was ruining my life. I half-expected her to immediately have me sectioned. But she listened, intently. In fairness, it's not every day someone walks in off the street and tells you that. At least it was interesting.

Alicia interpreted my balance issues as a literal manifestation of the delicate balancing act I had carried out throughout my life – that as the child of two unreliable parents, I had sought to provide stability, to hold things together. She found a poeticism in my condition that at first, I'll admit, irritated me.

'It's not a metaphor,' I'd protest, 'It's an illness.'

While I considered the symbolism a bit crude, in time it did help me to understand that there was some correlation between the physical and the emotional, to figure out that the way I thought was affecting the way I felt.

I could not believe that this was my story. I had never felt more of a failure, more distant from my pre-eminent grand-father. But talking about it, and talking about him, began to bring me closer.

Round Nine

CELEBRITY

In May 1966, American glossy magazine *Status* published a photograph of what they called 'The Group – a memorable assembly of England's contemporary luminaries'. The picture was taken in a London studio by the celebrated photographer Patrick Lichfield, with the twenty-one subjects arriving in a convoy of Rolls-Royces, Minis and motorbikes.

Among them were famous faces from all walks of British life. From the arts, the painter David Hockney, Dave Davis of The Kinks, and film director Roman Polanski. Some came from the upper classes: Prince Dmitri, nephew of the last Tsar of Russia, and Lord Douglas, Marshal of the Royal Air Force, sandwiching the Armenian oil magnate Nubar Gulbenkian. And there towards the back, a retired boxer with a budding business empire: one Terry Downes.

It gives an indication of the standing he held and the company he kept. If boxing made Terry a household name, it was his personality that made him a star. His prowess made him part of the firmament, but his charisma kept him there.

It would be fair to say I haven't been celebrated by the media in either the UK or US to quite the same degree. Probably the closest I've come to that recognition was when a video of me pranking Camille went viral in 2017 and the *Metro* ran a story with a headline: 'Is this the world's most annoying boyfriend?' *

Terry was indisputably, unquestionably famous. In 1961 he was the Sports Journalists' Association's Sportsman of the Year, and as his career went on he became accustomed to appearing on the front pages as well as back. He was the kind of character that transcended sport, partly because he fitted a convenient stereotype of the wise-cracking cockney. I suspect he knew that and played into it. Even as an older man, I noticed how his register would shift when he was recognised. A boxer has to know how to sell a fight, and to sell themselves.

One of the ways in which Terry managed to maintain a public profile was through acting work. Yes, that's right, not content with his towering sporting legacy, Terry thought he'd wade into the territory of theatre and television too. And guess what: he was substantially more successful than me. Terry took up acting as a hobby and achieved more in that field than I have managed in a lifetime of trying. He had a varied career as a performer, capped by starring in as many as five feature films. He even appeared alongside icons of sketch comedy Peter Cook and Dudley Moore in *Not Only . . . But Also*. At the time of writing, the most lucra-

---

* The prank consisted of me going around Mallorca saying, 'Got enough?' over and over again. 'Got enough apples?', 'Got enough forks?' It was every bit as infuriating and inane as it sounds. I compounded this by making the 'Got Enough Holiday Memories?' video the centrepiece of my wedding speech, insisting that the real reason we had all been gathered to celebrate was the fact it'd now reached one million views on YouTube.

tive acting job I have ever done is an advert for TUC crackers which aired in Belgium and the Netherlands.

According to IMDB, Terry's acting career began in 1957, in the brilliantly titled but sadly now lost ITV detective series *Murder Bag*. He went on to play a cameo role in Jack the Ripper movie *A Study in Terror*, popping up as Chunky, a muscle-bound butcher, in a scene with a young Barbara Windsor. He appeared in a French/Italian co-production called *Five Ashore in Singapore*, in which 'five CIA operatives are sent to Hong Kong to investigate a soldier's disappearance in this spy actioner . . . the group is kidnapped and drugged before being introduced to a Harvard-educated madman. The scientist freezes his victims before brainwashing them and hopes to sell his process to an enemy of the United States.' It's about as good as it sounds.

In the Seventies, he played a regular role in BBC series *Gangsters*, a drama about a former SAS officer recruited by the police to work as an undercover agent in Birmingham. Terry played a character called Roy Studd who, somewhat surprisingly given his name, is a bodyguard and not a porn star. Plotlines dealt with racism, drug addiction, bent coppers and organised crime, and the visual style of the show took cues from Asian gangster movies and Bollywood. Some say it was ahead of its time; others that it just wasn't very good.

The TV bit-parts kept on coming. As late as the 1980s, he appeared alongside Charles Dance in TV drama *The Secret Servant*. His final acting credit came in 1990, playing a character called Purvis in *The Bill*. There's a pattern here: military men and criminals. Terry was a kind of proto-Vinnie Jones: a sporting hard man who went on to play tough guys on screen.

Was he good? Ah, well there's a question. It feels unfair, given that Terry is not here to judge my footwork and punching power,

that I should cast aspersions on his acting. I'll say this: he's enthu-
siastic. He seems to be having a good time, stomping around sets
and chewing the scenery. 'He just loved it,' says my grandma.
What's more, he had something I haven't been gifted: good looks,
and raw charisma. On screen, that can count for a lot.

Like Jones, he certainly lacked range. My acting skills have
seen me dubbed 'The Chameleon', although some argue that's
just because my eyes point in different directions. Chunky, Roy
Studd and all his other characters were very obviously Terry
Downes – same look, same mannerisms, same indecipherable
accent. To be honest it's amazing they didn't subtitle him.

Spencer Tracy offered some famous advice on acting: 'Know
your lines, and don't bump into the furniture.' Terry at least
managed half of that. 'He did a play at the Mermaid Theatre
in the West End, *Shadow of a Gunman*,' recalls Barb. 'The
first time he walked on he nearly knocked the whole set over.

'I just had to shout and holler and bully people,' Terry said
of the job. 'It was quite good. I had one part as a prison warder
with Bernard Miles at the Mermaid Theatre and they paid me
£13 a week. The cab fare cost me more than me wages.'

For Terry though, this wasn't about money. He approached
his acting roles with the same discipline that had come to define
his entire life. 'I remember him locking himself away in his
office doing his lines,' says Grandma. 'I'd hear him shouting
away. He'd be in there hours.'

His most famous role came working with Roman Polanski.
Terry and the Polish-born director were both part of the *Status*
magazine shoot in 1966, and were reunited a couple of years
later for the comedy horror *The Fearless Vampire Killers*.
Polanski was apparently captivated by Terry's face (if not his
talent) and decided he would cast him in his parodic horror.

'He saw me in a television interview and liked the look of me,' Terry explained. 'Or maybe he *didn't* like the look of me. He cast me as a bloody monster, a hunchback with a deformed face and a club foot as big as anything.'

'I remember one time he came home from filming in all the hunchback gear, false teeth and all,' recalls Barbara. 'He jumped out from behind the curtain, frightened the life out of me. I wouldn't have minded, but I was eight months pregnant! I nearly had the baby then and there.'

During filming, Terry struck up a friendship with Polanski and his then girlfriend Sharon Tate. The director and Tate had met on set and began a relationship during filming. When they were married in 1968, the reception was held at the Playboy Club, and the Pathé News cameras were there to capture it. Review the footage and amid the bunnies and the bubbles, between Joan Collins and Michael Caine, are my grandma and Pop.

Polanski's reputation has taken a justifiable battering since the heady heights of his fame, but my grandma still speaks of him with a degree of reverence. 'Such a clever man,' she says. I guess he must be to have avoided arrest for this long. When the news of Tate's murder by the Manson Family broke in 1969, Barbara remembers Terry being 'devastated'.

It seems mad that Terry had these ties to Hollywood. To me, it is another world entirely – and suffice to say, by the time I came along those connections were not in place to provide me with a leg-up in the industry.

He admitted he would have enjoyed the chance to play a romantic lead 'for the birds', but he had no pretensions to serious acting. 'I played parts which fit my face,' he said. That much we have in common.

'Anyway,' Terry added, never slow to send himself up, 'I can't talk proper.'

I remember playing football in the playground at school when I was about sixteen. My friend Joel came up to me and said, 'If you were a footballer, you'd be one of the famous ones'. It may sound like an odd thing to say, especially in relation to someone who has all the footballing talent of a slug, but strangely enough I knew what he meant. I had a performative streak that bled into anything I turned my hand (or foot) to. I guess I was a show-off.

I think I wanted to be famous too, certainly in my youth. To someone with aspirations of an acting career, fame seemed simply a byword for success. For an actor, the ultimate goal is freedom of choice – to be in a position where you're able to select the roles you play, rather than rushing to endorse which-ever brand of crackers is prepared to pay the highest price.

I've not always had the breaks. My first agents out of drama school were the unconvincingly titled 'Backdoor Management'. It's about as bad a name as you can possibly imagine, even if you manage to set aside the fact that it sounds like clinical interven-tion for chronic haemorrhoids. The semantics are problematic too; the name implies its clients have to sneak in through the industry's 'back door'. Let's at least pretend we might get in through the front door, or ideally the stage door.

Bizarrely enough, Backdoor Management did have links in the world of boxing. They made a habit of signing former fighters who were considering a second career as performers. In my time there, they had former Olympian Richie Woodhall and Irish former world champion Steve Collins on the books. Backdoor would organise weekly screen-acting workshops for their clients, so I'd get to sit and watch these ex-fighters under-going a very different type of training. I'd say they were about as good at acting as I am at boxing.

Despite this promising willingness to invest in their talent, Backdoor was not a good agency. A particular example springs to mind. One afternoon, I received a call from one of the agents there, asking if I was free to pop along to an audition in the next couple of hours. Another of their clients, a young actor by the name of Jazz Lintott, had been due to attend but was now no longer available. Jazz was a nice guy who would later join the cast of BBC show *The Real Hustle*; a television programme which educated the general public in how to successfully commit petty crime. Now ordinarily I would be loathe to attend an audition at such short notice, but Backdoor explained this particular casting was for a new production of *Macbeth* – a show I had recently starred in at drama school. I had a few monologues still up my sleeve and so was good to go. I reasoned I'd turn up, bust out a few bars of iambic pentameter, and head home with the job in the bag. I accepted the audition, on one condition: 'Make sure you let them know to expect me.'

Spoiler alert: they did not know to expect me. I arrived at the audition, pacing up and down the waiting room 'tomorrow and tomorrow and tomorrow'-ing under my breath, but every time the casting director's head popped out the door she asked for another actor instead of me. After a while, it became obvious that I was being ignored. I noticed the other guys auditioning seemed to have a slightly different look to me, but that didn't put me off. I'd just played Macbeth in drama school; surely I had the edge. I got a distinction, for God's sake. And yet my turn never came. After waiting for almost two hours, I decided to take matters into my own hands. As one auditionee left the room, I sprung up and snuck through the doorway to accost the waiting panel.

'Hi guys,' I said, in as breezy a tone as I could muster. 'Just checking you've got me on your list. My agent said they'd let you know I was coming down, I'm a replacement for Jazz Lintott.'

In their faces I immediately detected surprise and, worryingly, anger.

'Did my agent not let you know?' I asked. 'They told me they'd definitely let you know.'

One of the panel coughed. Another looked at the floor. The third spoke. 'I'm not sure you're quite right for what we're looking for,' they said.

This did not put me off – lest anyone forget, I had just played Macbeth at drama school, producing the performance of an adolescent lifetime. It brought the house down; it was the talk of the campus. My dad had referred to my acting as 'quite a bit better actually'.

That, it seemed, wouldn't cut it with these guys. Increasingly aggravated by my insistent presence, the director explained that my agent should not have sent me to this audition. After all, she said, this production of *Macbeth* was to be one of the first in London to have an all-black cast.

Images collided in my mind as, like some half-witted Holmes I pieced together information that corroborated what she'd just said. Jazz was indeed black, as had been every other actor who'd passed through that waiting room. I probably allowed myself a brief moment of self-congratulation for not even noticing.

And then I did something that haunts me until this day. I imagine that when I inevitably die, this moment will flash shamefully across my consciousness, reminding me that the world will be a fundamentally better place once I am gone.

Instead of retreating in disgrace, tail between my pasty white legs, I thought for a moment and then asked, 'Well, do you mind if I have a go anyway?'

Can there be a greater example of white privilege than that: believing that you possess a talent so transformative it will dissuade a production team from proceeding with their plan for an all-black production. 'I understand you intend to cast a black actor, but bear in mind you haven't seen me, a gifted white man, yet.' *Macbeth* is the tale of a man whose ambition sees him lose his grip on reason and reality. Perhaps I really was perfect for the part.

To the panel's enormous credit, they had the patience and pity to let me go through with it. They probably reasoned that sitting through a two-minute monologue was the most expedient way to get rid of me. I finished my declamatory soliloquy to an awkward silence, and then sidled out into the night.

Remarkably, I stayed with Backdoor Management beyond that. Ultimately, I had nowhere better to go. I did once threaten to leave, which led to me being called in to meet one of the senior agents in their West End office. The agent in question was an archetype made flesh, a loose-tongued socialite who seemed to know everyone and yet hold no influence with anyone. In conversation she dropped names like Gretel trailed breadcrumbs, leading you down a delicious yet ultimately fruitless path. Crucially, I was naive enough to be easily bamboozled. She'd never got me any work, which made me doubt her, but she had taken me for lunch at The Ivy, which convinced me she knew what she was doing.

The meeting took place in the opulent Soho headquarters, premises I still don't understand how they could afford. When I was shown into the agent's office by her secretary, the agent was leafing through a pile of bound scripts on her desk.

'Sorry!' she said. 'I was just in the middle of reading through these for you!'

Quite the coincidence, but seemingly a good start.

She then proceeded to explain her plan to transform me from out-of-work theatre actor into A-grade Hollywood superstar. This all sounded fantastic and entirely logical to me – and she didn't even mention the need for a hair transplant. She also rejected a number of calls that came through on her mobile, signalling to me that for that twenty minutes, I was her absolute priority. I did think it odd, then, that she allowed her secretary to interrupt our meeting to say a call had come through on the landline. 'Sorry Jamesy,' she explained in characteristically over-familiar tones. 'Gotta take this one.'

The call apparently was from a casting director at the BBC. 'David – thanks for calling me back,' she breezed. 'I was just getting in touch to tell you about this up-and-coming actor we've got on our books, James McNicholas – I think he'd be perfect for some of your new projects.' Encouraging.

She hung up and we continued our chat. Plans were hatched and promises were made, and I left ebullient and full of enthusiasm. It was only when I called my mum to tell her how the meeting had gone that the reality dawned on me: the scripts, the phone call, the BBC – it was all staged. She might as well have been flicking through the Argos catalogue. As for 'David', the timing of that particular phone call was so convenient as to be practically implausible. It's amazing how ego leads you to be flattered into believing things that are plainly too good to be true. How could I be so stupid? The short answer is: because I wanted it so, so badly.

There were other bad auditions. I once attended a casting for a Cadburys Creme Egg advert, in which they made me act out various scenarios including drunk disco dancing, talking down a suicidal person from a ledge and getting on the floor and barking like a dog. I saw the ad a few months later; none of that was required. I have friends who work in advertising, and I have occasional anxiety-inducing daydreams about them uncovering some of those tapes.

I kept going to advert auditions though, however humiliating. As an out-of-work actor, you don't have much choice: a fee of several thousand pounds, often for just a day or two's work, is a considerable carrot to dangle. In the course of my career I have featured in commercials for products including Goodyear Tyres, Crunchy Nut Cornflakes and Sony PlayStation. I appeared in a viral ad for McDonalds as 'Australian backpacker' – a non-speaking role, so presumably they just felt I looked sufficiently Australian.

There have been some false starts. In 2017, a director I'd briefly worked with got in touch to say he'd written his first feature film and considered me ideal for the lead. That was a big deal: getting any role in a movie is difficult, let alone the main part. This, I thought, might be my big break! He explained the basic premise: a psychological thriller in which a polite middle-class homeowner called Jamie is tormented by his aggressive, bullying builder. Of course, it was the former of these two characters I was under consideration for.

I read through the script, excitedly envisaging myself portraying this harassed, troubled man – until, that is, I got to page 87. By now the builder has verbally humiliated Jamie, he's superseded him in the pecking order of the house, he's even bedded his wife. On page 87, however, the psychological torture plumbs new depths. At the film's climax, the builder coerces Jamie into, and there's only one way to say this, wanking off his dog.

When I failed to respond to the director's emails, he called me to assure me that the dog-wanking would happen off camera, and that the shot would instead be focused on my face throughout. Oh, much better.

Perhaps the most disturbing part of the whole project was that the writer had confided in me the script was loosely based on his own experience. I politely declined the part. As far as I'm aware, the project remains 'in development'.

It's not that I haven't achieved anything in my acting career. There have been things I'm really proud of. I played a leading role in a production of *The Importance of Being Earnest* that transferred to the West End's Theatre Royal, Haymarket. Working with my mates Ciarán Dowd, Owen Roberts and director Tom Parry, we made and performed sell-out comedy shows in London and Edinburgh as sketch act BEASTS. It has been a joy to join the cast of CBBC's celebrated *Horrible Histories* series. We even won a children's BAFTA, which I'm delighted to tell you is precisely the same size and weight as a grown-up BAFTA.

But only recently have these acting jobs come together to constitute what you might call 'a living' – especially so given the financial demands of living in London. In the course of my 'career' I've done countless other jobs. My dad got me a job as a caretaker at his office, where I had to manually scrape weeds out from between tiles in the drive. I've sold wine, spouting expertise on products I wasn't able to either afford or pronounce. I was a telesales person for Viking River Cruises, and later Hillarys Blinds.' I'll never forget the day I rang up one old bloke and said, 'Hello, it's James from Hillarys Blinds.' He was obviously slightly deaf, as he gasped in horror and shouted back, 'Hillary? My wife?! She's blind?!'

As stated, the highest paid acting job I have ever done remains that commercial for TUC crackers that aired in Belgium and the Netherlands. Hop on to YouTube and type in 'TUC Totally Crackers' and you'll see me there, sporting a polo neck and a pair of trousers so tight that it wouldn't surprise me if the Low Countries have pre-emptively registered me as a sex offender. This, in financial terms at least, is the high point of my acting career to date. Meanwhile Terry, a man with no formal training and arguably less talent, worked with Polanski! Granted, the director might have faced accusations of paedophilia, but artistically at least he has retained some credibility. Meanwhile, I've appeared in a Belgian cracker ad, utterly devoid of credibility, in full paedophile regalia.

Acting, we've established, is not a stable profession. Terry presumably recognised that and made sure to pursue other business interests in his 'retirement'. He invested in property and made for an unscrupulous landlord. Terry tended to collect rent himself – there's nothing to encourage paying up like a world champion boxer knocking on the door. 'You get a bit heavy-handed,' he admitted later. 'You do a bit. No wonder you lose your temper. One bloke is lying in bed, smoking, drinking a bottle of beer and he owes me seven quid. I hung him out of the window and I nearly got locked up.' All for just dangling a man out of a window and threatening certain death. Where's the justice?

In May 1961, the same year as Terry became world champion, The Betting and Gaming Act allowed betting shops to open in Britain. Terry recognised that opportunity and began opening betting shops of his own. By 1964 he had almost thirty, turning a working profit of £87,000 per year – around £1.5 million in today's money. Behind the cockney bonhomie was a shrewd business mind; he was as fiscally skilled as fistally skilled.*

---

* To those of you booing this admittedly torturous line: I will not apologise for who I am. No regrets, YOLO etc.

'We run the shops like an army,' the former US marine told *World Sports* magazine in 1964. 'I'm the general, so now and again I nip round and have an inspection. You've gotta be sharp to be up to the dodges of some of these punters, but we have a pretty good checking and security system which has seen us all right so far.'

'I was in the second-hand car business, but the bottom was falling out of it. I just had an idea that betting shops would pay off. I didn't know anything about them – no one did, 'cos they were something new. But the first one went like a bomb. Everything started from that.'

You certainly knew those shops were his: his name was written in neon above the door. When Terry Downes opened a bookmakers, he called it 'Terry Downes Bookmakers'. When he took ownership of a racehorse, he was similarly uncomplicated. Equine nominative convention dictates that horses are generally named things like 'All Sold Out', or 'Pardon Me Madam'. Racehorses frequently sound like crossword clues. They often have names which sound more like they're intended for sustainable perfumes: 'Gypsy Rain' or 'Willow's Cry'.

Not Terry Downes' horse. Terry Downes' horse was called 'Terry Downes'. Beautiful. Why complicate matters? It's gloriously simplistic. Maybe he just wanted to hear a commentator saying, 'and Terry Downes has cleared the last fence and is heading into the final straight'. The record books already had Terry Downes listed as a boxing world champion, maybe he fancied seeing that name under Grand National winner too.

It was the same naming policy Terry adopted with his first two sons – Terry Downes Junior (R.I.P.) and Terry Downes Junior (hello Uncle Tel). Looking back, it's remarkable that my mum – the oldest of his four children with Barbara – ended up being called 'Wendy' rather than 'Teresa'.

It was the same with the fashionable nightclub he owned in unfashionable Harlesden: 'Terry's'. Some might suggest this kind of narrow naming strategy is the work of a maniacal megalomaniac. And they'd have a point. An element of self-regard and narcissism often seems to be present in exceptionally high achievers. I suspect Terry thought that sharing his name was a marvellous honour. What better name could there be than Terry Downes? He didn't stop for a moment to think of the expectations it might pile on a young son trying to live up to his world champion father – or indeed the pressure it might place on a plucky young horse with a dream.

There's an element of tradition to all this. In the Downes family, it's not just the pugnacious nose that is passed down: it's names too. As previously mentioned, the family tree shows around a dozen people called Walter, each with their own soubriquet: big Wally, little Wally, old Wally, young Wally, Wally the footballer and Wally Junior. In my family, it's less 'Where's Wally?' and more 'Which Wally?'

There's something quite primal, quite unreconstructed about wanting to stamp your name all over the world. It's part of the patriarchal obsession with legacy. In a pre-Google world, bestowing your name on objects, animals and children was a way to endure. No one needs a gravestone now because they've got a Facebook page.

I'm not above any of that. After all, I'm not writing this under a pseudonym. Ask any writer about the appeal of writing a book, and they'll doubtless mention the satisfaction of creating something which could outlast you. When I'm long dead, this book will live on, resting on bookshelves and toilet cisterns across Britain.

The name of a world champion can be a heavy burden to bear. Terry Junior was a very promising sportsman in his own right, before back and knee injuries put paid to those ambitions. I have mentioned elsewhere a feeling that I'm permanently cast in the champ's shadow – I can only imagine how that is emphasised by sharing the same name.

As for the horse, it never won anything of note. Terry bought and named it before he'd ever seen it race, telling the media: 'I just hope it's got four legs and a head like the others.' Nevertheless, the name decision worked well from a business perspective. Terry knew that the horse would help promote his betting shops: an equine sandwich board, an advertising hoarding with hooves.

It's no coincidence that Terry, whose own father was a prolific (and problematic) gambler, should choose to open a book-makers. When I was young, I found it strange that a man who never really gambled himself, should go into that particular business. I asked him about it once, and he told me: 'It's easy money – I knew that the bookie always wins.'

Smart maybe, cynical certainly. I suppose, as the child of two alcoholics, it would be like me turning round and deciding to open a brewery. Somehow I can't see myself out there trying to flog people a cold foamy pint of 'James McNicholas'.

Opening the betting shops wasn't purely a cynical act, how-ever. Terry's dad Dick would frequent one of his shops, and Terry would regularly cover his losses. It provided somewhere he could keep an eye on him, close at hand – if he couldn't break his habit, he could at least manage it.*

---

* As it happens, the opening of betting shops actually had a severe impact on the greyhound racing tracks on which Terry's dad had once been so hooked. Between 1961 and 1969, twenty-one national greyhound racing clubs closed. Dick was at least now gambling on Terry's turf.

Terry made his name in boxing, but it was in bookmaking that he arguably made his fortune. He eventually sold his shops to William Hill – a company with an equally unimaginative, progenitive name bestowed by its founder. That windfall enabled Terry to keep living the highlife long after his boxing days were over.

He counted on a number of celebrity friends. After Terry's appearance on *Not Only . . . But Also*, he and Peter Cook struck up a close friendship, as did their wives Barbara and Wendy. That relationship granted them access to the social circle around The Establishment club.* Terry and Barbara once attended an intimate dinner party to celebrate Cook's birthday, where guests included John Lennon and Paul McCartney of The Beatles, actors Peter O'Toole and Tom Courtenay, and the designer Mary Quant. After a candlelit meal round the kitchen table in Peter's Hampstead home, they talked 'politics and prizefighting, painting and poetry, theatre, de Gaulle and President Kennedy, the Chelsea Flower Show and the summer sun in Spain.'†

'Peter gives the finest parties I've been to,' Terry told Harry Thompson in his Cook biography. 'It might be Michael Caine or John Lennon, or one of these top people you see on TV, but everybody's mixin'. It boils up to a great evening. Peter never makes himself too busy, never makes himself Jack the Lad. He looks after everybody, especially the women, gives them that little bit of extra attention. My bird's knocked out by Peter. He's a real hundred per cent diamond person.'

---

* The Establishment club was a nightclub on Greek Street, Soho, that became particularly associated with comedy and satire.
† Lin Cook, 1996, *Something Like Fire: Peter Cook Remembered*, Arrow, UK.

If there was a time to be famous, the Sixties were surely it. Terry and Barbara frequented a number of iconic nightspots – The White Elephant, The Astor, Sleepeazy. Barbara became a famous face in her own right, even appearing alongside Joan Collins on *The Eamonn Andrews Show* – an ITV programme which pioneered the American chat show format in the UK.

As a nightclub owner himself, it was perhaps inevitable that Terry would come into contact with some of the murkier aspects of London life, and so it was that he struck up a relationship with the infamous Kray twins. Reggie and Ronnie Kray ran a huge crime empire that spanned London in the Fifties and Sixties. Their gang, known as The Firm, were associated with murder, armed robbery, arson, protection rackets and assaults. 'They called them the Swinging Sixties,' Ronnie Kray wrote in his autobiography *My Story*. 'The Beatles and the Rolling Stones were rulers of pop music, Carnaby Street ruled the fashion world . . . and me and my brother ruled London. We were fucking untouchable.'

The twins and elder brother Charlie were celebrities in their own right, photographed by David Bailey and interviewed on television. Their West End nightclubs were the haunts of politicians like Lord Bob Boothby and Tom Driberg, prominent entertainers such as Frank Sinatra, Judy Garland and George Raft, and sporting celebrities including champion boxers Freddie Mills, Terry Spinks and my grandfather.

The link between boxing and the criminal underworld is no great secret – and perhaps no great surprise given that this is a sport where the combatants tend to emerge from poverty; a sport where legalised violence and gambling are helplessly intertwined. Ronnie, Reggie and Charlie were all professional boxers in their youth and retained an interest in the sport.

As both a boxer and nightclub owner, it was inevitable that Terry and the Krays would cross paths – and that he would have to keep them onside. It seems he certainly managed that. This professional acquaintance blended into the personal: my grandma Barbara says the Kray family and the Downeses would exchange annual Christmas cards.

It wasn't worth the risk of upsetting them. When the Krays were made to feel unwelcome, they were dangerous. When match-maker Mickey Duff banned the twins from attending a private members' boxing show, he received four dead rats in the post. Then in 1968, when the Krays were arrested before their famous murder trial, Duff was contacted by police. It seems that when authorities apprehended Ronnie Kray, they had found a list of names in his pocket under the heading 'These Men Must Die'. 'Duff' was on the list – as was 'Downes'. Duff famously quipped, 'I hoped they were going to kill us in alphabetical order!' It's unclear what had moved Ronnie to put Terry on such a list, but fortunately those embryonic plans never developed any further.

When their mother Violet passed away in 1982, the Kray twins were released from prison for the first time since their trial in 1969 in order to attend her funeral. The procession drove through Bethnal Green, where Violet's father, 'Cannonball' Lee, the boxer, used to lick a white-hot poker to earn money from market crowds. It went past Vallance Road, where the Kray family home, known as Fort Vallance, stood. The carriage then weaved through Hoxton, where the twins were born over a shop in 1934, and Cazenove Road, where they killed Jack 'The Hat' McVitie in 1967 because he had called Ronnie 'a fat poof'.

After almost an hour, the cortege arrived at Chingford Old Church where the twins were waiting, along with the classic Kray coterie of celebrities and high-calibre criminals.

The Great Train Robber Buster Edwards had sent a wreath. There was a heap of chrysanthemums and lilies from 'all the boys in Parkhurst Prison' and another from 'all your friends at Parkhurst Hospital'.

Two of the Nash brothers, the most prestigious club owners in London's East End, were in attendance, as was the film star and singer Diana Dors. And there, stood by the grave with the Krays' father Charles and their Aunt May, was Terry Downes.

When the Krays needed a favour, Terry was understandably happy to comply. When one of Britain's most infamous inmates, Charles Bronson, was in Broadmoor, he attempted to strangle his cellmate Gordon Robinson with a silk scarf. Although Robinson survived, Bronson was sent to Norfolk Ward – a section of the hospital which he claimed 'houses the cream of the madmen. One had decapitated his mother. He was caught on the bus with her head in a shopping bag.'

While there, Bronson became depressed and suicidal, tearing up his photographs and destroying many of his letters – so the Kray twins arranged for a surprise visitor. 'Who was it that come to see me, but ex-middleweight world champion Terry Downes – one of my boxing heroes!' writes Bronson in his book *Silent Scream*. 'What a boost it was for me, what a visit, what a lovely man coming to see someone like me.'

Bronson is a former East End bare-knuckle boxer with convictions for armed robbery, wounding with intent, criminal damage, grievous bodily harm, false imprisonment, blackmail, and threats to kill – but that wasn't enough to put Terry off. In another book, *Broadmoor: My Journey into Hell*, Bronson describes Terry as 'a proper loved and respected cockney. He grabbed my hand and whispered, "Ronnie Kray's concerned about you, so we've come to see you're okay. What do you need?"

'A guard clocked this and marched over. A big fat twat I didn't like. He said to Terry, "Wasn't you the British champion?" Terry winked at me and smiled, then said to the fat twat, "The world, sonny. Get it right. The world." It didn't stop him asking for a signed photograph. Terry said, "On your way, mate, I'm talking to my pal here." It was a priceless moment, to see one of the nasty fuckers taken down a peg or two. He made him look a right prick.'

Ronnie Kray was right to feel sympathetic towards Bronson – he would later end up in Broadmoor himself, suffering with paranoid schizophrenia. I don't quite know how I feel about these connections, even if I think we can assume they weren't all entirely voluntary. The associated violence is obviously grim, but there is a certain glamour to it all that's undeniably alluring. But then, isn't that boxing all over?

Terry was, of course, no angel. He, I have discovered, had his own run-ins with the law. In 1966 he appeared at the Old Bailey to testify against a group of men who'd attacked his friend George Hollister outside his nightclub on Curzon Crescent in Willesden. Newspaper reports said that Terry had become embroiled in the fight 'when there was a shout that somebody had an axe'.

In 1970, he attended Hendon magistrates, accused of causing bodily harm. Nineteen-year-old Christopher Holloway had been hospitalised for five days with a fractured jaw after 'a motoring incident'. The *Evening Chronicle* reported the accuser's account: 'Mr Holloway said that on 17 September at Hendon, a sports car overtook him on a narrow road causing him to break and swerve. He chased the other car and stopped it. The driver, who he later discovered was Downes, got out and asked him if he wanted a fight. Mr Holloway said: "He swung a punch at me and missed. I still had my glasses on at the time. I took them off and then hit him two or three times. He then hit me once."'

He had glasses? Immediately we know this isn't a fair fight. I'm tempted to side with young Christopher here. Terry's side of the story, unsurprisingly, varies slightly.

'Downes said he was going to overtake Mr Holloway's saloon car, when Mr Holloway "obviously took the needle". The saloon pulled out and there was "a slight tap". He stopped to inspect any damage, when the other car came up.

'"They came from behind and swerved in front of me as if I was a bank robber," added Downes. Asked by Mr Victor Lissack, defending, if he intended to fight, Downes replied: "Certainly not. I don't go around fighting people. I used to fight people, but only for money."

'Downes said Mr Holloway "swung a punch". He pushed Mr Holloway back, but Mr Holloway came at him and swung a couple of blows.

'"I only hit him once. I wasn't looking for any world championship. I only gave him a light punch to stop him, so we could talk."'

Terry was cleared, the court chairman stating: 'Evidence is conflicting on many points, but we do accept Mr Downes' statement that he was quite obviously reluctant to use the skill with which he possessed. We are satisfied that the unfortunate blow was not struck with any malice, and, therefore, the case must be dismissed.'

'It is a relief,' Terry told the media afterwards. Then, with the same sense of inevitability with which he discussed his title wins, he added, 'Although I knew I was innocent from the very start.'

Three years later, he was arrested by police after a punch-up, but released without charge. 'The row had started in a restaurant at Clifton, Bristol,' said the *Daily Mirror* in a brief article. 'Downes stormed out, and restaurant owner Joseph Panazistou followed him to his hotel. Then a fight started.' The report culminates in a fashion that feels, rather appropriately, like a punchline: 'Mr Panazistou was treated for facial injuries.'

There may be more. Suffice to say, these are stories I've had to investigate myself – they're not shared as readily among family. Terry did have a short temper and was never one to back down. However, I think it's also worth considering that as a celebrity, and a fighting one at that, there was quite a considerable target on his back. As unwise as it might seem, there are plenty of fools who want to come away with a story of the time they fought the champion of the world. The likelihood is that Terry had to show considerable restraint: if he'd really wanted to hurt people, he would have ended up in a lot more trouble.

Even when Terry wasn't operating outside of the bounds of the law, he was a bit of a troublemaker. One story tells of Terry going on a joyride through the gates of Buckingham Palace, doing donuts in the front drive, all with a friend locked in the boot of the car. When police and guards understandably intervened, they recognised Terry and simply gave him a rap on the knuckles.

While he charmed his way out of any issues with police constables, he certainly fell foul of the PC brigade. Veteran boxing PR Geraldine Davies recalls chaperoning Terry on a flight to watch a big fight in America. When the German pilot came on the tannoy, Terry reportedly got up and started goose-stepping up and down the aisle.

He attended plenty of fights in retirement, although his shouts of 'encouragement' from the back of the hall weren't always well received. His trademark growl could be heard telling fighters they were 'bleeding useless . . . My old woman punches harder than you!'

Only once did he suffer a verbal counterpunch. A rather precious MC was taking a long time introducing celebrities.

'And now a big hand for the wonderful, the inimitable, the one and only . . .'

From the darkness came a raucous: 'Get on with it, you old poof!'

The MC paused and sniffed: 'Not so much of the old, Mr Downes.'

It's not clever, it's not right, but it is absolutely what he was like. To omit that aspect of his behaviour would be an over-sight. He was firmly stuck in his ways, and resolutely resistant to change. If he had remained in the public eye, he would certainly have been 'cancelled'.

My grandma, meanwhile, has her own explanation for his aberrations. 'It's all down to the fact that he couldn't handle his drink,' she explains. 'He'd spent so long not drinking as a youngster, on account of all the training, that he'd have a couple of pints and end up pissed. Then all bets were off.'

In another era, would his drinking have been characterised as problematic? Had I grown up as Terry's son, rather than his grandson, would I have observed in him the same lack of control I witnessed in my own parents? It's something I think about.

Terry's fame also provided him with a platform for his charity work. Derek O'Dell was a member of the Uppercut Club, a charity organisation of which Terry was chairman. 'We raised a lot of money and distributed to ex-boxers and their families when they were in need of help,' says Derek. 'At the same time, Terry was instrumental in raising thousands of pounds for the Variety Club Sunshine Coaches which took handicapped children on outings. To see the fuss he made of these children and the joy it brought to them made me so proud of him.

'These were well publicised charities, but I was even more impressed by what he did out of sight of press reporters, or even those of us who knew him. I saw him once quietly handing out cash to old-time fighters who were on a coach outing. And then there were times when I was working for Ricky Porter Promotions and we had benefit nights for an ex-policeman who was crippled, and another old-timer suffering from terminal cancer. We asked Terry to appear and he accepted immediately, asked for no money and made those two unfortunates feel like royalty. It was touching to see the fuss he made of them.

'And there was one final charitable act,' he adds. 'When my wife died some fourteen years ago, the first telephone message of condolence came from Terry. The man was 100 carat.'

Citing someone's charity work, however impressive, has a whiff of cliché: I have no desire to deify Terry. His good deeds are part of a fuller, complicated picture of an undoubtedly complicated character. The process of writing this book has been one of unpacking the family legend, of getting to know the man behind the myth. For better or worse, I find myself grateful for that opportunity. Few people come to know their grandparents as well as this.

Celebrity never quite dies, it just fades. Even as an old man, Terry made a habit of carrying around a few signed photographs in case he was recognised. It happened surprisingly frequently – at garden centres, car boot sales and pubs. The difference is that the people coming up to you get older, providing a reflection of your own advancing years. There comes a point where you can see in their approach a surprise and delight that you're still alive.

I am lucky enough to be recognised on occasion. I say 'lucky', it's not always particularly fun. I remember in the midst of a break-up, crying my eyes out down the phone on a park bench, only for a man to tap me on the shoulder and say, 'Sorry mate, hope you don't mind me interrupting, but I recognised your voice from a podcast.'*

I don't know if I expect that to endure, though. There's something about the particular nature of my diluted version of 'celebrity' – maybe modern celebrity in general – that feels somehow cheap, and certainly transitory. The irony is that although podcasts and YouTube videos and tweets are housed on servers forever, they all feel so throwaway. They're tomorrow's digital chip paper. Maybe that's why I've wanted to write a book. Maybe that's why, deep down, I've always wanted to win something – something that matters, something that really lasts.

It's mad nevertheless to think of Grandma and Pop as properly, actually famous. I feel very fortunate that my grandparents are so eminently googleable. Not everyone can peer into their past quite so easily.

It's difficult too to reconcile the party-going superstar with the kind but cantankerous old man I knew. My grandparents were famous in a different era, too. Terry and his celebrity cohort behaved in a way that simply isn't possible now. The advent of social media has put a curb on that kind of hell-raising, at least in public. Terry's partying and bingeing with

---

* It goes without saying that he immediately followed up with, 'Oh, you're a lot taller than I expected.'

the likes of Oliver Reed would today be plastered all over the internet. Woke culture, rightly or wrongly, would have left Terry in its wake.

The closest I've probably come to being celebrated on a national scale was with my 2019 show at the Edinburgh Fringe, *The Boxer*. This was a dramatisation of Terry's life – the show that led to me writing this book. After a series of positive reviews, it ended up being named in *The Guardian*'s ten best comedy shows of 2019. It was my show, yes – but it was Terry's life. The greatest acclaim I've received was for a show in which I told Terry's story. Only with him in my corner could I become a true contender.

IN MY CORNER

As I edged closer to a diagnosis, the parameters within which I lived my life became increasingly more defined, more specific. Doctors provided me with a list of dos, and a significantly longer list of don'ts.

By now my symptoms were being vaguely classified as atypical chronic migraine. I was encouraged to embrace the 'migraine diet', which meant eliminating a list of food including eggs, tomatoes, onions, dairy, wheat, citrus fruits, alcohol, caffeine, additives, chocolate, cheese, and nuts. Really, it would have been much quicker to tell me what I could eat. (No word of a lie, suggestions on the pamphlet included 'orange, yellow or green vegetables' and 'carbonated, spring or tap water'. Oh Monsieur Neuro-otologist, with these menu options you are spoiling us.)

The limitations went way beyond my diet. I was handed a list of potential triggers that could worsen my condition that included reading, watching television, crowded spaces, loud music, supermarket aisles, bright lights, cinemas, planes, trains and automobiles – and, of course, boats. I didn't follow all these guidelines, because frankly it seemed entirely impractical, but it meant that so many experiences left me feeling either ill, or guilty.

That wasn't the worst of it. There were two pieces of advice that had particularly significant ramifications. Doctors explained that, in order to avoid overly-stimulating environments, I should stop exercising, and stop going on stage.

Eliminating exercise didn't bother me initially. As the previous chapters have demonstrated, I am no natural athlete. But as time wore on, as I lost confidence and gained weight, it began to create a disconnect between my emotional and physical self. I didn't trust my body, and nor did I like it. I felt unattractive, and emasculated. It's hard to feel like a man when you feel like a buoy.

Performing was admittedly a perfect storm of potential triggers: it came with the unholy trinity of bright lights, high pressure and crowded spaces. Maybe it was for the best. I was now so miserable I'd begun to wonder how funny I might be. I was less sparkling wit and more snarling misanthropy. On the occasions I had tried to get on stage, it had been an overwhelming experience, a blur of lights and faces and throbbing pain. It's difficult to do stand-up when you can't stand up. My dizziness was robbing me of my very identity. These two restrictions fed each other: the more out of shape I got, the less I wanted to be on stage, or on camera.

I should have been starting the best chapter of my life, with the perfect wife and doing the kind of work I'd dreamed of. Instead, it was unravelling around me. The celebrity and success I had wanted would never be mine. You feel thwarted, and you don't know where to discharge all that anger. You're fighting something that you can't hit.

I thought back to the Indian Ocean, to the comparison I had drawn between Terry and me. The man who seemingly had it all, and his grandson, who seemingly had it all taken away. I cried, and I thought of where it all began.

On that fucking boat.

Round Ten

LOSING THE TITLE

In 1962, Terry once more travelled to America by boat. As the familiar rugged New York skyline loomed into view, he would have had ample opportunity to reflect on the change in his circumstances. It was the same journey from Southampton to New York he'd taken as a teenager, but this pugilistic pilgrimage was re-enacted in substantially more style. A decade prior, he had arrived to help his sister in an emergency, the unknown brother of an injured circus performer. This time, he landed in the States as champion of the world. This time, he was aboard the lavish RMS Queen Elizabeth, training in a dedicated personal gym by day and dining with the captain by night. If he wasn't quite so pronounced a cockney, you'd say it was the American Dream realised, bound up in a belt round the waist of this quintessential Londoner.

He was en route to face Pender in Boston once more – a third and final fight for the title. Terry had refused to fly, in part because Barbara was pregnant again, but also because he was all too familiar with the tale of Michael Cerdan, the French world middleweight champion who'd died in a plane crash in 1949. Cerdan had been engaged in a high-profile affair with compatriot and singer Édith Piaf, and had boarded a flight from Paris bound for a rendezvous with her in New York, before it crashed into a mountain in the Azores. Whatever her most famous lyrics might suggest, I bet Piaf bloody regretted him getting on that plane.

The crossing took four days – in the scheme of things, a small delay. Terry had originally been due to meet Pender again just two months after his Wembley triumph. In the end, it would be nine months before they would fight again – long enough for either man to gestate a baby, although due to biological barriers, Terry left that to Barbara.

The fight had been held up by a bizarre run of injury and illness. Just a few weeks before Pender and Downes were set to settle their score, it happened to be my mum Wendy's second birthday. Creeping down the stairs of their Mill Hill home to prepare her presents, Terry tripped and fell. It was an injury sustained due to paternal instincts rather than the toil of training. In all his years fighting, Terry's infamous witches brew had prevented him sustaining a single hand injury, and yet this tumble nearly cost him a thumb. A simple sprain led to a course of injections, which in turn led to an infection. Ultimately, he came within a few hours of emergency amputation. Frankly, it all sounds like something more likely to happen to me.

An absurd accident perhaps, but this was potentially a career-ending injury. Think about it: you don't see many boxers without thumbs – they even have that special bit of the glove for them. Can you clench a fist without a thumb? I broke my thumb in that skiing accident, and I have never boxed professionally. Coincidence, much?

For the next two months, Terry attended a clinic daily for electrotherapy on his mangled thumb. Just as it was starting to work sufficiently to make him an opposable opponent for Pender, he suffered another setback: a severe chest infection. It seems the champ had no choice but to take a medically advised eight-week holiday in Mallorca. I suppose there are worse medicines.

If you think that sounds like an improbable series of events, you're in good company – when Terry delayed the bout, Pender's camp were certainly suspicious. The Americans suspected foul play and sent a delegation to inspect Terry's thumb in the grossly swollen flesh. Personally, I don't think there's much chance Terry was trying to duck the fight – he wasn't really one for ducking anything, hence all the cuts. As world champion, his earning power per fight was greater than ever. He was probably itching to beat Pender a second time and go on to bigger paydays.

But he definitely had his reservations about returning to Boston. In their previous match there, he'd felt he'd been fighting uphill – he knew the Yanks would be determined to bring the belt back to American soil. At this point in time, no Brit had ever gone to America and come back with the world title. 'We boxed in Boston once and Pender won, we boxed in London once and I won,' said Terry. 'I think it's only fair that this rubber match should be on neutral ground. There's absolutely no question of me being afraid to fight Pender again – let's face it, I want some money, and they've got a lot of my money tied up. I want to get this fight over with as soon as I can to make some more title defences and make some big money, but I'm not prepared to go to Boston again at no cost.'

His concerns were not without precedent: in 1961, the world heavyweight champion Floyd Patterson had refused to fight

Tom McNeeley, a far inferior fighter, in Boston if the commission insisted on appointing a Boston referee. When the local authorities refused to budge, the fight was moved to Toronto. Terry pushed and pushed for a neutral setting, such as New York, but was unsuccessful. The odds were against him again, figuratively and literally.

I find his fears over a possible plane crash to be revelatory – a rare moment of superstition from someone so self-determined, an instance of insecurity from a man usually so utterly fearless. His paranoia about the prospect of returning to Boston is palpable too. On his last trip, lest we forget, he had insisted on bringing his own water into the arena, as well as his own doctor. This time he campaigned for a new referee. He feared he was being set up.

Any jangling nerves weren't helped by the fact that Cuban welterweight world champion, Benny Paret, had died from injuries sustained in the ring just a month prior. Maybe the thumb injury and the chest infection led Terry to wonder if the belt was somehow cursed. Since winning it, he'd been kept out of the sport he loved for three-quarters of a year. He wanted to be champion, yes, but a fighting champion – to him, boxing mattered more than the belt.

Was he, on some subconscious level, dragging his heels back to Boston? Seeking to somehow delay the inevitable? How he must have savoured those final four days crossing the Atlantic – king of the world, aboard the Queen's finest vessel.

Raja and his crew of Sri Lankan sailors use a trimaran boat – a deviant of a catamaran, with a two-tiered observation deck well suited to its purpose. It is not quite the RMS Queen Elizabeth, but does boast a small kitchen and 'western-style toilet'. The boat departs Mirissa Harbour at 6.30 a.m., with trips lasting four hours, rather than four days. A $54 ticket comes with a money-back-guarantee, applicable only 'in the rare event' that you do not see whales.

We had been in Sri Lanka for about a week – the first leg of a honeymoon that would involve a whistle-stop tour of Sri Lanka and India. The destination was Camille's suggestion. I don't mind admitting I was somewhat daunted by the prospect of visiting South Asia: the people I know who've returned from India tend to fall into one of two camps. On the one hand, you've got people who come back all spiritually inclined, telling you how it changed their life and they've realised possessions are meaningless. And on the other, you've got the people who come back, but all they talk about is the fact that they've spent the best part of a month shitting themselves. I did not want to be either of those people: I like my possessions, and I like my pants.

Going to India must be the only holiday where when someone returns, it is legitimate to ask them whether or not they shit themselves. If they've been to Marbella and you ask them, you're just weird. If they've been to India, it's somehow fair game – dig deep, get into the specifics. Another factor which put me off was the cost of the flights. However, Camille was insistent she wanted to go somewhere exotic – and apparently my suggestion of Center Parcs just wouldn't cut it.

Our trip was delayed too. We were married in September 2017 but didn't go on honeymoon until New Year's Eve. Admittedly, this was due more to the Sri Lankan climate than anything else – but nonetheless that period between the wedding day and our honeymoon, a time when I should have felt absolute bliss, had its difficulties.

As you know, it was in this period that Terry passed away. In truth, Terry had been suffering difficulties with his health for some time. In the 1980s, he contracted polymyalgia rheumatica – an auto-immune condition which causes chronic muscle pain, a cruel irony to see a man once so strong rendered so weak. The condition would ultimately lead to him requiring two hip replacements. At one point he was taking as many as seventeen steroid tablets per day. 'I was popping more pills than Maradona,' he quipped.

In his seventies, he had battled bladder cancer – a fight he won, but not without taking a bit of a beating from the radiotherapy. His memory was fading too, the years and the punches finally taking their toll. Nevertheless, he always seemed to bounce back. But this time, it was different. It felt ominous, it felt final.

And six weeks after we were married, he died. Admittedly, it was no tragedy. He was eighty-one – a good age, especially for a boxer. My anecdotal experience is that men who spend their lives fighting have all the longevity of a pair of Apple earphones.

But it was still desperately sad, and a huge loss to us all. The night he died, boxing arenas up and down the country marked the occasion as tradition dictates: ringing ten bells for the fallen champ. It's a mournful, solemn sound: the final ten count that you can't beat.

'I remember you really crying,' says Camille. 'You said you felt like you'd grown up at their house – that you'd spent so much time with them, almost as much as your parents. I remember you saying it felt like the head of the family was gone. And I remember feeling sad that I hadn't know him better, and that you never really knew my grandad.'

I didn't process it right away, I don't think. I grieved, I felt sad, I certainly wept, but I didn't accept it. The funeral was a procession of characters from the fight game recounting stories about Terry, some of which feature in the pages of this book. Although his life had been quite private, in death he somehow seemed to belong to other people. It's a strange sensation to open a newspaper and read an obituary about your own grandfather. I acknowledged that Terry Downes, world champion, had died; I don't think I fully accepted that Pop had too.

Then there was the fact that Camille and I had just got married. A bit like falling down the stairs a month into being world champion, this wasn't exactly an ideal start. Maybe I was guilty of simply biting down on my gumshield and putting on a brave face. Perhaps between the wedding bells and the honeymoon, I felt an obligation to try and bridge the gap, to keep spirits up, to mask my pain.

I think I was doing a pretty good job. I knew too that it would be good to get away – and fortunately I had the TUC crackers cash burning a hole in my back pocket, so that covered a good chunk of the costs. We were scheduled to visit both Sri Lanka and India, starting on that southerly island.

I loved Sri Lanka: the food, the people, the scenery. If you haven't been, it's lovely. It's sort of like a decaf India. And while it was Camille who'd picked the part of the world to visit, it was I who had insisted we get up early to see the whales.

I love a boat, you see. Before we married, Camille and I talked about living on a houseboat. It was one of those vague dreams you have in the first flush of love, like living abroad or opening a dog-grooming salon. There was also a pragmatic element: being artists in London, a boat is one of the more affordable ways to live.

It seems crazy now. Because after that day with the whales, 7 January 2018, I'll never get on a boat again.

Being a champion brings with it its own pressures. It must've been strange: Terry, a perennial underdog, suddenly had it all to lose.

A lot of the headlines in Boston surrounded Terry's growing betting empire. By this stage, he had seven shops, with another two in the process of opening. With sports betting still illegal in America, the papers found his dual status as both sportsman and bookmaker fascinating. 'We'll take bets on anything,' Terry boasted to local reporters. 'Even on this fight. We'll have it even because it's in Boston. But I'll win. I don't know if I'm the better fighter or not, but I'll win. I'll win easily.'

Whether he believed that or not is another matter. Certainly, he knew that Pender had plenty to prove. His decision to quit in London had drawn criticism on both sides of the Atlantic – knowing he already had a rematch in the bag, he had faced accusations of both cowardice and cynicism.

After Paret's death in the ring in New York, boxing was under scrutiny in the States, and consequently Terry and Pender were asked to keep a lower profile while promoting the fight. That wasn't easy for Terry, whose braggadocio – a stark contrast to Pender's stoicism – won him both friends and enemies in Boston. Never one to avoid confrontation, Terry even incorporated a jog past Pender's family home on the route of his daily run. The Downes family were accompanied everywhere by Bob Hall and Joe Walsh, two local police detectives who were detailed to help ensure the champ didn't talk himself into any trouble. Never one to miss an opportunity for a wind-up, Terry got them to 'arrest' manager Mickey Duff on gambling charges when he arrived in Boston.

This family of mouthy Londoners made quite the impression in Massachusetts. One report in *The Boston Globe* reads somewhat unkindly:

'The cockney accent is not easily understood under any circumstances by a plain New Englander, but it was almost a foreign language in the Downes [hotel] suite, with the TV playing a kiddy drama, Wendy kissing daddy first on this cheek and then that, and the carpet still smouldering from a loose cigarette butt.'

My mum, two-and-a-half at the time, made a more positive impression elsewhere. Arthur Siegel of the *Globe* wrote:

'Wendy Downes of England may be boxing's answer to Caroline Kennedy. The blonde daughter of Terry and Barbara Downes is an unabashed starlet with photographers, reporters and the world at large . . . She made a fist for the camera and wasn't disturbed by the quick flashes or the floodlights. She popped Daddy with a right hand and, when asked if she could fight, turned loose a barrage of left and rights.'

Pender was the sort of fighter who turned up to weigh-ins in a bowler hat and with an umbrella under his arm – erudite, well-read, softly-spoken. Compared to this, the Downes family turning up felt like the circus had come to town. Before The Gypsy King, there was The Cockney Prince.

It was my mum and grandma who first took me whale watching. I was ten, and we were in Iceland (the country, not the shop). I love whales. I think there's something intrinsically awe-inspiring about big animals. It's nature on its grandest scale. We can't resist elephants, rhinos – there's even something faintly inspiring about a really massive duck.

Whales certainly offer that spectacular sense of scale, plus their submarine environment adds an element of mystery. What are they up to down there? We're told they sing, and yet so few whales enter *The Voice*. Like I said, mysterious. I'd love to see that though: imagine Will.I.Am. turning round on his chair, only to see a sperm whale on stage belting out *Mustang Sally*. That's prime-time telly.

I'd loved whale watching in Iceland. I remember seeing whales breaching the North Atlantic as the midnight sun threatened to set yet never quite did. With such fond recollections, I was determined to go again during our honeymoon, even if only to hear what 'Thar she blows!' sounds like in a Sri Lankan accent. But here's the thing: I'd been quite young on my previous whale-watching escapades, and I think that had resulted in me having a somewhat rose-tinted memory. When you see a whale in the wild, it's majestic, even magical – so much so that you actually tend to forget some of the broader frustrations of the whale watching experience.

How best to explain . . . Well, the fundamental issue with whale watching is that you are on a boat, but the whales are under the water. You're in something keeping you above the surface, and they are spending ninety-nine per cent of their time beneath it. It's completely illogical, like going bird-watching in a submarine. The bit you see is them breathing – it's like paying fifty dollars to watch a bunch of snorkellers.

They shouldn't call it whale-watching, they should call it water-watching. You watch the water and then someone shouts out that they've seen a bit of a whale peep above the surface. Everyone hurries over to that side of the boat to try and catch a glimpse before it disappears back into the depths. It's like whack-a-mole but bigger and wetter.

And you've got to go out really early to see the whales, it's the only time you'll see them. They're the postmen of the ocean. Judging by the timing of these trips the whales sack off the day around lunchtime. 'Sod all this swimming about, let's get down the pub.'

There's a guy on the boat with binoculars who's apparently a whale expert; he knows where the whales like to hang out (the sea). If he spots one, he shouts out something like, 'Whale! Twelve o'clock!'. I'm there thinking, 'Christ, it's only quarter past seven now, this is going to be a long day.' It's supposed to be the photo opportunity of a lifetime. Is it? If you get anything, you get the very top of their head. It'd be like having a photo of me that only showed my bald spot.

But we did see whales, or at least bits of them. We saw a whale shark which is the biggest fish – and then a blue whale which is bigger, but isn't a fish.* Apparently you're very lucky if you see a blue whale. They didn't say why but I'd imagine it's the camouflage. I knew whales were intelligent but being blue and living in the ocean? That's genius. If you want to see one yourself, pop down to Kensington: at the time of writing they've got a blue whale replica hanging fifty feet in the air in the entrance hall at the Natural History Museum. It's spectacular, but misleading: based on the evidence I have managed to accumulate, a blue whale cannot fly.

We chose a company called Raja and the Whales (despite the

---

* Another one for the pedants to pick over.

name, as far as I'm aware the whales and Raja do not have a formal business arrangement), as unlike some other companies they made sure to keep their distance from the wildlife and not disturb or stress them.

It was a windy day, with choppy seas. On Raja and the Whales' website, they warned about the conditions, saying: 'The Indian Ocean is not a calm ocean. There is always at least a light swell. If you tend to get seasick or if it is the first time for you on a boat in the Indian Ocean, we advise you to take seasick pills on the morning of the trip (about one to two hours *before* you enter the boat).'

To help combat any seasickness, the crew also give out ginger biscuits – apparently ginger settles the stomach. Personally, I wasn't feeling any ill effects, so I just tossed mine overboard – for the whales, obviously. Disappointingly, they showed no interest. Admittedly, it'd be difficult to eat a biscuit in the sea. Presumably it'd just disintegrate, like when you dunk a digestive for too long. Maybe that's what sand really is.

But as the ocean swelled and the sun rose, I thought about my recently passed grandfather. About his achievements and his story, about the journeys he made across an ocean to make his name and fulfil his destiny. I thought how outlandish, how impossible it all seemed. I knew I'd never pull into harbour a world champion; that compared to his, my life would always seem ordinary. But with Camille by my side, and the sun on my back, I thought, 'I'm doing okay.'

The build-up to the Pender fight was overshadowed by talk of Paret's death. The sport was under fire, with calls for boxing to be banned. From the moment Terry stepped off the boat, until the moment he stepped into the ring, he faced questions from the media about what had happened in New York.

Paret, the Cuban fighter nicknamed 'Benny the Kid', had been fighting US Virgin Islands native Emile Griffith. As with Downes and Pender, this was a third and final fight in a trilogy – a decider for the world welterweight title. Over the course of the three bouts, a vicious enmity had developed between the two Latin Americans. Griffith had been incensed by Paret's actions at the weigh-in for their second fight, when he touched Griffith's buttocks, flashed a limp wrist, and whispered '*maricón*' in his ear – a Spanish insult roughly equivalent to 'faggot'. Paret then rubbed salt into the open wound by winning a controversial decision in the fight. At the weigh-in for the fateful final bout, there were more of the same homophobic taunts: Paret slipped behind Griffith, thrusting his pelvis crudely against his backside. 'Hey, *maricón*,' Paret cooed, 'I'm going to get you *and* your husband.'

Griffith had faced rumour and innuendo about his sexuality for some time. Some cited his gentle manner and high-pitched mellifluous voice as evidence he was gay. Others queried the fact that he worked in a factory which produced women's hats. There was seemingly an unresolvable tension between Griffith's softly-spoken persona and his profession as a fighter. For a boxer to be willing to exist outside of traditional masculine norms challenged some people, and infuriated others. Even in the liberal Sixties, such things were incompatible, irreconcilable.

The homophobic abuse was a heavy price to pay. To a boxer – and a Latin American one at that – the insults were potentially career-threatening. They would destroy his credibility and popularity. Paret had turned to these slurs out of desperation. He saw them as a way of winning the psychological battle. Ultimately, that decision would cost him the fight, and his life.

In the twelfth round of their final contest, an enraged Griffith caught Paret with a flurry of blows to the head. The referee might have stopped the fight then and there, but saw fit to allow the contest to continue. In a devastating burst, Griffith was able to land eighteen punches on Paret in just six seconds – the culmination of a run of twenty-nine unanswered blows. When the referee belatedly stepped in, Paret slid to the ground and slipped into a coma. With his right hand caught over the middle rope, he hung limp and heavy like some grotesque crucifixion. Ten days later, at Manhattan's Roosevelt Hospital, he died from massive brain haemorrhaging. In the aftermath of the fight, doctors speculated that Paret had still been suffering from the heavy beating sustained in his previous match against Gene Fullmer. Had he been tested properly, he might not even have been permitted to fight.

The novelist Norman Mailer, who was in attendance that night, wrote: 'As he took those eighteen punches something happened to everyone who was in psychic range of the event. Some part of his death reached out to us . . . As he went down, the sound of Griffith's punches echoed in the mind like a heavy axe in the distance chopping into a wet log.'

Mailer summed events up with the solemn words: 'Paret died on his feet.'

Paret's death spared him the censure he deserved for his homophobic behaviour. Reports of the event stated he had called Griffith an 'anti-man' – the most generous translation imaginable of the hateful '*maricón*'. This was no kind of justice, though – there were no winners here. For decades afterwards, Griffith was haunted by nightmares – torturous dreams of Paret walking down the street towards him, extending his hand, only for it to turn cold and lifeless in Griffith's palm.

Conjecture over Griffith's sexuality continued, but it was

another thirty years before he was outed in the most violent fashion possible. In 1992, he was viciously assaulted while leaving a gay bar called Hombre on West 41st Street, New York. Some reports suggested he'd been beaten with steel bars, others that his body and head had been repeatedly shut in a car door. Either way, the damage was every bit as devastating as the beating he'd given Paret. Somehow, he survived. In the aftermath, he said he considered himself bisexual. 'I like men and women both,' he told *Sports Illustrated*. 'But I don't like that word: homosexual, gay or faggot. I don't know what I am. I love men and women the same, but if you ask me which is better . . . I like women.'

Griffith's fateful punches reverberated well beyond the walls of Madison Square Garden. New York Governor Nelson Rockefeller created a seven-man commission to investigate the incident. There were just three days between Paret's hospitalisation, and Terry and family landing in New York. Inevitably, he faced a barrage of questions about what had happened. 'It doesn't do boxing any good. It's unfortunate. But it's one of those things,' he told reporters. 'Men get killed playing football – your football – don't they? And car racing kills drivers – and ten or fifteen spectators too.'

One of the criticisms levelled at the New York commission was that Paret had not undergone sufficient medical testing before the fight, to ensure he had recovered enough from the comprehensive beating he'd taken from Fullmer. Would Terry take an electroencephalogram before the 7 April fight, if asked by the Massachusetts Boxing Commission?

'You mean one of these things on your nut?' he said. 'Sure. It's for your benefit.' He then added in typically tactful style: 'If your brains are scrambled, you shouldn't be in there fighting.'

Terry was as good as his word. On arrival in Boston, he

posed for the cameras at Carney Hospital, a metal helmet fitted to his head as the electroencephalogram monitored his brain activity. Pender did the same. Both men were declared healthy and fit to fight. Four days before the big night in Boston, Paret died in hospital.

The boat didn't particularly agree with Camille. She was making the same face she makes at the end of a night out, a sort of leering smile that also suggests she might vomit at any moment. She had refused to take the seasickness medication, suggesting it might make her drowsy. I had said that would probably be okay – it's not like she was expected to drive the boat – but nonetheless she had declined. I felt fine. Suspiciously fine.

We disembarked and returned to land, stopping at a beach bar with Wi-Fi to upload photographs to Instagram and prove we were indeed #livingourbestlife. And it was sat there, sipping on a pina colada, that I noticed the floor appeared to be moving – and this wasn't the gentle sway of drunkenness, but almost an exact replication of the undulations we'd experienced aboard the boat. Suddenly I, who hadn't experienced any seasickness at all on the boat, was 'landsick'.

'You kept saying, "I still feel like I'm on the boat,"' says Camille. 'You didn't seem too worried at that point, just very confused. I thought it'd just go away . . . but it didn't.'

At the time, we were one week into a three-week honeymoon. We had cars, trains and planes still to catch. I felt horrendous but I couldn't bear to cancel our bookings, to declare the honeymoon over. Plus, the thought of the journey home filled me with dread. If this is what four hours on a boat had done, how might I fare after nine hours on a plane?

On reflection, the decision to soldier on, to continue with the charade of the honeymoon, was a mistake. Our balance is so fundamental – taking it away almost literally pulls the rug out from underneath your feet. Everything is difficult, everything is awkward.

Over the course of our holiday I got worse, and then worse still. The constant motion brought with it the now-familiar symptoms I have tried to describe to you: the splitting headaches that are with me to this day, intense sensitivity to light and sound. Before long, I had that constant accompaniment of a high-pitched ringing in my ears. A more recent addition has been a constant tingling in my face, as if someone is passing an electric current through my skin.

I know that even after all my explanations, the whole thing must sound mad, fantastical even. It felt like that too. Like a trip, like my reality had suddenly been altered. It seemed to be an unsubstantial, illusory horror made real. I tried and tried again to convince myself this was just a figment of my imagination, that if I just looked long and hard enough at the horizon, everything would stop moving. Every time I got out of a car, or off a train, I hoped my vestibular system would somehow reset. I remember catching the plane back to England, convincing myself that this was all a psychosomatic response to my anxieties about travelling to India, that having home soil under my feet would steady the ship. But it didn't. It just went on and on, the endless rocking.

In lighter moments, I saw the absurdity in my condition. I marvelled at how bizarre the body could be and railed at how I'd never heard of this before. Why aren't there warning signs on boats: 'By the way, be aware there's a small chance you'll feel like you're on here forever.' How many other mysterious conditions were there out there? Are there people who feel like they're trapped watching infinite television, or who are stuck strapped to an imaginary motorbike?

But as time wore on, I became worn down. I had searched for answers in doctors' surgeries, internet forums and the spiritual realm. I don't wish to be critical of doctors: my particular set of symptoms is rare and poorly understood. The advice was invariably that such a condition would surely 'settle down', which is doctor-speak for 'please go away and come back in a bit'. I kept coming back, looking for answers.

'You didn't want to go out as much,' says Camille. 'You weren't as social. You were more irritable, more tired, more depressed. Before you were very happy-go-lucky, but then everything seemed hard and heavy. It took away your lightness, your freedom.'

I remember distinctly the moment that, in my desperation, I began punching into Google variations on the phrase 'still feel like on boat'. Eventually, I came across a news story in science magazine *Nautilus* with the headline, 'What to Do When Your Brain Insists You're Always on a Boat'. I instantly clicked through to read. The article began thus:

'Last July, Chris Perry went on an Alaskan cruise with her family to celebrate her parents' fiftieth wedding anniversary. When she boarded the massive Norwegian Sun cruise ship, she felt "a little woozy and weird" from the boat's gentle rocking, she remembers, but the sensation quickly faded. Perry didn't feel seasick at all during the rest of the cruise, and spent a happy week marvelling at the glaciers. But while standing in the Anchorage airport to catch her flight home to San Francisco, she suddenly felt the ground moving under her, undulating with the gentle rhythm of waves.

'Many people have experienced this sensation after getting

off a boat; they may sway or stagger until their vestibular system re-adapts to stationary ground and they get their "land legs" back. For most people, the feeling vanishes within minutes or hours. But in rare cases, and for mysterious reasons, the illusion persists for months or even years. Perry is one of those unlucky ones, a sufferer from the disorder rather poetically dubbed "Mal de Débarquement Syndrome".'

Mal de Débarquement Syndrome, I later discovered, literally translates as 'Disembarkation Sickness'. I experienced a panicked recognition at the mention of 'months or even years'. Another frantic google brought me to a page for the MdDS Foundation. The opening paragraph on their website reads as follows: 'You're standing in a small boat tied to a dock, waves moving you back and forth, up and down, and side to side. Now, imagine that you feel this way all the time, even without the boat. You can't concentrate. Your head hurts. You've never felt so fatigued in your life. You don't know what's wrong and you need help. Your diagnostic tests are all returning as normal. After several months of symptoms, you start to wish that you had a brain tumour just to have an explanation. Nobody, neither you nor the physician, made the connection that your symptoms started after you returned from that last vacation during which you were in a boat all day. Welcome to the world of someone with Mal de Débarquement Syndrome.'

Even amidst all the bobbing and rocking, there was a moment of sudden stillness as the realisation dawned on me. This was it. It fitted absolutely. When you know, you know.

Boxing tradition dictates that the challenger enters the ring first. For Terry, that meant another few precious minutes as champion. Having made his way to the ring, he stood in the corner waiting for television commercials to end, the live transmission to begin, and that first bell to ring. A travelling English fan, a few rows back, shouted some words of support. 'Terry!' he yelled. 'There's no danger!'

'No,' Pop replied dryly. 'Not for you.'

It was an awkward fight – Terry had spoken beforehand of Pender's tendency to hold, a habit that earned him the nickname 'The Boston Crab'. In an effort to dissuade Pender from getting too close, Terry aimed an early headbutt at the challenger. A dirty trick – but Terry had come to retain the belt, not win the moral high ground. Pender showed a willingness to bend the rules too, hitting Terry with a right hand after the bell had rung to signal the end of the second round.

The veteran seemed buoyed by the home crowd. In the seventh round, Terry began to bleed from the nose. In the eighth, a loss of balance saw him tumble between the ropes and land hard on the outside of the ring apron. For the boxing writers at ringside, it brought up grim memories of Paret's limp body hanging from the ropes. For a brief moment, Terry was woozy, ears ringing, eyes flashing, head buzzing. Punch drunk, presumably: all at sea.

Pender continued to slow Terry down by leaning on and grabbing at him. He used every inch of his experience. Afterwards, Terry would complain that Pender had been grabbing him 'like a leech' – based on my admittedly limited understanding of their biology I presume that means mouth first, sucking on his leg. The *Daily Mirror* said Pender 'was a pair of handcuffs on legs, walking manacles, a man who used his hands as much to hold as to hit.'

The contest went the full fifteen rounds – today, fights are limited to twelve, to reduce the risk of life-threatening brain injury. Terry was surprised Pender had it in him to last that long. In the final round, both men let loose, unforgiving punches leaving their faces bleeding and bruised. Terry fought on through the fog of blood and haze and pain. At the bell, he felt he'd done enough to retain. The judges disagreed, scoring it as a win for Pender, who became only the fourth middleweight in history to reclaim the crown.

The belt didn't bring him much luck, either – just a few weeks later, he was hospitalised with a severe scalp injury after crashing his car into a New York fire hydrant. After six months as champion, he was stripped of the title entirely after refusing to fight the New York Boxing Commission's nominated number one contender. Who can blame him: it was Dick Tiger.

After the fight, Terry visited Pender in his dressing room.

'Good luck,' Terry said, before offering an acid-tinged, 'I guess you have to make a living.'

He joined Pender in his shower – two gladiators under the water's balm. In the grim aftermath of the Griffith-Paret affair, the irony of this homosocial moment was, one imagines, lost on everyone.

'We've been together all night, Paul, why stop here?' Terry said, his blood and tears running down the drain, and his title reign with them.

'I thought I won,' he admitted ruefully to *The Independent*, half a century later. 'But then I always did.

'And I got my own back on Pender.' The subsequent pause, displaying a natural comic timing, somehow softens the apparent callousness of what follows. 'He's dead. I outlived him.'

*   *   *

Aside from my own symptoms, I was dealing with a lot of guilt. Guilt for ruining the honeymoon; but also guilt about the husband I had become. Suddenly, I felt like a burden – I may have been stuck on that boat but, as my wife, poor old Camille was lashed to the mast, along for the ride. You say 'in sickness and in health' on the big day, but no one expects to be held to that promise within a matter of months. She knew I was accident-prone, but she didn't sign up for this. I felt as sorry for her as I did for myself.

Certainly, I was depressed. That much is clear now, even if I didn't know it at the time. I knew I was sad, sure – but to me it was just a rational response to my circumstances. I never *wanted* to kill myself, I never planned it, but it began to present itself as one of my better options. Continuing like this, I believed, was intolerable. I'd wanted to live on a boat. How wrong I had been.

And perhaps above all else, I struggled with the fact that it was my brain letting me down. My body, I would have accepted, I was used to that. But my brain was supposed to be the bit of me that worked; the bit I had come to rely on. Without that, what did I have?

People say that dealing with situations like this makes you stronger. I didn't feel stronger. I felt weaker with every passing day, unable to do the simplest things. The sensation wasn't transitory – it didn't come and go, there weren't good days and bad days. There was no port in this storm: it was twenty-four hours a day, seven days a week. Pain in the temple, pain behind the eyes, and perpetual motion. I felt cursed.

Before the boat, one of the things Camille had said she loved about me was my ability to take pleasure in the small things in life. In her speech on our wedding day, she spoke of how could I relish a sunset, a beautiful tree, a plate of beans on toast. I lost that, almost overnight. I remember noticing after a few weeks of suffering that I'd stopped remarking on the light, stopped finding the beauty in the ordinary. A shadow had been cast over my life.

I could see no end in sight. Those online support groups were full of stories of people who suffered for a lifetime, or who achieved remission only to relapse after another 'motion experience' – anything from a boat to a car to an escalator. I despaired.

The weeks turned to months, the spring turned to autumn. Time ticked on, and the world kept moving. Terry returned to Britain by boat, and disembarked in Southampton, no longer a champion.

At least he disembarked.

IN MY CORNER

I never told you about the end of the Tyson Fury vs. Deontay Wilder fight, and how it affected me.

You see, it wasn't Fury hitting the canvas that moved me to tears. It was what followed.

Having detonated a left hand on Fury's temple, The Bronze Bomber clearly considered the contest over. He turned towards his corner, arms aloft in celebration. The giant had been slain.

Or had he? As the referee began the count, something extraordinary happened. Fury's eyes stopped lolling in the back of his head and found their focus. He took a breath, looked up into the referee's face, and clambered to his feet.

Somehow, when all appeared lost, he got up. Whether due to reflex or will or some kind of supernatural intervention, he rose up out of despair, like a six-feet-nine Mancunian phoenix with love handles.

As Fury got to his feet and fought on, I found myself fighting back tears. Every punch he threw weakened my resolve – and when he roared back towards Wilder the dam was broken. Before long, I was blubbering. At this point in time I didn't even really like boxing, nor Tyson Fury, and yet I was so moved by that moment that I collapsed into heavy, cathartic sobs.

It spoke to me, I guess. It was an act of defiance. Fury beat the clock and beat the odds. He refused to lie down and accept his fate. In the end, the contest ended as a draw. A fitting finish: neither man deserved to lose. Fury hadn't won the fight, but he had vanquished some of his demons.

As replays rattled round the television screen, I continued to cry, until the spell was broken by a light switch turning on. My wife looked more concerned for my well-being than Fury's did at ringside.

'What's the matter? What happened?'

I looked at her, tears still tumbling down my cheeks.

'He got up.'

Round Eleven
THE COMEBACK

Terry's defeat in Boston led to questions over his future. Peter Wilson, one of the most respected boxing writers of the day, openly called for his retirement in the *Daily Mirror*. The headline read: 'Quit Terry – You Can Only Go Down Now'.

'Terry Downes, ex-middleweight champion of the world, should now, in my opinion, make a thoroughly honourable retirement from boxing. It is not only my opinion, but that of his father, who was at ringside to see his son lose decisively over fifteen rounds to Paul Pender, and who said afterwards: "Terry has had a lot of hard fights. He doesn't need the money now, he's got other businesses. His mother and I would both like to see him give it up."

'Terry's wife, Barbara, who will be presenting Terry with another offspring shortly, was also at the ringside, in an eye-sheltering sort of way. And I'm sure she would be the happiest of the lot if betting shop proprietor Downes in future concentrated on laying the prices instead of taking the slices.'

This must have been a testing period. Terry had always made a point of saying he knew he'd be world champion; he'd visualised winning the belt a million times or more. How many times had he considered the inevitability that he'd someday have to give it back? For a man with such a determined winning mentality, how much space did he permit himself to contemplate defeat?

Wilson was right: Terry was already a rich man. He had no need to fight again. Yet within six weeks, he was back in the ring. Within six months, he was facing Sugar Ray Robinson – arguably the greatest pound-for-pound boxer of his generation. Two years later, he would contest another world title. They say it ain't over until the fat lady sings – and Terry's was determined his story would only be over when that last bell rings.

People say in a crisis it's fight or flight. Terry wasn't conditioned to see those things as mutually exclusive. He grew up watching Spitfires soar overhead – they flew and they fought. He believed that could still be his destiny; travelling the world, taking on all-comers as a champion again.

If there's anything he left me, it's that: the understanding that life'll try to knock you down, but you've got to roll with the punches. You duck, you weave, you sweat, you grieve, and you get up and you fight again.*

From this point on, Terry didn't fight for the money. He didn't fight to prove a point. He did it because he loved it, and because it was who he was. Because if his sister could cope with losing an arm, he could surely lose a belt. Because he knew that the title didn't define him – and that the mark of a true champion is to get back up when it feels for all the world like you can't.

*   *   *

---

* When life gives you drama, make dramalade.

The rocking went on, but my life as I knew it had stopped. The simplest things became difficult. A trip to the supermarket was such a claustrophobic sensory overload that it felt like under-going a fully body MRI – or alternatively, like flying Ryanair. I grew insular and isolated.

There will be people reading this book, who feel they know me quite well, who will be surprised by all this. Chronic illness is a pernicious thing, because it's often relatively easily disguised. If you look fine, people assume you are fine. And most of the time you won't want to dissuade others of that opinion. Very few people actively seek pity.

The exercises given to me by physio Nicola Harris provided a pathway to potential recovery. To an extent, they worked: the more I trained the better I felt. Nicola helped get me back on my feet, step by uncertain step.

It was Nicola who introduced me to Dr Shura Surenthiran, my consultant neuro-otologist. Dr Surenthiran recently con-ducted a survey of fifty of his patients – he found that on average they have been unwell for forty-four months before they see him, and in that period they have seen at least two other hospital specialists, around five times each, with an average of eight visits to their GP – all without substantial improvement. I first saw Dr Surenthiran after about five months – I was one of the lucky ones.

Somewhat controversially, Dr Surenthiran makes no great distinction between MdDS and other vestibular disorders, treating it in the same way he would chronic migraine, with a combination of drugs and physiotherapy. By this point, I was regularly displaying typical migraine symptoms: blurred vision, facial tingling, tinnitus and that endless headache.

Initially, I was resistant to taking medication. This was in part due to the side-effects: I knew they came with the risk of fatigue, dry mouth, and weight gain. Given that I already felt exhausted, and that the condition had robbed me of the energy to either a) exercise, or b) bother to get up and get a glass of water, I decided these were risks I could tolerate. There was also the stigma, though: by taking medicine, it felt like a concession I was really ill. It felt a little like defeat.

The proposed drugs were usually old tricyclic antidepressants, the kind that haven't been in regular use for that purpose since the 1970s. The idea was that, in small doses, they could effectively dampen down the faulty messages careering through my nervous system, reducing the intensity of my symptoms. Dr Surenthiran described the medication as a 'sticking plaster' – something necessary to give my brain time to rehabilitate. After a bit of trial and error, I eventually found a tolerable cocktail of drugs in Nortriptyline and Gabapentin – medicines typically prescribed for depression, chronic pain, epilepsy and seizures. The Venn diagram of my symptoms had enough overlap with these conditions to offer some success. It wasn't ideal, but by this point I was desperate enough to compromise. If Terry could take seventeen steroid tablets per day, I could swallow a few brain pills.

I was lucky enough to have some correspondence with Dr Viviana Mucci, an extraordinarily impressive researcher with a passion for physiology and vestibular science. She had done her MSc in Space Physiology and Health, studying the effect of microgravity on astronauts in space. Now she had turned her attention to the phenomena of MdDS, becoming one of the world's leading experts on the condition. Along with her scientific mind, Viviana has a fantastic capacity for empathy. She understands the bizarre nature of the disorder and the sense of loneliness it can engender. She works by the maxim, 'You don't get it, until you get it'.

At the University of Antwerp, she had conducted an exhaustive retrospective study of MdDS patients, as well as working at the forefront of experimental treatment. She collaborated with New York's Mount Sinai hospital, who had pioneered a form of treatment intended to readapt the vestibulo-ocular reflex.

The results of this experimental treatment were good – it promised improvement, if not a cure. Even those who experienced remission from symptoms faced the constant risk of relapse. The Mount Sinai official website warns recovered patients: 'It is not safe to be in or on natural waters such as an ocean, rivers, lakes or even ponds, not even to swim in an ocean or river. Swimming in a pool is okay as long as you are not spending time on a floating device (i.e. raft). MdDS is different for each patient, so walking on a beach is okay for some but not for others. Avoid virtual reality and driving simulator experiences. If you are still experiencing symptoms, it is recommended not to walk on a treadmill or to use an elliptical machine.'

And that was the crux – it wasn't just the sensation that was getting me down, it was everything the condition had robbed me of. As far as I could see, I might never be able to go travelling again. With no exercise and limited performing, I became sedentary and uninspired. And so I withdrew. It felt like the only choice.

Viviana was kind enough to offer me the opportunity to undergo the vestibular-ocular therapy, if I could just make it to Antwerp. At the time, however, the idea of catching a plane or train to travel abroad seemed simply unthinkable.

While doctors had varying approaches to my condition, there was a consensus that one thing would be incredibly beneficial: walking. And I could, just about, do that. And so I did, stumbling along the pavements of north London, slowly teaching my body to put one foot in front of the other, pushing forward despite the relentless motion of the waves. It wasn't quite Rocky running up the steps to the Philadelphia Museum of Art, but it was a start.

For Terry, the gym always represented sanctuary. Even on the boat home from America, he kept up his rigorous training regime. Terry used to say that when the chips are down, you've got to get back on the horse – he didn't mince his words, but he did mix his metaphors.

Just forty-five days after tasting defeat in Boston, Terry faced a palette cleanser in Don Fullmer. Don was the brother of Gene Fullmer, the fighter who'd given Benny Paret such a ferocious beating it was feared it had contributed to his death in the ring against Emile Griffith.

Terry won a gruelling fight, but more hardship was around the corner. A scan on a sore knuckle revealed a fracture that required surgical intervention. Meanwhile, there was more turmoil in his private life. In June 1962, Barbara gave birth to their second child six weeks premature. Having lost one baby at birth already, the worry was almost too great for the young couple to bear.

'They came up and they told me he had only a fifty per cent chance of living,' says Barbara. 'He couldn't breathe, his lungs hadn't expanded. I was in a private clinic in London, the Welbeck Street Clinic. They got a top paediatrician down from Great Ormond Street, Eddie Hart.'

'He was born late at night, and Terry went out with Auntie Elsie and Uncle Cyril to the Astor Club to celebrate. He only realised the baby was ill when he came back the next morning to see me.'

'He weighed four pounds – but he was so long, he was just skin and bone. Poor little thing, I mean you should've seen him. They didn't tell me he was going to be okay for forty-eight hours. I didn't see him in all that time, he was in an incubator in a special unit.'

Ultimately, Terry Junior would spend a full fortnight in intensive care. 'I remember Terry's dad turned round to me and said, "He's going to be alright. Don't worry, he's going to be alright".'

For once, Dick's gambling instincts were right. 'Once he started to get better, he went on in leaps and bounds,' says Grandma. Fortunately, Terry Junior inherited some of his father's tenacity, growing to be six-feet-two and an impressive athlete in his own right. Sixty years later, he has recently survived a daunting battle with cancer. The fighting spirit is strong in him.

With his mind clear, and fist healed, Terry Senior could now focus on the contest with Sugar Ray. What better way for Terry to mark a comeback than by facing his idol? There was not a fighter he admired more in the world. Terry felt Robinson might well have been the best boxer in history – an opinion shared by Muhammad Ali. 'That man was beautiful,' said Ali. 'Timing, speed, reflexes, rhythm, his body – everything was beautiful. I'd say I'm the greatest heavyweight of all time, but pound-for-pound, I still say Sugar Ray Robinson was the greatest of all time.'

This was not, admittedly, Sugar Ray at his height. By the time an agreement was struck, he was either forty-one or forty-two – frankly, he wasn't sure. Terry was still only twenty-five.

Nevertheless, that brought its own pressure. Lose this, and the knives would be out for Downes again. As Frank McGhee put it in his *Mirror* column: 'If he can't beat a forty-two year old who, on his own admission, is over the hill and on the way down, bookmaker Terry might be well advised to listen to those who have been telling him to concentrate on the punters rather than the punchers.'

This time, Terry wasn't arguing. 'If Sugar Ray Robinson beats me I might feel like jacking it in,' he told the *Evening Standard*. And then he flashed that grin, and the bravado flooded back into him. 'Not that I can honestly see it happening. Sugar Ray has been a great fighter, at the top long before I started and he's still up there. But if I thought he was still anywhere near his best, promoter Harry Levene couldn't pay me what I'd ask to fight him! The only way I can see me losing at Wembley next Tuesday is if he knocks me out. No one has ever managed it and I don't think he'll be the first.'

Both men may have been written off by quarters of the industry, but crowds still flocked to Wembley to see these two great entertainers in action. This was boxing with all its razzmatazz – Sugar Ray and Terry held a glamorous press conference at Park Lane, decked in their finest attire. In between interviews, Sugar Ray entertained journalists with impromptu piano recitals. British fight fans were captivated by Robinson for the duration of his three-week stay.

'For once in his boxing lifetime, Terry Downes has had to take second place to his opponent in the pre-fight personality build-up,' said the *Evening Standard*. 'Each and every one of the 10,500 tickets were sold.'

In the ring, it made for an interesting clash of styles – a mismatch of technique against tenacity. 'Robinson is a colourful living legend,' wrote McGhee. 'He has always operated with surgical skill, on the simple theory that the way to get to the top and stay there is to hit the fellow without getting hurt.'

Pop was an altogether different type of fighter, as McGhee attested: 'Downes sometimes appears to have a diametrically opposite belief. His idea of blocking a left jab is to stick his face in the way, feeling that if you keep walking into and through what your opponent is throwing, you will break his heart.'

The aficionados will go for a fighter like Robinson every time – but as Terry's grandson, I can't help but swell with pride at the thought of a fighter who was propelled by bravery as much as skill, by courage as much as class.

Robinson showed there was still plenty of fight left in him, mind. In the fifth round, he unleashed a peach of a left hook that made Terry's legs and teeth rattle. Although Terry dominated, the dying moments of the fight saw Sugar Ray somehow rejuvenated, letting loose an explosion of punches, desperately fighting to defy the clock, to defy time itself.

Terry was the younger, stronger man however, and was awarded the decision. He would later say that sharing the ring with Robinson, let alone beating him, meant more than any world title.

And it provided an opportunity for a touching moment of humility. 'It'd be a liberty to say I beat Sugar Ray Robinson,' Terry told reporters after the fight. 'I didn't beat Sugar Ray. I beat his ghost.'

And in doing so, Terry laid a few ghosts of his own to rest too.

One of the things that has struck me in writing this book has been the degree to which the same names recur across stories.

In an industry such as boxing, or indeed comedy, there is a degree to which that is inevitable. By their very nature, these worlds feature a small, revolving cast of characters.

Some encounters, however, feel fated – and one such case is that of Terry Downes and Willie Pastrano. They first met during Terry's time in America, when Pastrano refereed him during a Marine tournament. When Terry fought and beat Phil Edwards for the British title, he shared a dressing room with Pastrano, who topped the bill. And now, as Terry's career entered its final act, it was a fight with Pastrano he sought above all others. Perhaps this story was always destined to come full circle.

Pastrano was, at the time, the world light heavyweight champion. With his slender build and wiry legs, Terry was not an obvious choice to step up a division. However, having conquered the world at middleweight, and beaten his hero in Robinson, he needed a new challenge. What do you do once you've climbed the mountain? The only option, Terry had concluded, was to climb a bigger one. It turns out you always have to go again.

Some said Terry was too small to challenge Pastrano, but Terry felt every inch the bigger man. Pastrano was from a higher weight division, but Terry believed he was a class above. Once again he prepared to face an American champion, looking to lay some stripes on his adopted nation's star. Once again he sought to make the home of the brave cower before the cockney kid.

Several months earlier, Terry had been stripped of his British title after refusing a third showdown with 'Cowboy' John McCormack. He didn't fancy risking his reputation and his face against the Scotsman's awkward left hand. What's more, he saw himself competing at international level now. 'Being British champion doesn't hold any glamour for me anymore,' he told

World Sports magazine. 'Once you win the title, the Board of Control become your manager. They tell you who and when to fight. I'm not being pushed around like that anymore.' He was still a proud patriot, but saw a second world title as the best way to 'put the old country back on the map'.

Pastrano's story has echoes of my own. He grew up a chubby boy in New Orleans, convinced his size would prevent him fulfilling his sporting ambitions. His childhood nickname, somewhat incredibly, was 'Fatmeat'. When he joined a gym to lose weight, the other boys laughed so cruelly at his efforts that he borrowed a key and took to working out alone at night. Terry had better watch out: hell hath no fury like a fat boy scorned.

Eighteen months after joining the gym, Pastrano was in good enough shape to start amateur boxing. He lied about his age to turn pro at fifteen.

'I got the taste for it,' he explained. 'The taste of the applause, the taste of being in shape.'

I've been there, Willie. Except it was live comedy instead of boxing, and my shape was: spherical.

Once again, Terry was tested by tragedy away from the ring. In the summer of 1964, Terry's dad Dick succumbed to a long battle with lung cancer. It was a body blow to Terry, and the first of a one-two punch: just a week after his father's funeral, Sylvie's daughter Judy – Terry's niece – drowned. Again he toyed with retirement, but was determined to have one last hurrah.

Terry won three warm-up fights at light heavyweight and secured himself a shot at a second world title. At the weigh-in, it looked a mismatch. Pastrano had fought as an out-and-out heavyweight in the past, and came in just a quarter pound inside twelve stone seven pounds. A puffed-up Terry was twelve stone three, soaking wet.

Pastrano was trained by Angelo Dundee, who achieved legendary status by being in Muhammad Ali's corner for all but two of his fights.* Pastrano had shown himself to be a good traveller, winning fights in the UK, Italy and South Africa. A cold night at Manchester's King's Hall held no fear for him. He began the night as comfortable favourite over Terry – but once the bell rang, looked anything but. Terry had worked himself into the shape of his life. What's more, he felt more confident than ever. What he sacrificed in weight he made up for in mobility. This was him at the peak of his powers. Steadily, the Manchester crowd began to believe they'd see the title change hands.

In Pastrano's corner, Dundee was apoplectic. Terry's name was ringing around the arena as the inevitable approached. And then, just before the eleventh round, Dundee let loose.

'What are you doing, you son of a bitch?' he yelled at Pastrano. 'Why are you screwing around out there?'

Some eyewitnesses say Pastrano was so incensed he shaped to hit Dundee, who instead told him to take it out on Terry.

As the bell rang, Dundee gave Pastrano a final slap on the behind. It seemed to do the trick – just as it had when he'd launched a verbal assault at Muhammad Ali during his victory over Sonny Liston.

Pastrano found a second wind, when all appeared lost. A tasty left hook sent Terry to the canvas. The challenger remembered the lessons he'd learned against Dick Tiger, taking his time getting to his feet, attempting to get his breath back. When the fight restarted, Pastrano came again, sensing this was the

---

* Dundee and Ali, then Cassius Clay, actually first met during one of Pastrano's training camps.

moment. Either he took Terry out now, or he surrendered his title. Terry knew this was the critical hour too – comfortably ahead on points, he simply had to survive until the end of the fight. Terry could have held on to Pastrano, but it went against his instincts. Instead, reeling from another blow, he dropped to his knee to buy time to recover.

He bought more time than he bargained for. Interpreting Terry's kneel as a knockdown, the referee stepped in to end the fight. Terry shot to his feet and then toppled back in shock. It was over. Pastrano escaped with his title, but Terry took the plaudits.

Sid Bailey called it 'the most amazing turnabout I have seen in the boxing ring ... Twenty-eight-year-old Downes, the Londoner, born in the slums of Paddington but now in the Rolls Royce class, the Cockney kid who fights because he loves it, gave everything he had. It looked like being enough but in the final reckoning, it wasn't.'

Even in defeat, Terry's humour never deserted him. Asked by journalists if he could have gone on, he said, 'Course I could, but the ref's getting old, you know. He can't last fifteen rounds.'

The controversy led to talk of a rematch, but there was never a real chance of that. In the moments after the fight, Terry decided that it was over. This was his best performance, his great effort, the fight of his life. He had more to give, but nothing to prove. He couldn't fight better than this, and he didn't want to fight worse. He retired at twenty-eight, a world title-contender, and the wealthiest boxer in Britain.

Terry didn't need to be champion. He'd already won.

When I set out on this journey, I made a decision not to tell my trainer Rowan about my condition. I didn't want any special consideration – if his philosophy was to train amateurs in the same way he trained pros, then that's the experience I wanted.

It amused me whenever he complimented me on my balance. He said I had a good natural stance for a boxer, that I could plant and pivot and move without becoming unstable. He attributed that to some inherent talent, perhaps something acquired from Terry's champion DNA. In all likelihood, the reality is it was simply down to the hours and hours of work I'd put in, learning how to stand and walk again. My balance is pretty good now – I might still have the sensation of swaying internally, but externally it appears, for all intents and purposes, as if I've finally moored.

Everything I have done to write this book – every hour at the laptop, every session in the gym, that grim weekend at a military boot camp in Wales – I have done while suffering with MdDS. Sometimes it was okay, other times it made me feel worse. I say this not to impress, but to remind myself of how far I've come. For a long time, I felt sure this would be impossible.

My initial goal was to fight a true boxing match; to go one-on-one with an opponent. Covid regulations put paid to that – if you're not a pro, it's impractical to fight right now.

And I've realised, I don't need competition to prove anything. The last few years have been my fight. I'm not my grandfather, and I never will be. I don't need to box to be a champion. I've already won.

IN MY CORNER

In the boxing movies, it's a wizened old fighter, or wily coach, who usually provides the catalyst for the comeback. Inspiration can, however, be found in other places.

It's true that watching Tyson Fury get up from Deontay Wilder's devastating left hand was a pivotal moment for me. It demonstrated the capacity of the human will to overcome. Small gestures helped too. In the weeks after that, my brother offered to accompany me to the gym to get me back exercising. It was his way of saying, 'I'm here, and I can help.'

Along with the drugs and physical therapy, talking helped me most. Sometimes it would be on a personal basis – I was touched by occasional enquiries from friends, or Camille's seemingly limitless patience. The therapy, too, helped. Having an outlet to contextualise what was happening to me, to discuss my fears and pain without burdening those closest to me, was invaluable.

Inevitably those sessions touched on the trauma of previous years – on Terry's death, on my feelings of being an alien in my own family. Steadily I began to piece together the idea that would form the basis of this book, my condition only serving to emphasise the physical frailty I felt in comparison to my grandfather. As I placed myself within that archetypal boxing narrative – that of the rise, the fall and the rally – I began to psychologically reframe my own story. What if this wasn't the end, but merely the comeback?

Real-life interaction with people who had some sense of how I might be feeling proved invaluable. Through Camille, I was put in touch with friend-of-a-friend, Holly, who was suffering with post-concussion syndrome. She too had picked up her condition while travelling, but in altogether more dramatic fashion: while taking a business flight, a suitcase fell out of an overhead locker and landed on the back of her head and neck. There was considerable overlap in our treatment and medication, but more importantly in our emotional experience. She was essentially a stranger, and yet in her company I felt entirely understood.

I also reached out to an old school friend, Adam Jacobs. When we were eighteen, Adam went to Nottingham University – only to be struck down during freshers' week by his first-ever migraine. The following week he had two migraines, the next week three. Before long he was suffering with intense migraine, twenty-four hours of every day. Soon his sensitivity to light, sound and even touch were so extreme that he was forced to spend two years lying in a darkened room, with the curtains closed and sunglasses on.

Occasional visitors would have to remove their shoes before entering, and whisper. Adam could not even eat a meal with his family, as the hubbub of conversation and clinking of cutlery sounded to him like a steam train going past. 'All I was able to do was jigsaws, paint by numbers and listen to the radio – mainly podcasts and Spurs matches – on a very low volume,' he says.

I spoke to Adam over Skype. He'd been through the same labyrinth of misdiagnoses and scepticism. He was wrongly diagnosed countless times.

Along the way, he'd encountered many of the same doctors as me – good and bad. He spoke glowingly of Nicola Harris, the vestibular physio who was helping me literally get back on my feet. Ultimately though, he took the decision to brave a flight to America to seek the best possible treatment.

When Adam was twenty-one, he travelled to the Michigan Headache & Neurological Institute in Ann Arbor. The journey cost him dear. He spent six weeks on an IV drip before drugs and physical therapy got him to the point where he could begin rehabilitation. A stay that was planned to last a month lasted five years. Eventually, his condition was diagnosed as Postural Orthostatic Tachycardia Syndrome – a rare disease of the autonomic nervous system, contracted after a bout of food poisoning.

Over time, he steadily regained his freedom. As he ventured back into the outside world, he began taking photographs as a distraction from the pain. Wearing earplugs, soundproof headphones and a beanie hat, he would snap pictures of his Michigan surroundings.

He found his sensitivity enhanced his ability as a photographer. 'My condition causes all of my senses to be constantly heightened,' he explains. 'It's like the volume switch is always turned up, meaning my sensitivity to light, sound, smell and touch are all elevated. Given that the etymology of 'photography' stems from 'painting with light', I can definitely see things in a different way now. My eye picks up on shadows and highlights in ways that I would not have previously noticed. Nuanced colours are perceived as more vivid to my system.'

One day when he went to get his photos developed, a lady

working in the shop asked him if he was a professional. She passed the images on to a contact and set in motion a chain of events that led to Adam becoming an internationally renowned photographer. He has photographed sporting contests from college football all the way to the World Cup. He's photographed stars like Mick Jagger, Andy Murray and boxer Amir Khan. He even took candid shots of Nelson Mandela and Bill Clinton together in the former South African president's office.

Against all expectations, he managed to complete his degree remotely, graduating just twelve months late with the highest mark in his year group. From the wreckage of his situation, he'd salvaged not just a life, but a career.

Looking back through my phone, I found a message I sent to Adam in February 2007 – two and a half years on from his condition starting, while he was still almost totally confined to darkness. It read simply: 'Ad, you will get better. I know you well enough to be certain of that. X.'

He'd proved me right.

Round Twelve
CONSEQUENCE

The brains typically arrive in an innocuous cardboard box. Inside that is a polystyrene cooler packed with ice, inside that a series of plastic bags, and inside that a human brain – as 'fresh' as physically possible.

We are in Boston, not in 1962, but in 2003. Dr Anne McKee has received a call to attend an autopsy. This brain is fresher than most, having been donated by a patient from the neighbouring Alzheimer's clinic. There is a buzz in the hospital: the subject of the autopsy was apparently something of a local celebrity. His widow had taken the difficult decision to donate his brain to Boston University, hoping to find clues as to why her husband had deteriorated so dramatically after the age of fifty.

His diagnosis had been Alzheimer's disease, but neither he nor his family were convinced, especially given his profession. That widow's name was Rose Pender – and her husband, Paul, had been Terry's opponent in his three world middleweight title bouts.

It was Pender's short-term memory that disappeared first, as he entered his sixth decade. A man who could once quote

Shakespeare at will found himself searching for the most basic words. Later, he would suffer with outbursts of rage and confusion. 'Something's wrong with me, I don't know,' he would repeat to his wife. 'I just don't know, but something's wrong.' Ultimately, Rose became his full-time carer, committed to helping a declining Pender retain his dignity.

The clinicians who diagnosed Pender with Alzheimer's were well-respected. They felt it was impossible that Pender's boxing career had caused his cognitive issues – after all, he had retired at thirty-two, shortly after facing Terry that third and final time. His symptoms didn't seem to present for the best part of twenty years.

Dr McKee had been studying Alzheimer's and other types of dementia for more than two decades, with a particular interest in tau – a protein found inside corrupted brain cells that is associated with neurodegenerative disease.

The process is always the same: first they weigh the brain, then they photograph the external surfaces. Then they do a series of dissections, taking more photographs and making microscopic slides. For McKee, these practices had become routine. She had seen thousands of brains over the course of more than two decades. Yet she had never seen anything like Pender's.

'When I looked at his tissue, it was this florid, very unusual pattern I'd never seen,' she says. 'It was very clearly not Alzheimers. He had tremendous amounts of this tau protein, inside nerve cells throughout his brain. He had such an extraordinary disease. You know, for a person who looks at patterns and different pathologies, this was something I had never seen before. I became fascinated and wanted to understand more.'*

---

* Dr McKee was speaking in the film *Unforgotten: The story of Paul Pender* (2016), an illuminating if troubling documentary about his life and illness.

The autopsy provided as many questions as answers. McKee had never seen degeneration quite like it. 'It's like you're just knee-deep in it trying to figure it out,' she explains. 'And then you wade through the previous literature, and you try to put it in its place. Has this been described before? How does this fit in with what we know? And it really seemed much more expansive than anything that had ever been described before.'

It's long been known that blows to the head could have a severe impact on the mind. The Ancient Greek physician Hippocrates wrote of 'commotio cerebri' – a loss of speech, hearing and sight that could result from 'commotion of the brain' – a vigorous shake or blow to the skull.

In the tenth century, Persian physician Abu Bakr Muhammad ibn Zakariya al-Razi is believed to have been the first to distinguish between the kind of dramatic brain injury that killed someone, and a more subtle type – the sort that caused dizziness and perhaps even loss of consciousness, but was not fatal. He termed it a 'cerebral concussion'. Six hundred years later, Italian anatomist Jacopo Berengario da Carpi speculated that this 'commotion of the brain' could be caused by the squishy organ being bounced off the inside of the solid skull. It was a prescient theory, but one difficult to pursue: until recently, obtaining brains for autopsy has not been straightforward. There is an understandable cultural sensitivity around giving up the brain, the part of the body in which the personality – the person – seemingly resides.

In truth, modern science has danced around this diagnosis for a century, like a boxer circling their opponent without landing the crucial blow. In the early 1900s, two New York neuropsychiatrists – Michael Osnato and Vincent Gilberti – theorised that concussion was more than just 'an essentially transient state'. They believed there could be long-term reper-cussions.

It was in the 1920s that the crude classification of ex-fighters as 'punch-drunk' emerged. That was the title of a seminal study by Dr Harrison Martland, a Newark pathologist in 1928. Martland described multiple cases of ex-fighters showing signs of wear and tear from the ring, be it slurred speech, erratic behaviour, or short-term memory loss. 'I am of the opinion that in "punch-drunk" there is a very definite brain injury due to single or repeated blows on the head or jaw which cause multiple concussion haemorrhages in the deeper portions of the cerebrum,' he wrote. 'The condition can no longer be ignored by the medical profession or the public.' But, for the most part, it was.

Shortly afterwards, the syndrome was rebranded as 'dementia pugilistica'. It has had other names. In the Thirties, people called it post-traumatic encephalopathy. In the Forties and Fifties, people called it chronic traumatic encephalopathy. In 1973, British neuropathologist J.A.N. Corsellis conducted studies on the brains of fifteen former boxers who had died of supposedly natural causes. He observed irregular folds and patterns in the brain – clear evidence of brain damage. Crucially, however, he also observed 'neurofibrillary tangles' – build-up of the same clumpy tau protein found in Pender's brain.

Dr McKee's attempts to label what she found in Pender were helped when she saw a report from Dr Bennet Omalu, who had conducted an autopsy on former NFL centre Mike Webster just a few months prior. Webster had died suddenly and unexpectedly at fifty, following years of struggle. Many athletes have trouble adapting to life after competition, but this was different. Webster suffered with cognitive and intellectual impairment, mood disorders, depression, and drug abuse. He became destitute, and attempted suicide multiple times. He got lethargic. He forgot to eat. One day he peed in the oven. His teeth started falling out, so he superglued them back in. He bought himself a Taser and used it to zap himself into unconsciousness, just to get some respite.

Although Bennett's brain was not obviously distorted, examination under microscope revealed the same proliferation of tau proteins. Dr McKee determined that Pender's cognitive problems, like Bennett's, had been caused by CTE: chronic traumatic encephalopathy. 'CTE is similar to Alzheimer's but is triggered by progressive head trauma,' she says. 'It's linked to very specific distinct lesions in the brain.'

'What we see are isolated lesions in the cortex or brain matter of the brain. That's the mildest form we see in the youngest individuals. When it gets more severe – and it gets more severe with ageing – it tends to spread to other parts of the brain matter. Eventually it becomes quite a devastating disorder with abundant tau proteins in many lesions of the brain.'

The symptoms of CTE vary. They can entail personality shift, mood change, aggression and violent behaviours, impulsivity and a short fuse. Other symptoms include memory loss, difficulty organising and planning, and a loss of attention span. Some patients describe 'mental fogginess . . . a feeling like they've lost control over their brain'. That struck a chord with Pender's friends and family, with some even attesting to him displaying symptoms during his boxing career. In a sportsman whose strongest asset was his brain, the decline was all the more pronounced.

In the years since Pender's autopsy, diagnosis of CTE has become endemic in contact sports. The NFL initially denied that the sport had produced Webster's condition, but since 2009 have since taken steps to combat CTE. They have changed concussion protocols, invested in research and adapted policies about when athletes can be cleared to play again. Dr McKee has become a central figure in the ongoing debate over CTE, and Pender remains her patient zero – the case study to which she compares the countless brains she has examined since. Boston University School of Medicine, in Pender's hometown, is now home to the Centre for the Study of Traumatic Encephalopathy.

As other sports take steps to lower the risk of brain injury, the question persists as to whether boxing has done enough. One of the issues is that while NFL players are unionised and united, boxing is made up of self-interested individuals. It is more difficult to galvanise collective action.

Within the sport of boxing, the subject of brain trauma remains somewhat taboo. There have been a few athletes prepared to take a stand. In 2015, former Olympic gold medallist Audley Harrison retired due to brain damage. In a statement, he revealed: 'I looked at the latest research into concussions and Traumatic Brain Injuries [TBIs]. After years of denial and sticking to my guns, I'm finally getting out of my own way. As tough as it is to say this – it's time to stop. I've suffered a few TBIs and will have to work hard to reverse some of the effects taking punches to the head has brought to my overall health.

'I have vision problems, vestibular injuries that lead to balance disturbances, and have bouts of serious irritability and moodiness that come with TBI recovery.'

Harrison's willingness to speak out is atypical. There is a passive acceptance in boxing that brain injury comes with the territory. There is a moral quandary that hangs over the sport, one that has preoccupied me throughout the writing of this book. Its critics claim the sport is a barbaric celebration of brain damage. It is an argument best summarised by sports-writer Simon Barnes, who explained that when deaths occur in sports such as horse racing or Formula One, it is because things have gone horribly wrong. 'When they happen in boxing it's because things have gone horribly right.'

It's a sport which can be a matter of life and death. Between 1890 and 2011, it's estimated that 1,604 boxers died as a direct result of injuries sustained in the ring. That is an average of thirteen deaths per year. How many more could be ascribed to the long-term effects of CTE? Brain injury is absolutely an occupational hazard for a boxer. The American Association of Neurological Surgeons estimates that ninety per cent of boxers will, at some point in their career, suffer a concussion.

Pender boxed forty-eight times, losing on only six occasions. This was not a fighter who spent a lot of time on the floor, or even on the ropes. His trilogy with Terry was the final chapter of his career. It is strange to think what damage punches thrown during those three fights might have done, how they might have contributed to the cumulative effects of CTE.

'How do we come to grips with the fact that boxing is dangerous? That for some people, the consequences are terrible?' asks Dr McKee, herself somewhat susprisingly a fan of contact sports. And, she ponders, how do athletes reconcile the risks with the rewards? 'Ultimately it's hard for people to think, when they're young, that this could happen to them.'

I asked myself over and over again: 'How could this happen to me?'

But of course, if I look back, I have had bangs on the head. I've skied into trees, fallen off bikes, I've been assaulted in one of London's most affluent boroughs. These are injuries acquired through idiocy rather than bravery. The kind of thing more befitting a Chuckle Brother than a champion boxer. I never thought they would lead me to here – to a neurology department, in Gillingham. Gillingham, of all places! The link between concussion and MdDS is debated, but the majority of my specialists referenced it as a possible contributing factor.

It felt unfair. A guy whose spent his entire life purposefully avoiding getting into fights, and yet accidentally stumbled into neurological problems. Call me naive, but I just didn't see this coming.

Nobody gets on a boat expecting consequences like these. Boxing is a different matter. When you box, you're taking a calculated risk. You know there's a possibility of coming to harm, but you weigh the odds of an injury against the payday and the glory. And if there's anyone who understands odds, it's a bookmaker.

Even if Terry backed himself to the last, there's no doubt that fighting took a toll on both his body and his mind. But think of the rewards that came in exchange: fame and fortune, a world title, fifty years retired. Now my brain had backfired, and what did I have in return? A few quid for a cracker advert and a load of blurry photos of the postmen of the ocean.

My consternation at ending up in this particular boat was relatively reasonable, according to Dr Mucci. After all, her experience suggests I am not your typical MdDS patient. I was youngish, I was seemingly healthy, and above all else: I was and am a man. Dr Mucci's studies have revealed MdDS is primarily a problem affecting women, particularly in the pre-menopausal period. If my sense of masculinity was threatened beforehand, being diagnosed with a rare disorder that typically afflicts middle-aged women hasn't exactly helped.

I know what you're thinking: is this just because middle-aged women seem to spend so much time on cruises? However, Dr Mucci's research suggests there may actually be a hormonal component to MdDS – some patients experience remission during the first three trimesters of pregnancy, for example. I guess all I need to do is get pregnant. Wish me luck.

It's Dr Mucci who asks me another question – one that ultimately proves even more pertinent than the one about banging my head. 'When the MdDS began,' she asks, 'were you stressed?'

I want to say, 'No'. I was on honeymoon, I was #livingmybestlife. And yet, I did feel under intense pressure. A pressure to enjoy myself, to be the perfect husband, to relax. And, of course, I was still reeling from Terry's death, a matter of weeks before. Dr Mucci believes it could have played a part.

'One thing we need more research into, but I think it's very important, is the prevalence of depression and anxiety among patients,' says Dr Mucci. 'In the main, when you speak to patients you discover the symptoms always begin at a rough period in their lifetime.'

These emotional disturbances, she believes, could disrupt the patient's hormonal balance – in comparable fashion to something like pregnancy. 'I had some patients who were playing with hormones due to steroid abuse or some who were suffering with burnout,' explains Dr Mucci. 'If you have depression or similar, your neurotransmitters and your hormone level won't be balanced. We need more data, but the indications are that that could predispose you to being susceptible.'

There is a direct link between the part of your brain that

governs emotion, and that which governs balance. 'In the brain you have a part that controls emotions, the limbic system, and that part is constantly in communication with the rest of the brain where there are the receptors for the balance and vestibular system,' she explains. 'The balance system and the limbic system communicate very closely.'

This proximity between the limbic (or emotional) system and the vestibular system also explains the traumatic emotional impact contracting MdDS can have on sufferers. In the absence of balance, they feel . . . well, unbalanced.

'It's very important to explain to patients, because maybe physicians don't: it's fine if you feel weird or you have anxiety,' she says. 'The most primitive sense that we have is balance. We just learn to walk and from that moment, a moment you don't even remember, you always know when and where you're stood – okay, maybe apart from when you're drunk. But you never have to consciously adapt it. It's the most prominent primitive thing, it's solid, it's at the core of consciousness, it's where you stand.

'So, of course, if you play with it and all of a sudden you start to have these crazy sensations, you feel dizzy and out of space. It's absolutely normal that you feel scared. You lose control.'

And I did.

Terry became physically vulnerable when he was still in his fifties. As I mentioned, he suffered from a rare disease of his own called polymyalgia rheumatica – it effectively caused muscle wastage in his legs. For a man who had been pounding the pavements for decades, having to walk with a stick was quite the adjustment. The absence of muscle support meant his hip joint would grind like a pestle in a mortar. On the second of two hip replacements, he insisted on being awake, just 'to check what they were doing'.

'I have my good days and my bad days,' he told an interviewer when he was in his seventies. 'It don't get better. It just stops and then I get it again. If I mow the lawn I feel it the next day. I have no stamina and no body strength. I used to be able to load a lorry, easy as anything. Now, I have this stick and bloody pills.'

Inevitably, he slowed down, his world grew smaller. The Terry I knew – my Pop – was more concerned with television than titles. When I was a kid in the Nineties he had three TV sets, each with its own VCR recorder. He would obsessively tape and catalogue anything that was of interest to him. In my memory, he was forever taping repeats of *The Bill*. I have no idea how much of it he ever watched – maybe he was trying to catch his cameo. It was as if, in the absence of a training schedule, the TV listings provided a structure for his life.

There were other little rituals too. We'd go for a Sunday roast at his favourite carvery. He'd book the table for 12pm, the very moment they opened, and would be queueing outside. He began collecting elaborate decorative clocks, and would go around his house winding them up, as if somehow wishing to turn back time to his fighting days. At the weekends he'd mow the lawn, or yell instructions at me while I did it for him. My abiding memory is of him sat in a deckchair in his front garden – flat cap on, pipe in mouth, shouting indistinguishable greetings at terrified passers-by like Oscar Wilde's Selfish Giant. Behind that coarse exterior, however, was a cuddly grandad.

He smoked a pipe incessantly, cigars occasionally. His car, a red Nissan Z-car which was his pride and joy, was lined with the delicious stink of tobacco. He still watched boxing, but with the cynicism you'd expect from the older generation.

'Half of them can't fight,' he told the *Daily Mail* in 2011. 'I take *Boxing News* every week, but I don't know half the names in there – most of them I can't pronounce anyway. They're all bloody foreign-sounding. Mind you, I do like that Manny Paccy-whatsit. Brilliant. Those Klitchkies aren't bad either.'

But ultimately, it was still the same sport he'd always loved. 'How can you change two blokes fighting, eh?' he said. 'They can't do nothing except fight. There are only so many ways to hit each other. They ain't got ray guns or nothing. The will to win matters so much.'

Being an old man suited him. Having retired from his primary profession so young, he'd been waiting to be one for ages. And, in many ways, he belonged to a different time. He was a man from a different world, a different era. But he was happy, too. He adored his grandchildren, doting on them. He'd often joke candidly about waiting to die, but when he contracted bladder cancer in his early seventies, I saw him fight to live. He enjoyed his retirement.

'Now life treats me the same way I treat life,' he told an interviewer in 2005. 'It wakes me up in the morning, and I do what I want with life, which is absolutely nothing, and it does nothing to me.'

There is seemingly no particular timeline for the recovery of MdDS patients. Some experience spontaneous remission within a few months, others suffer for years on end. I'm happy to say that after two years of hell, I began to find some respite. Slowly, the waves subsided. I don't know if it was due to medication or therapy or time, but I found some semblance of equilibrium again.

I'm not perfect. My life is changed irrevocably. Headaches

are a constant companion rather than an occasional inter-loper. My life is scored by the persistent hum of tinnitus. A perceptible current jolts through the nerves on my face. It's like being constantly tickled with a Taser. Weekend getaways are pointless: if I catch a flight, I know it will take me several days to recover. I have huge wraparound goggles I am supposed to wear while watching television or working. Like a wanted buccaneer, I have been advised never to set foot on a sea-going vessel again. Camille's sister wants to get married on a boat. If she does, she can count me out.

But things have improved. I spent two years feeling like I was one of those pirate ship rides at a theme park. Now it feels like I'm sat on the deck of an enormous vessel like the Titanic. There is perpetual, perceptible motion – but it is nowhere near as violent as it once was.

At one stage I couldn't look at a computer screen for more than twenty minutes; now I have written a book. I couldn't walk without feeling like the world was about to capsize; now I can survive boxing training (just about). I may never feel 'perfect' – but that's okay. The society we live in seems to think good health is a right; that we should all expect to be free of physical and mental ailments. That isn't realistic, and it stigmatises illness. I may always be unfixed, but that doesn't make me broken.

Crucially, I have reached a point of acceptance. My condi-tion has forcibly slowed me down, it's made me consider my mortality. I'm grateful for that. Would I like to get rid of it? Sure. Would I change the path that's taken me to this point? That's harder to say. The storm has subsided, the clouds are clearing. The waves are gentler now. I am happy.

* * *

In the final years of his life, Terry's memory began to fail. It always seems somehow sadder for someone to lose their recollection of a life so richly lived.

Terry retired from boxing at twenty-eight, feeling he'd got out of the game before any serious damage could be done. Recent studies suggest otherwise: a combined project from researchers in Denmark and America demonstrated that patients who suffered a traumatic brain injury in their twenties were sixty-three per cent more likely to develop dementia in the next three decades than someone who did not sustain one. If people experienced the same head injury in their thirties, the risk over the same time period dropped to thirty-seven per cent. The young may feel invincible, but they are far from it.

Terry regularly used to say that if he began to lose his faculties, he didn't want to be around. Speaking to the *Daily Mail* in 2011, he said: 'I don't want to end up doddering and be a nuisance to people. It's difficult for a man who has been so fit.'

Away from reporters, in the confines of his own living room, he'd put it rather plainer: 'Boy, if I start going doolally, stick a pillow over my head, or take me out the back and shoot me.'

I think he meant it, too – at the time. One of the kindest and cruellest things about dementia is the way it thwarts any euthanistic ambitions. The longer you suffer the illness, the more you forget your promise.

I don't know for a fact that Terry had CTE. We do now know that being hit on the head repeatedly can't have helped. With Terry, a formal diagnosis never really came. This was in part down to his ability to deceive others. I said earlier that he wasn't much of an actor – but when it came to disguising dementia, he was Lawrence Olivier. As with his sister Sylvie, some of that was down to a sense of humour that never deserted him. He could still throw out a one-liner. It's a reflex that he never lost, like throwing a right hand. Just as plastic surgery had masked the scars to his face, his wit masked the scars on his mind.

It wasn't just family that Terry fooled – it was doctors, too. That's no slight on them. He was able to compensate for his deficiencies. Whenever he faced a memory test, that competitive spirit kicked into gear.

My grandma was complicit too, the perfect foil. She evolved so seamlessly from companion to carer that nobody really noticed it happening. She was protecting him; protecting the pride of the champ. It was well-intentioned, if not well-advised.

Nevertheless, this man who once bestrode the world saw his own world begin to shrink. Public appearances became more fleeting, his short-term memory faded. He could describe in depth a fight fifty years ago, but not always remember what he'd had for breakfast. But, crucially, he remained content. He was one of the lucky ones.

We live in a time where there's increasing awareness of the risk incurred by all contact sports. Boxing is an obvious example, but even gentler games incur an element of danger. Recent studies have demonstrated a concerning link between professional footballers and dementia. I was struck, however, by the response of Jamie Carragher in his *Telegraph* column:

'If I suffer from dementia in my old age and research suggests that is because of my football career, I will have no regrets. I would not change my life or the moments I enjoyed on the pitch for anything, whatever the long-term cost. If fate determines that was part of the deal, so be it. Even if I had been made more aware of statistics suggesting I am more likely to be afflicted, I would make exactly the same decisions and do it all again. Whatever the future holds for me, I accept personal responsibility.'

Throw in a few percussive expletives, flip the accent from Scouse to cockney, and those words could've come from Terry's mouth. Terry was insistent to the end that he had no regrets. With the coming of the coronavirus pandemic, we live in a time where that tension between risk and health, between freedom and safety, is more pronounced than ever. Ultimately, Terry saw fighting as his own risk to take. To him, this was just an occupational hazard.

Would he have swapped a world title, fulfilling his dreams and sporting potential, for a few more years on the planet? No. For a clearer memory of the history he made? I don't think so: his job was to live it, not recount it.

Of course, it's entirely possible Terry would have developed memory problems even if he'd never boxed. His mum, Hilda, suffered with Alzheimer's disease – his sister has dementia too. This, of course, has implications for his children and grand-children. It may be these degenerative disorders are coded into my DNA in a way some of Terry's other attributes plainly aren't.

It's certainly alarming to know that, from the age of thirty-one, my brain's synapses have already been misfiring.

What's more, the medication I'm taking to manage the condition has been linked to a substantially increased risk of Alzheimer's and dementia. There is a plan to wean me off the tablets gradually, but what if that causes the swell to rise again? I keep swallowing pills to keep the waves from swallowing me. Currently my condition is imperfect but tolerable. Like Terry, I face a dilemma of short-term profit against long-term risk. The prize in my sights isn't a world title, or a place in the history books, but simply a semblance of normality. To live the life I want now, what price am I prepared to pay?

THE SCORECARDS

Terry was in hospital for about six weeks before he died. He was cared for at Watford General; the very place where I'd been born some thirty-one years before. Endings and beginnings, jumbled into one.

A few months prior, he'd been in for a few days after a fall, but came out growling and grinning. This time, it was more serious. Initially he went in with a bladder infection – the cancer had made him prone to them. The longer he stayed in, the more he declined. When he was unable to attend my wedding, I grew more concerned. It wasn't like him to miss a chance to steal the show.

He was attended on by a rotating vigil of family, and friends from the fight game. My grandma Barbara practically moved into the ward, as did my sister Rosie. I was there as much as the bustle of newlywed life permitted, but I think deep down I still expected him to pull through. He'd survived a world war, military training, countless fights, radiotherapy – I didn't fully believe anything would keep him down.

In the end, it wasn't one thing. He stayed on Bluebell Ward – a dementia ward – but in truth was suffering with a variety of ailments. His battles with polymyalgia and cancer had worn him out. He was still strong, but he was tired.

There were, as always with Terry, moments of levity. The infection made his dementia worse. One day when I brought Camille to visit him, he latched on to her name and kept asking, 'Who's that French maid?'* On another occasion my mum came to visit, only for him to ask, 'Where's Barry?' – the husband she had divorced some fifteen years earlier. I remember at one point him sitting bolt upright and saying, 'Right, let's pay the bill and get going, I've had enough of this restaurant.' Some might suggest it's cruel to laugh at someone suffering with illness. I'd ask them, what's the alternative?

Towards the end, he was in and out of consciousness, that old reflex for staying in the fight gradually deserting him. Even at his most frail, Terry was still delighted by simple things: cards from old friends, getting the daily paper, a spoonful of ice cream. It was, in some respects, a very happy time – a chance for family to talk and share memories. In those moments, nobody spoke about fights and titles. He was remembered as a father and grandfather, as a friend.

Eventually, the doctors explained there was no more they could do, and that they were moving to palliative care. Even then, Terry fought on for another week. He never did like a quitter.

By this time, my brothers and sisters and I were holed up at my mum's, effectively on a visiting rota as we prepared for the

---

* Camille isn't French at all. She's actually Guyanese-English but raised by a Turkish father, but good luck to anyone who tried to explain all that to Terry.

inevitable. On the night of 5 October, I left the hospital late, taking the opportunity to get a few hours of sleep. Moments after I got into bed, I received a phone call from my sister, urging me to come back.

It was too late. The bell had tolled. By the time I'd rushed back to hospital, he was gone. Waiting for someone to die is a bit like watching a boxing match – turn your back for a minute, and you might miss the knockout blow. In the end, he had only been with my sister Rosie, his eldest granddaughter, when the moment came. The nurses say it's often like that. Terry wasn't ever going to die in front of a crowd. I wish I could say the same regarding my comedy career.

In the end it was kidney failure that killed him. It didn't feel right: you can't strike the kidneys in boxing, it's against the rules.

I had the job of collecting his things – his slippers, his glasses, his blanket. I put them in a bag for my mum; she still keeps it in her bedroom. She's too sad to ever open it, too sad to throw it away. Her dad was her hero. Still is.

I think he's mine, too – even if the process of writing this book has led me to have a more rounded appreciation of the man he was. He was complex, and frequently difficult. We excuse high-achievers things in life that we would not tolerate in others. Terry wasn't perfect, but there is a sense in which he was perfectly himself, uncompromising in everything he did. Could he have lived like that in this day and age, and escaped judgement? Perhaps not. Is that a bad thing? Perhaps not either. By 2017, Terry was in every sense a man out of time.

I asked my grandma what sort of husband Pop was, and she said 'unusual'. She's definitely right there: after all, this was a man who'd buy her beautiful jewellery, then chuck it at

her in a brown paper bag. He was an unusual father too, and
sometimes an absent one. According to my mum, he once tore
around the house trying to kill a bat with fly spray. He insisted
on naming his eldest son Terry, then spent the next fifty years
calling him 'boy'. When Paul showed him a huge blister he'd
got from chopping firewood, he bit into it, sprinkled some salt
on the raw skin and growled at him to get back to work. He'd
visit Richard at university in Coventry, ostensibly under the
guise of checking up on his studies, but end up out all night
painting the town red.

He was an unusual grandfather. As toddlers he'd insist on
feeding us Tabasco. He'd lock us in 'The Grip' – a kind of
torture tickle from which there was no escape. Almost before
I could speak, he embarked on a personal project to teach me
to say, 'Pop's car's the best'.

And he was an unusual friend. He wasn't a great one for
planning – if he decided he was taking you to Barcelona, you
were going. If you haven't told your wife, leave her a note.*
But wherever he went, he'd show you a good time.

My grandma summed him up perfectly. 'Unusual' is a brilliant word for my Pop, because there was absolutely nothing
ordinary about him.

He was a wonderful contradiction – a man who hung out
with film stars and royalty, but treated the dustman with just
as much respect. A bookmaker and uncompromising landlord,
but a tireless charity worker. He was a stern disciplinarian who
couldn't say no to his kids; a hard man who adored babies and
animals; The King of the Ring who performed at the Royal
Court Theatre. Someone ferociously independent, but fiercely

---

* This isn't a hypothetical example. This actually happened.

protective of his family. A man with the highest standards who always managed to be so proud of his grandchildren, whatever we did.

There was always something giddy, something childlike about how he saw the world. Even in his seventies, he'd insist on opening all his Christmas presents on Christmas Eve – he just couldn't bear to wait until the next day. That's how he fought, and how he attacked life – like he had to have it all, immediately.

He was unusual, yes – extraordinary too. In and out of the ring, he only knew how to go forward. He never conformed, and he never compromised. He did it all, and he did it his way. He lived truly unapologetically, for good and bad.

I try to learn from his example. To walk into rooms like he walked to the ring. I do have a little of that: I believe in myself. Maybe that's easier when you know the story of his fairytale life; when you know for a fact that the wildest dreams do come true. Is there anything I could have taught him? Again, I will stress, a few acting lessons wouldn't have gone amiss. But aside from that, I don't know. Maybe only that it's okay to not be okay; that there can be strength in vulnerability.

What would he think of me writing this book? He'd probably say that I was being soppy. But deep down, I think he'd be flattered too. This, after all, is the man who bought the papers on the way home from winning the world title. He'd quite enjoy being on the cover of a hardback in 2021. There's a lot I would have liked to ask him, but I'm not sure he would've answered. Part of the challenge here is unpacking the emotional life of a professional hardman.

I do think he was proud of me. He wasn't the type to say it, but I think he was. I think he accepted me, in every version of myself: the fat one, the one with long hair, the one dressed like a hippy, the student, the actor, the journalist, the pontificating podcaster. My life has been easier than his, but he never resented me for it. That's what he wanted. He hoped he'd fought so we wouldn't have to.

I wish I'd told him, explicitly, how proud I was of him. I can't imagine how he would have received it – reluctantly, I suspect, at least outwardly. I toyed with the idea of writing it down in a letter; it was the only way I could imagine him being willing to listen. Now I guess I've written it down in a book. It is, in some respects, too late.

Terry and I are wildly different. But that's by his design. His sacrifices gave me access to things he didn't have: comfort, security, an education. Why apologise for those, when he bled for them?

I think it's clear I'm never going to be a world champion, and that's okay. I think even Rowan accepts that now. I might not even be a prize-winner in my chosen field. But life is full of smaller fights, smaller victories, that add up to provide meaning. A champion is someone who gets up when they can't. Like Terry's sister Sylvie, recovering from losing an arm to rejoin a circus and raise a family. Like my parents, who overcame their drinking problems to rescue their relationship with their son. Like Shaine, who has dealt with the trauma of losing his father and is now prepared to chase his own dream, however fanciful.

And my grandma is a champion: Terry's finest opponent, and his best match. They don't give out world titles for grandparents, but if they did, surely she'd be a number one contender.

I remember telling my grandma that I was working on a project about me and Terry – about how, despite being from the same family, we're so very different. She thought for a few seconds. I was worried she was going to tell me the whole thing was a bad idea. And then she spoke.

'You're not that different,' she said. I've still got the recording. In it, you can hear me almost laugh. I think I thought she might be joking.

'You're not,' she went on. 'You're like him because you're single-minded . . . You do what you want to do.'

I warm ever so slightly to her theme. 'Right, yeah.'

'Nothing would have stopped him being a boxer. Nothing would have stopped you being an actor, being a writer. You've got to set your goals in life and you go for them.'

'I can just see it,' she said. 'He would've been so proud of you doing that one-man show, or writing a book. That's like a fighter. You're on your own.'

On my own perhaps, but I've rarely felt more part of something than at that moment.

'So, in actual fact, out of all my grandchildren, you're probably the one most like him.'

Another pause.

'Except he couldn't write, and you can't box!'

Acknowledgements

I want to thank my family – the Downeses, the McNicholases, the Ucans – all of them. Writing a book about your family is a delicate, dangerous thing. The stories contained within are very personal and often sensitive. I have felt a twin responsibility to honour Terry's extraordinary legacy, while also painting a truthful portrait of the man we knew – to be as open as possible, and as honest as possible. I recognise that a huge amount of faith and trust has been placed in me. I sincerely hope I have done you all justice.

I'm especially grateful to my mum and dad, Wendy and Barry. I can't imagine any parent dreams of having a son who grows up to write a book about his upbringing. Nobody really wants the foibles or failings of their parenting held up for public dissection. When a life is viewed through a comic prism, there is an inevitable fear of caricature. Frankly, they could have said, 'No'. That they didn't, and that they were prepared to let me tell my story – warts, chicken kievs and all – is testament to their courage and their love. They have always supported my idiosyncratic ambitions; they've let me pursue every dream I've ever had. And deep down, I really do appreciate the sacrifices they made for me. I might be uneasy with my expensive education, but I know I've almost certainly fared better for it. Thank you, mum and dad, for everything. Even when I'm seemingly being stupid, I'm still trying to make you proud.

My siblings, Charlie, Rosie and Ella, have been a constant source of support. As a big boxing fan, Charlie has provided a particularly valuable sounding board for the book. My brother and sisters have a tremendous knack for building me up when required, and knocking me down when necessary. I feel so lucky to be one of this four.

I'd like to thank my grandma, for the cups of tea, the crumpets, the madeira cake, the trips to the Harlequin Centre, the handmade 'Baloo the Bear' outfit, the endless conversations about the BBC's *Antiques Road Trip*, and so much more. The similarities she sees in Terry and I are, at best, debatable – but they come from a place of such love. Thank you, grandma. You, as I'm sure you are well aware, are the best.

And of course, I thank Terry, for being my inspiration. It is such a thrill to me that more people will know your story.

A word too for my other grandfather, Tommy McNicholas, who we all miss terribly. I have many happy memories with my paternal grandparents, Tommy and Margaret, and am equally proud of them.

I want to thank everyone who contributed an anecdote, story or reflection towards this book – and apologise to those whose offerings were left on the cutting room floor. There have already been two books about Terry's remarkable life, but there is arguably still room for several more.

Before this book, there was a show. My trip to Sri Lanka meant that for the best part of 2018, I was physically and emotionally reeling. Then, at the start of December, I had that epiphanic experience of watching Tyson Fury get up from that Deontay Wilder left hand. Over the following days, an idea formulated in my mind for a comedy show about boxing. And I knew exactly who I wanted to work with on it: director Tom Parry. Within a matter of days I had pressed him into meeting me for a drink.

As absurd as it may seem, my initial idea was to write something primarily fictional: a kind of *Rocky* parody, with only occasional allusions to my grandfather's story. It was Tom who persuaded me to drop that, and to delve instead into the personal. I guess, until then, I had been scared.

If you're working with Tom on a show, there is no need to fear anything. He has such an intuitive understanding of story, of structure, and of empathy. This book is built on the bones of a design that Tom and I carved out together.

He's a clever bloke, but what I love about him is that he's all heart. Within our industry, there is a belief that comedy exists to make you laugh and think. Tom subscribes to the belief that comedy should make you laugh and feel – and it is a belief I have subsequently inherited.

It was Richard Roper, my editor at Headline, who asked me whether I'd considered turning the show into a book. He'd seen me perform in Edinburgh and London, and spotted some potential. I was excited by the idea, and not especially daunted – I assumed that, having performed an hour-long one-man show on the same subject, I'd already done most of the legwork. Imagine my horror when I printed out the script for the show, only to discover it was just thirteen pages long. Apparently, that is not sufficient length for a hardback book.

And so, Richard led me through the process of turning *The Boxer* into the book. What started as an adaptation of the show has, by necessity, developed into something altogether different. It was Richard's instincts that helped shape that, curbing my tendency to punctuate every paragraph with a joke, and every moment of reflection with cynical self-deprecation. Through panicked late-night emails, impulsive rewrites, and missed deadlines, he has been so generous and entirely unflappable. The fact he is an excellent author in his own right means he is perfectly positioned to lend support and advice. The faith of Richard and the wider team at Headline has propelled me towards the finishing line.

I'm grateful to everyone who helped turn this from a typo-laden

Word Document into an actual book. Justyn Barnes was my patient copy editor, and Katie Field my eagle-eyed proofreader. Patrick Insole designed the cover, taking inspiration from the authentic posters from Terry's career that hang in my office. Idil Sukan and Murdo MacLeod lent their outstanding photography skills, and Feyi Oyesanya kindly scanned an unwieldy folder-full of family snaps. Thanks also to the team at Heavy Entertainment who helped produce the audiobook, particularly Alfie Thompson, who spent the best part of 20 hours listening to me wrestle with trying to reproduce Rowan's South African accent.

I'd like to say thank you to Rowan Katzew himself, who was open, patient and never patronising. Thanks to Trudi and Scott Lowndes for their hospitality at Higher Tregerest. Thanks to The SF Experience and their special forces boot camp for a) permitting me to join them, and then b) permitting me to quit. Alicia, my therapist, acted as an unwitting editor for this book, organising my neuroses into chapters and paragraphs.

I want to thank my team at United Agents – Millie Hoskins, John Hyslop, Isaac Storm and Freddie Best. They took a chance on me when others wouldn't. Millie, my literary agent, gave me a whistle-stop induction to the publishing industry, and countless nuggets of advice. John, Isaac and Freddie, meanwhile, have been endlessly forgiving about the fact that, for the past twelve months, I'd had my head trapped in a book.

I'm grateful to my employers at *The Athletic*, particularly my editors Alex Kay-Jelski and Kev Coulson. For a long time, I feared there would be an irreconcilable tension in my life between my love of sport and my love of comedy. Their understanding has enabled me to strike a delicate balance. Thanks also to Andrew Mangan of Arseblog, whose advice on everything from first drafts to dog ownership is always invaluable.

My oldest friends – Jack Hartnell, Danny Fisher, Jonny Burch, Robert Samuelson and Thomas Penn – have helped keep alive the memories of my school days, enabling me to draw upon them for this book. Jack also went beyond the call of duty, producing a professional-standard copy edit in his spare time. Truly, what a wonderful nerd he is.

A number of other friends also kindly agreed to read advance copies of the book: James Acaster, Rob Beckett, Greg Jenner, Mae Martin, Suzi Ruffell, Phil Wang and Josh Widdicombe. I'm flattered, grateful, and sorry about all the spelling mistakes in that early draft. Darren Richman lent his expertise on the life and times of Peter Cook. Thanks also to Mike Costello, the BBC's voice of boxing. During the run-up to the 2019 Edinburgh Fringe, he was kind enough to come and see a ramshackle preview in a pub. I was half-tempted to hand him the mic and let him commentate over the top of it. Afterwards, he promoted the show via his podcast. To get that kind of approval from someone within the fight game was so precious to me.

I owe my sketch group brethren, Ciarán Dowd and Owen Roberts, an awful lot. Without BEASTS, I would not have crossed over into the world of comedy. Without BEASTS, I might still be stuck in a call-centre, spending my breaks furtively looking for castings in Elizabethan-Jacobean theatre productions. And without BEASTS, I would not have met my wife.

It is difficult to find the words to explain my gratitude to Camille. Her tolerance, kindness, and generosity know few bounds. Practically, she's read several drafts, and talked through countless more. Emotionally, her support is the reason I am still here, still functioning, still okay. Through the nightmare storm of MdDS, she has been my lighthouse – a beacon of brilliant hope. This book may be dedicated to my grandma, but would not exist without Camille. It is her who has kept alive my dream of a happy ending.